RALPH WALDO EMERSON

Bloom's Classic Critical Views

RALPH WALDO EMERSON

Edited and with an introduction by
Harold Bloom
Sterling Professor of the Humanities
Yale University

BLOOM'S
LITERARY CRITICISM
An imprint of Infobase Publishing

Bloom's Classic Critical Views: Ralph Waldo Emerson

Bloom's Literary Criticism
An imprint of Infobase Publishing
132 West 31st Street
New York NY 10001

Library of Congress Cataloging-in-Publication Data
  Ralph Waldo Emerson / [edited by] Harold Bloom.
    p. cm. — (Bloom's classic critical views)
  A selection of important older literary criticism on Ralph Waldo Emerson.
  Includes bibliographical references (p.   ) and index.
  ISBN-13: 978-0-7910-9559-1 (hardcover)
  ISBN-10: 0-7910-9559-2 (hardcover)
  1. Emerson, Ralph Waldo, 1803–1882—Criticism and interpretation. I. Bloom, Harold.
II. Title: Bloom's classic critical views : Ralph Waldo Emerson.

  PS1638.R283 2007
  814'.3—dc22

                                    2007014944

Series design by Erika K. Arroyo
Cover designed by Takeshi Takahashi
Printed in the United States of America
Bang EJB 10 9 8 7 6 5 4 3 2 1

This book is printed on acid-free paper.

Contents

Series Introduction

Bloom's Classic Critical Views is a new series presenting a selection of the most important older literary criticism on the greatest authors commonly read in high school and college classes today. Unlike the Bloom's Modern Critical Views series, which for more than twenty years has provided the best contemporary criticism on great authors, Bloom's Classic Critical Views attempts to present the authors in the context of their time and to provide criticism that has proved over the years to be the most valuable to readers and writers. Selections range from contemporary reviews in popular magazines, which demonstrate how a work was received in its own era, to profound essays by some of the strongest critics in the British and American tradition, including Henry James, G.K. Chesterton, Matthew Arnold, and many more.

Some of the critical essays and extracts presented here have appeared previously in other titles edited by Harold Bloom, such as the New Moulton's Library of Literary Criticism. Other selections appear here for the first time in any book by this publisher. All were selected under Harold Bloom's guidance.

In addition, each volume in this series contains a series of essays by a contemporary expert, who comments on the most important critical selections, putting them in context and suggesting how they might be used by a student writer to influence his or her own writing. This series is intended above all for students, to help them think more deeply and write more powerfully about great writers and their works.

Introduction by Harold Bloom

As I approach my seventy-seventh birthday (hoping for good luck), the thought of Emerson heartens me. Towards Emerson I feel nothing but admiration: he gave me as much self-reliance as I know. Out of Emerson came Walt Whitman, Henry David Thoreau, Margaret Fuller, William James, and John Dewey. In a more antithetical way, Emerson provoked creativity in Herman Melville, Nathaniel Hawthorne, Emily Dickinson, and Henry James. During the twentieth century, the catalog becomes too large to list. But as representative figures I would cite Robert Frost in the direct line of descent and Wallace Stevens as a rather rueful literary grandchild of the Sage of Concord.

After Emerson, every strong American writer and thinker has been an Emersonian or an anti-Emersonian but not indifferent to him. This is because he became the Mind of America, much as Dr. Samuel Johnson became the Spirit of England or Montaigne the master of all French skepticism. Though he derived from Montaigne, Emerson can be seen now as being like his younger contemporaries Nietzsche and Walter Pater. Nietzsche is the clearer analogue, partly because he overtly admired Emerson. Pater certainly read both Nietzsche and Emerson yet never mentioned them, but he also kept silent about his closest model, Ruskin.

Emerson was blocked from major accomplishment as a poet by Wordsworth, and had no impulse at all towards storytelling or stage drama. He became the greatest writer of wisdom-essays since Montaigne, outpacing even Sigmund Freud in this genre. Though Freud asserted he was a scientist, he was in fact a literary essayist, in the sage-like mode of Emerson, Carlyle, and John Stuart Mill.

I myself began to read and reread Emerson when I was in Dante's "middle of the journey," aged thirty-five. My rather classic mid-life crisis involved a blank-like deep depression, during which I read and thought my way through Emerson, Freud, and much of Gnosticism and Kabbalah. These religious stances were mediated for me by Hans Jonas and Gershom Scholem. Those sages were alive; I sought them out and listened for many hours. Jonas I encountered in American academic circles, and later he introduced me to Scholem in Jerusalem, the two being lifelong close friends.

Freud gradually has abandoned me, and I have gone on to ruminate endlessly upon the Gnostic texts expounded by Jonas, and the Kabbalistic writings magisterially interpreted first by Scholem, and then by his revisionist, my close friend Moshe Idel. And yet Emerson is with me daily, more frequently even as I age, for I need his highly individual wisdom so that I may survive. He insists, in his central essay, "Self-Reliance," that we can gain from other minds no tuition but only provocation. If I betray him at all, it is in my relying upon him for perpetual tuition.

So vast is Emerson's wisdom that I seek it even more in his journals and notebooks than in his essays, which he quarried, together with his lectures, from his daily jottings of his own aphorisms and perceptions, and from his reading, which covered the world's cultures. His favorite authors, after Montaigne, were Shakespeare and Plato, who to me seem antithetical to each other. Emerson had an Eastern orientation, particularly to ancient Persian and Indian literature. His stress upon balancing antitheses is more Indian than Iranian, and his desire to reconcile differences in one transcendental vision is more Platonic than Shakespearean. Yet to him Shakespeare was more than a poet-dramatist, but the writer of the text of modern life.

My investment in Emerson is so large that only Shakespeare is more my concern. Shakespeare gave us a unique cosmos of human forms, more persuasive as presences than all but a few beings I have known. Emerson realized he could not do that: inventing personalities was beyond him. Even with Shakespeare, Emerson could not be content; the genius of the shores of America longed always for a poetry still to be composed. That longing accounts for Emerson's wonderful reception of Walt Whitman's first *Leaves of Grass* in 1855. We have no American Shakespeare, except perhaps by merging Emerson, Whitman, and Henry James. Even our best dramatists—Eugene O'Neill, Thornton Wilder, Tennessee Williams—are lesser literary imaginers than the triad of Emerson, Whitman, and Henry James.

Emerson fathered our national philosophy of Pragmatism by his rich essay "Experience." The central formula of Pragmatism, as developed by

William James, C.S. Peirce, and John Dewey, is that only a difference that makes a difference is truly a difference. In my own generation, the tradition inaugurated by Emerson was carried on by the brilliant Post-Pragmatist, Richard Rorty, who taught us that philosophy, like poetry and the other arts, is governed by contingency, our struggle with inescapable precursor-figures. Emerson, most inevitable of American forerunners, is the Angel with whom we must struggle if we are to win the blessing of a new name, whether it be the American Scholar or some twenty-first century equivalent.

BIOGRAPHY

RALPH WALDO EMERSON
(1803–1882)

Ralph Waldo Emerson was born in Boston on May 25, 1803. His father, a Unitarian minister, died in 1811, leaving the family in difficult financial circumstances. Emerson attended the Boston Public Latin School (1812–17) and Harvard College (1817–21), and in 1825, after several years of teaching, entered Harvard Divinity School. He received a degree in divinity in 1827 and became junior pastor of Boston's Second Church in 1829, the year he also married Ellen Tucker. In 1831 Emerson's wife died, and in the following year he resigned from the Second Church, feeling he was unable to believe in the sacrament of the Lord's Supper. During 1832–33 he traveled in Europe and while in England met Samuel Taylor Coleridge, William Wordsworth, and Thomas Carlyle.

After returning to the United States, Emerson became active as a lecturer. In 1835 Emerson married Lydia Jackson. They lived in Concord where they had four children between 1836 and 1844 and where Emerson first formed, in 1838, a close friendship with his neighbor Henry David Thoreau. During these years, Emerson also began to evolve the new quasi-religious concept of transcendentalism, expressed in his essay "Nature" (1836). In 1837 he delivered his influential lecture the "American Scholar," in which he called on America to assert its intellectual independence. This was followed in 1838 by the "Divinity School" address, also delivered at Harvard, which forcefully argued the principal tenet of transcendentalism, that knowledge of reality is derived from personal intuition and not from objective experience.

In 1840 the *Dial* began publication. It was the literary organ of the so-called Transcendental Club, which had been meeting informally at Emerson's house and elsewhere since 1836. In the *Dial,* edited first by Margaret Fuller (1840–42) and then by Emerson himself (1842–44), Emerson published a number of poems, including "The Problem" and "Wood-Notes," and also the essays "Self-Reliance," "Compensation," and "The Over-Soul," gathered in *Essays* (1841). The second volume of *Essays,* containing "The Poet," appeared in 1844, after the *Dial* had ceased publication. This work was followed in 1846 by a collection entitled *Poems*. Throughout 1845 Emerson delivered a series of lectures on Plato, Napoléon Bonaparte, Emanuel Swedenborg, and others, collected in 1850 as *Representative Men*.

In 1847–48 Emerson traveled in Europe for a second time, visiting France and England. His experiences in England, where he was much admired, led him to publish his portrait of the English national character, *English Traits* (1856). From 1851 Emerson began actively campaigning against slavery, and throughout the 1850s he also continued to publish poems and prose, notably in the *Atlantic*. In 1860 he published *The Conduct of Life*, followed by *May Day and Other Pieces* (1866) and *Society and Solitude* (1870). In 1872–73 Emerson traveled in Europe and the Middle East, visiting France, Italy, Egypt, Greece, and the British Isles. The decade following his return from Europe was marked by a gradual loss of mental powers, but he nonetheless managed to publish a final volume, *Letters and Social Aims* (1875), written in collaboration with Ellen and James Eliot Cabot, and also had a hand in preparing the 1876 edition of his *Selected Poems*. Emerson died at his home in Concord on April 27, 1882.

PERSONAL

Thomas Carlyle (1833)

Our third happiness was the arrival of a certain young unknown friend, named Emerson, from Boston, in the United States, who turned aside so far from his British, French, and Italian travels to see me here! He had an introduction from Mill, and a Frenchman (Baron d'Eichthal's nephew) whom John knew at Rome. Of course we could do no other than welcome him; the rather as he seemed to be one of the most lovable creatures in himself we had ever looked on. He stayed till next day with us, and talked and heard talk to his heart's content, and left us all really sad to part with him.

—Thomas Carlyle, Letter to His Mother (August 26, 1833),
*The Correspondence of Thomas Carlyle and
Ralph Waldo Emerson*, 1883, Vol. 1, p. 4

Theodore Parker "Journal" (1838)

Proceeded to Cambridge, to hear the valedictory sermon by Mr. Emerson. In this he surpassed himself as much as he surpasses others in the general way. I shall give no abstract. So beautiful, so just, so true, and terribly sublime was his picture of the faults of the Church in its present position. My soul is roused, and this week I shall write the long-meditated sermons on the state of the Church and the duties of these times.

—Theodore Parker, *Journal* (July 15, 1838),
cited in John Weiss, *Life and Correspondence
of Theodore Parker*, 1864, Vol. 1, p. 113

Charles Sumner
"Letter to Lord Houghton" (1839)

Senator Charles Sumner's estimation of Emerson was set down in 1839, just three years after the publication of "Nature," and immediately follow-ing the "American Scholar" address and the "Divinity School" address. This may account for the biographical style of Sumner's entry. As a U.S. senator from Massachusetts, he obviously is interested in the life and background of this speaker from Boston who had become such a sensation.

Sumner's description of Emerson is important for students interested in him as a preacher and a public speaker, since Emerson's contemporary reputation was formed on the basis of both his lectures and his written work. Sumner's description is both factual and imaginative. His description of Emerson as an "Aeolian harp" (a stringed instrument that, when exposed to the wind or a current of air, produces sound) is an ideal metaphor for Emerson's manner and his thinking. Indeed, Emerson is "inspired" in the Latin sense of that term; that is, he is moved from within by a spirit (or wind), an image that conjures both divine inspiration and the "Aeolian harp" qualities Sumner wishes to convey.

———— ———— ————

Ralph Waldo Emerson is one of three brothers, all quite remarkable persons, and he is the only survivor. The other two died young, but everybody hoped great things of them. Their father, I think, was a country clergyman, passing rich on little more than £30 a year. They all, however, received good educations, and were distinguished scholars in our oldest and best University—that of Cambridge. Ralph must be now about thirty-eight years old. He has studied theology, has been settled (that is the American word to express the idea) as pastor of an Unitarian congregation in Boston; was much liked in this character, but speculated too deeply even for Unitarians; pushed his beliefs and unbeliefs very far; rejected much of the Christian faith; espoused much of the Swedenborgian; was disinclined to administer the Sacrament of the Lord's Supper; and then parted from his congregation in Boston. This was about six years ago; he then retired to a little country house at Concord, about twenty miles from Boston, within sight of the spot where the first British soldier fell in the war of the Revolution. Here he has kept ever since—thinking, reading, and writing; still regarded as a Christian clergyman, but without any charge. During the winter months delivering lectures in Boston, in character not unlike Carlyle's here, and to audiences brought together in the same way, and for the double purpose of spreading knowledge and getting money. A series of biographies formed one of his courses, and he has several times treated of the true nature and uses of history, and of the way in which it should be written. I need give you no hint about his style or his writings, for you know as much of both as I do. As a speaker in delivering his lectures, sermons, or discourses he is remarkable. His voice is good, his enunciation clear and distinct; his manner his own, but very striking. He is always self-possessed, and his strange fancies fall upon the ear in the most musical cadences. His voice is now low and then again high, like an Aeolian harp; but this is natural, not affected, and I think anywhere before an educated audience he would be deemed a remarkable speaker. In person he is tall and graceful. Some people think him slightly mad (one of his brothers died insane, and the other brother had been insane before his death), others think him almost inspired. Old men are not prepared to receive or listen to or read his thoughts. The young of both classes think highly of him. He has a great influence over many of the young minds of my acquaintance, who always couple him with Carlyle. I think him neither mad nor inspired, but original, thoughtful, and peculiar, with his mind tinged with some habits of speculation that are less practical than beautiful, and with a fearless honesty that makes him speak what he thinks, counting little any worldly considerations. In other times he might have been a philosopher or a reformer, but he would always have been tolerant and gentle, and he would have gone into uncomplaining exile if the powers that were bade him. I have hastily dotted down some things about Emerson according to your wish. I hope I have not said too much. When we meet in conversation I can explain whatever is left uncertain in your mind. I should not forget to state that he has been twice married. His first wife died young—under twenty, I think. By her he had a small property, which is to him an independence, enabling him to gratify all those "small desires which ask but little room," and which fill the life of a retiring literary man in all countries, and particularly in America. Emerson had no children by his first wife. He loved her and lamented her much, and cherished her memory in the Swedenborgian way. He has since married again a person who sympathises with him. When his child was born, about two years ago, men and women were astonished, and inquired if the infant has wings. This is enough.

—Charles Sumner, Letter to Lord Houghton
(March 2, 1839), cited in T. Wemyss Reid, *The Life, Letters, and Friendships of Richard Monckton Milnes, First Lord Houghton*, 1891, Vol. 1, pp. 237–39

JOHN QUINCY ADAMS (1840)

Adams's entry is typical of Christians suspicious of the mystical leanings of transcendentalism, and the effect such aspects will have on the Christian Church. Note that Adams's bias against transcendentalism is something of an ad hominem or personal attack, evident in the former U.S. president citing Emerson's "failing in the every-day avocations of a Unitarian preacher and school-master." Such sentiments express to a degree the anxiety Emerson's early work, such as "Nature" and the "American Scholar" and "Divinity School" addresses, caused contemporary religious leaders. Students interested in responses to Emerson's radical theology should note the tone of Adams's entry. Emerson resigned his position as minister of Boston's Second Church (rather than fail in his profession), but Adams's final claim—that Emerson "declares all the old revelations superannuated and worn out, and announces the approach of new revelations and proph-ecies"—is true enough.

—⁓⁓⁓— —⁓⁓⁓— —⁓⁓⁓—

It is the doom of the Christian Church to be always distracted with controversy, and where religion is most in honor, there the perversity of the human heart breeds the sharpest conflicts of the brain. The sentiment of religion is at this time, perhaps, more potent and prevailing in New England than in any other portion of the Christian world. For many years since the establishment of the theological school at Andover, the Calvinists and Unitarians have been battling with each other upon the Atonement, the Divinity of Jesus Christ, and the Trinity. This has now very much subsided; but other wandering of mind takes the place of that, and equally lets the wolf into the fold. A young man, named Ralph Waldo Emerson, a son of my once loved friend William Emerson, and a classmate of my lamented son George, after failing in the every-day avocations of a Unitarian preacher and school-master, starts a new doctrine of transcendentalism, declares all the old revelations superannuated and worn out, and announces the approach of new revelations and prophecies.

—John Quincy Adams, *Diary,* August 2, 1840

RUFUS DAWES "BOYHOOD MEMORIES" (1843)

Boston native Rufus Dawes, son of Massachusetts supreme court judge Thomas Dawes, attended Harvard but did not graduate. He attended law school and was admitted to the bar, but did not practice, choosing instead to become a writer, contributing essays and literary criticism to the *United States Literary Gazette.* As a child in Boston, he encountered the young Emerson, as he describes in this personal memory.

Dawes's entry is noteworthy because he gives us a striking image of Emerson as a boy. Dawes has the luxury of hindsight, thus the prophetic tone to his writing. But descriptions of Emerson as a child are rare, and students researching the young Emerson (perhaps in order to connect his demeanor with his thinking and influence) should consider Dawes's entry.

—⁓⁓⁓— —⁓⁓⁓— —⁓⁓⁓—

It is 8 o'clock, A.M.: and the thin gentleman in black, with a small jointed cane under his arm, his eyes deeply sunken in his head, has asked that spiritual-looking boy in blue nankeens, who seems to be about ten years old, to "touch the bell,"—it was a privilege to do this;—and there he stands! that boy—whose image, more than any other's, is still deeply stamped upon my mind, as I then saw him and loved him, I knew not why, and thought him so angelic and remarkable,—feeling toward him more than a boy's emotion, as if a new spring of brotherly affection had suddenly broken loose in my heart. There is no indication of turbulence and disquiet about *him;* but with a happy combination of energy and gentleness, how truly is he the father of the man! He has touched the bell, and while he takes his seat among his fellows, he little dreams that, in after-times, he will strike a different note, and call around him a school of the transcendental philosophy. He is RALPH WALDO EMERSON.

—Rufus Dawes, "Boyhood Memories,"
Boston Miscellany, February 1843, p. 60

HENRY CRABB ROBINSON (1848)

It was with a feeling of predetermined dislike that I had the curiosity to look at Emerson at Lord Northampton's, a fort night ago, when, in an instant, all my dislike vanished. He has one of the most interesting countenances I ever beheld—a combination of intelligence and sweetness that quite disarmed me. I was introduced to him.

—Henry Crabb Robinson,
Letter to Thomas Robinson (April 22, 1848)

ARTHUR HUGH CLOUGH (1848)

Arthur Hugh Clough was an English poet and lecturer whose work reflected the religious skepticism of nineteenth-century England. Clough and Emerson were contemporaries in this regard. After an invitation from Emerson, Clough delivered a series of lectures in Massachusetts in 1852.

An important assertion in Clough's letter is that Emerson is less "Emersonian" than his essays. This expression seems to echo or confirm other contemporary reports regarding Emerson's lectures that they were less mystical and more prosaic, and therefore less "Emersonian." Students examining Emerson's reputation as a lecturer should note this observation. Also, it is significant that Clough uses the term *Emersonian* to imply a quality of thinking peculiar to and identifiable in Emerson's writing. That Emerson's public addresses are less "Emersonian" than Emerson actually is in person, or in other modes, provides a clue as to how Emerson was defined in the public consciousness. That is, Emerson is defined by his essays; however else Emerson appears or is portrayed is in relation to the style of his writing.

⁓⁓⁓ ⁓⁓⁓ ⁓⁓⁓

The next topic is Emerson, whom I left yesterday on the deck of the Halifax steamer and saw pass rapidly down the Mersey on his way home. He came to Oxford just at the end of Lent Term and stayed three days. Everybody liked him, and as the orthodox mostly had never heard of him, they did not suspect him. He is the quietest, plainest, unobtrusivest man possible—will talk but will rarely *discourse* to more than a single person—and wholly declines 'roaring.' He is very Yankee to look at, lank and sallow and not quite without the twang; but his look and voice are pleasing nevertheless and give you the impression of perfect intellectual cultivation as completely as would any great scientific man in England—Faraday, or Owen for instance, more in their way perhaps than in that of Wordsworth or Carlyle. Some people thought him very like Newman. But his manner is much simpler. I told him I had sent my copy of his Poems to the Antipodes with you. Whereupon he gave me another. I have been with him a great deal, for he came over to Paris and was there a month—during which we dined together daily; and since that I have seen him often in London and finally here. I liked his Lectures (he gave six in London) better than either his conversation or his appearance. I should say, his appearance is common, in the Lectures he looked prophetic at times. They were all *read*. One thing that struck everybody is that he is much less Emersonian than his Essays. There is no dogmatism or arbitrariness or positiveness about him. However, I have perhaps talked enough about him. Your sister Mary was at the lectures and you will perhaps have her report too.

—Arthur Hugh Clough,
Letter to Thomas Arnold (July 16, 1848)

Herman Melville (1849)

Herman Melville was not a member of the New England literary circle surrounding Emerson, but he knew of Emerson's work and reputation. In this letter to his publisher, Melville conveys his general impressions of Emerson.

Melville refers to Emerson's reputation for borrowing material and taking his education at second (or third) hand. Melville suggests that this is not as important as Emerson's usage of influences, and the directions to which his reading takes him (for Melville loves "all men who *dive*"). This is a critical point in understanding Emerson's method of composition. He shaped his essays and lectures from material he recorded in his journals and notebooks, far-ranging ideas and thoughts taken from direct experience and from his readings as well. Thus, Emerson might be said to be something of a collagist; his shaping and utilizing material in support of his own unique claims marks his work. Students exploring the genesis of Emerson's ideas and essays might take note of this letter.

Melville also notes what he considers to be Emerson's "gaping flaw," that "had he lived in those days when the world was made, he might have offered some valuable suggestions." The passages in "Nature" regarding natural objects as symbols of spiritual intent, nature as a metaphor for the mind of God, the doctrine of correspondences (taken from Emanuel Swedenborg's idea that what exists in nature is exactly mirrored in heaven), or the well-known "transparent eyeball" segment (in which Emerson's ego is dissolved in nature) seem to speak to Melville's observation.

⸺ ⸺ ⸺

Nay, I do not oscillate in Emerson's rainbow, but prefer rather to hang myself in mine own halter than swing in any other man's swing. Yet I think Emerson is more than a brilliant fellow. Be his stuff begged, borrowed, or stolen, or of his own domestic manufacture he is an uncommon man. Swear he is a humbug—then is he no common humbug. Lay it down that had not Sir Thomas Browne lived, Emerson would not have mystified—I will answer, that had not Old Zack's father begot him, old Zack would never have been the hero of Palo Alto. The truth is that we are all sons, grandsons, or nephews or great-nephews of those who go before us. No one is his own sire.—I was very agreeably disappointed in Mr Emerson. I had heard of him as full of transcendentalisms, myths & oracular gibberish; I had only glanced at a book of his once in Putnam's store—that was all I knew of him, till I heard him lecture.—To my surprise, I found him quite intelligible, tho' to say truth, they told me that that night he was unusually plain.—Now, there is a something about every man elevated above mediocrity, which is, for the most part, instinctively perceptible. This I see in Mr Emerson. And, frankly, for the sake of the argument, let us call him a fool;—then had I rather be a fool than a wise man.—I love all men who *dive*. Any fish can swim near the surface, but it takes a great whale to go down stairs five miles or more; & if he don't attain the bottom, why, all the lead in Galena can't fashion the plummet that will. I'm not talking of Mr Emerson now—but of the whole corps of thought-divers, that have been diving & coming up again with bloodshot eyes since the world began.

I could readily see in Emerson, notwithstanding his merit, a gaping flaw. It was, the insinuation, that had he lived in those days when the world was made, he might have offered some valuable suggestions. These men are all cracked right across the brow. And never will the pullers-down be able to cope with the builders-up. And this pulling down is easy enough—a keg of powder blew up Block's Monument—but the man who applied the match, could not, alone, build such a pile to save his soul from the shark-maw of the Devil. But enough of this Plato who talks thro' his nose.

—Herman Melville,
Letter to Evert Duyckinck (March 3, 1849)

A. Bronson Alcott
"Fuller, Thoreau, Emerson" (1871)

Bronson Alcott's 1871 essay regarding Margaret Fuller, Henry David Thoreau, and Emerson is of particular value to students exploring Emerson's manner of composition. Rather than compose his essays and lectures from notes or outlines (or conceive of them in terms of developed arguments), Emerson relied on the observations recorded in his many journals or "commonplace books," in which he kept seemingly all of his observations, no matter how small. Emerson would work these comments and observations into essays and lectures. In this way, he was more like a sculptor than a philosopher, working the final shape of his essays from the raw materials contained in his notebooks.

Alcott also makes insightful observations on Emerson's attraction as a lecturer. Note the praise Alcott heaps on Emerson's style: "That is entirely his own. It is Emersonian; it is not imitable." Using the term *Emersonian* to describe Emerson himself seems like a tautology or needless repetition, but this is part of Alcott's point. Emerson's attraction *is* his style, which becomes inseparable from his content. This is true of his written work (prose and poetry) as well. There is no separation between Emerson's exquisite marriage of content and form, which helps account for his art, as well as the clarity and accessibility of his lectures. Given this estimation, it is no wonder that Emerson was such a highly regarded speaker on the Athenaeum circuit.

We come now to Mr. Emerson, . . . our central figure. I suppose the present company have all seen Mr. Emerson; perhaps not any of the others I have mentioned. He is a very plain, simple man, graceful manners, and fine culture, and modesty becoming his eminent talents. A scholar by genius, culture and habit, his books are more read, perhaps, by thoughtful persons all over the country than those of any other author, and it would not be an unfair test, in my judgment, if one were to go into any city and take the census of the readers of his books to find the number of thoughtful and earnest people.

I will tell you a secret about his method of composing books, since it will explain what a great many people have not comprehended, and will really show them how to read his books. It makes no difference, they say, whether you begin at the last paragraph and read backwards, or begin at what he meant for the beginning. There is some principle in that. There is, nevertheless, a thread running through all his writings; it takes a very subtle, fluent, and ingenious reader to find that thread; but be assured there is a thread on which he strings all his pearls; it is not accidental.

He is a man who lives for thought, and who is a thinker. He is a benevolent man, since, on all occasions when the town of Concord wishes his aid, Mr. Emerson is ready to perform any service for his fellow towns-people. On many great occasions, . . . he has given his voice to determine questions which arose in the history of our country, and if the speeches were collected which he made we should see how much he contributed in that way, perhaps more than any other person except Mr. [Theodore] Parker. He lives for thought, which means life, since those who do not think do not live in any high or real sense. Thinking makes the man.

How does he live, and what are his habits? Imagine a man who says: "Here is a day now before me; a day is a fortune and an estate; who loses a day loses life." Therefore he is alert, busy, awake. If he walks he sees what there is to see, and remembers it. He has a tablet in his pocket, and puts it down on the spot, not when he gets home. If he has visits to make, which is not often, any conversation that occurs goes into his commonplace book without order. If he dreams, and any thought occurs in his dreams, that goes down also. If he reads a book, and it suggests a thought, that goes down in his commonplace book. Whatever he hears, or sees, having all his senses awake, whatever product they give him, goes into his tablet; and any time he has an invitation to speak, or that he knows he is to speak, he sits down and reads what is in his commonplace book.

Perhaps some topic has been growing on his mind for some time. In every true man and woman things grow and get the ascendency, and all who are

fruitful will give birth to their thought. How shall it be clothed? is the next
question, since before the arrival we prepare the garments. The garments
are already partially prepared; the material, at least, is there for dressing
the thought. He finds what he has in his commonplace book; looks over it
and sees what passages he has written, perhaps during the last twenty or
forty years, touching the question. He copies them off; sees in what order
they can be strung together; perhaps spreads them before him. I remember
hearing of an instance when a neighbor went in to see him, and there was the
philosopher and poet leaning over his papers spread out on the floor before
him, singling out paragraphs, perhaps, or trying what would be best for the
introduction.

After going over many times, he goes to the lecture-room and reads to
see whether it has any connection or not. If the people think he is turning
somersaults and cannot get from one paragraph to another without some
explanation, he must continue to build a bridge, so that he may at least seem
to get across; how he gets across is a miracle to most people. Sometimes it
seems as if he had a bridge let down from above. He never falls or stumbles;
there he is on the other side, and how he got there is a miracle. When you get
acquainted with his style, however, you begin to feel confident he will pass
over, and that there will not be a fearful plunge into the chasm between his
paragraphs. I mention this for the information of those who read Emerson.
They see no connection between one paragraph and another; but there
certainly is, or he would not have classified them as he did.

Something has to be said about his style. That is entirely his own. It is
Emersonian; it is not imitable. It is ridiculous for young men and women to
try to imitate him; it cannot be done. The style is his, and entirely his, and we
are happy that it is so. A good style fits like a good costume. His thought is
deep and measures the intelligence of his readers. His suggestions are good.
He helps us most who helps us to answer our own questions. . . . He gets us
to do our work, does not do it for us. He does his work well, for he never
produces any finished piece of work. That is his great excellence.

By so doing, consider what a lesson he teaches those young authors who
rush into print with the first little essay they write, instead of keeping them for
years, and letting them ripen and mellow, and looking at them. A thing that
has not been slept upon and talked about is not worth printing. Sleep upon
it, talk about it, sit upon it, drink it, digest it, corporate it in your flesh and
blood, make it yours, and then it will do to print. Never show it to anybody. If
you ever write anything tell scholars that it is good, but by no means show it
to anybody; they will take all the charm out of it. The best of the great books

are so simply natural and fine that we don't know that we wrote them; we didn't write them, they wrote themselves. Such are all his books. When he has thought a thing and committed it to paper he stops. It is a great thing to stop; it is as hard to stop as to begin.

Mr. Emerson has certainly been a university to our people. Think of his value as a lecturer. For thirty years every winter he has travelled from East to West, and been heard by select audiences. Now no lecture-course in any State of intelligence is thought to be perfect without at least one lecture from Mr. Emerson for those who wish it and can enjoy it; because the best things are not enjoyed by all. I think we may say he made the lecture. The lyceum is Emerson's work really, since he began lecturing earlier than any one and holds his place as no other lecturer has. A great many of the lecturers have fallen away, but Emerson is still a bright star, and sought after, though now beginning to be 70 years of age. I will not speak of his verses particularly. I suppose they are less poetical, as a whole, than his prose. A poet by genius, he always writes poetry, though it be in prose form. A good deal of verse is made in that mood, but I think we will find less in Emerson than in any other writer except Henry Thoreau, who has none at all. He is as wholesome as spring. With him it is all fair weather, all out of doors. . . . His is a grand mind which is pretty nearly divinized.

—A. Bronson Alcott, "Fuller, Thoreau, Emerson.
Estimate by Bronson Alcott. The Substance of a 'Conversation.'"
Boston Commonwealth, May 6, 1871, pp. 1–2

WALT WHITMAN
"A VISIT, AT THE LAST, TO R. W. EMERSON" (1881)

Students might notice the careful, observing eye in poet Whitman's description of Emerson. Whitman's visit occurred in 1881, a year before Emerson's death. Whitman seems pleased to note Emerson's healthy appearance and most notably the "good color in his face, eyes clear."

The details Whitman provides are of interest to students examining Emerson's final years and the condition of his life after his most productive years had passed. Also notable in this remembrance is the company present: A. Bronson and Louisa May Alcott, Margaret Fuller, Henry David Thoreau. All of these key figures are represented in this volume. Also noteworthy is Whitman's description of the Emerson home, its

"democratic ease." This observation serves as an indication of Emerson's
sense of value, as reflected by how he chose to live.

—⁓⁓— —⁓⁓— —⁓⁓—

Never had I a better piece of luck befall me: a long and blessed evening
with Emerson, in a way I couldn't have wish'd better or different. For
nearly two hours he has been placidly sitting where I could see his face
in the best light, near me. Mrs. S(anborn)'s back-parlor well fill'd with
people, neighbors, many fresh and charming faces, women, mostly
young, but some old. My friend A. B. Alcott and his daughter Louisa were
there early. A good deal of talk, the subject Henry Thoreau—some new
glints of his life and fortunes, with letters to and from him—one of the
best by Margaret Fuller, others by Horace Greeley, Channing, &c.—one
from Thoreau himself, most quaint and interesting. (No doubt I seem'd
very stupid to the room-full of company, taking hardly any part in the
conversation; but I had "my own pail to milk in," as the Swiss proverb
puts it.) My seat and relative arrangement were such that, without being
rude, or anything of the kind, I could just look squarely at E., which I did
a good part of the two hours. On entering, he had spoken very briefly and
politely to several of the company, then settled himself in his chair, a trifle
push'd back, and, though a listener and apparently an alert one, remain'd
silent through the whole talk and discussion. A lady friend quietly took
a seat next him, to give special attention. A good color in his face, eyes
clear, with the well-known expression of sweetness, and the old clear-
peering aspect quite the same.

Next Day.—Several hours at E.'s house, and dinner there. An old familiar
house, (he has been in it thirty-five years,) with surroundings, furnishment,
roominess, and plain elegance and fullness, signifying democratic ease,
sufficient opulence, and an admirable old-fashioned simplicity—modern
luxury, with its mere sumptuousness and affectation, either touch'd lightly
upon or ignored altogether. Dinner the same. Of course the best of the
occasion (Sunday, September 18, '81) was the sight of E. himself. As just
said, a healthy color in the cheeks, and good light in the eyes, cheery
expression, and just the amount of talking that best suited, namely, a word
or short phrase only where needed, and almost always with a smile. Besides
Emerson himself, Mrs. E., with their daughter Ellen, the son Edward
and his wife, with my friend F. S. and Mrs. S., and others, relatives and

intimates. Mrs. Emerson, resuming the subject of the evening before, (I sat next to her,) gave me further and fuller information about Thoreau, who, years ago, during Mr. E.'s absence in Europe, had lived for some time in the family, by invitation.

> —Walt Whitman, "A Visit, at the Last,
> to R.W. Emerson" (1881), *Prose Works*,
> ed. Floyd Stovall, 1963, Vol. 1, pp. 278–80

A. Bronson Alcott (1882)

Amos Bronson Alcott was as important an influence on Emerson as any thinker in the transcendentalist hotbed of Concord. The Alcott and Emerson families were close, as is reflected both in Emerson's letters and in Louisa May Alcott's remembrances of Emerson. The excerpt below is from Alcott's essay on Emerson, privately printed and delivered to Emerson on the occasion of his birthday, May 25, in 1865. Alcott's advocating of religious and educational reform, as well as his personal ties to Emerson, make him, as well as his daughter, Louisa May, important touchstones for Emerson students.

Students might note that Alcott makes a distinction between Emerson, the "lover of his neighborhood, of mankind," and the Emerson who "is no recluse misanthrope." This discussion arises somewhat from the too-common perception of Emerson as a kind of intellectual hermit. Alcott writes that Emerson "likes solitude, and knows its uses." The key here is that Emerson realizes the *uses* of solitude; that is, he emphasizes the importance of solitude for specific reasons (as outlined in the first section of "Nature," as well as in other essays), but not in and of itself. Students exploring the distinctions (and possible conflicts) between Emerson the public figure and Emerson the private man should carefully consider Alcott's essay.

Alcott also offers insight into Emerson's process of composition, observing that Emerson contemplates and determines the scope of his essay, and then gathers the necessary material from recorded observations in his journals and notebooks. Such comments point to the importance the thesis plays in Emerson's essays and the emphasis he places on the clarity of his central arguments. Critic Stanley Cavell, for example, has remarked that, for Emerson, "every statement is a thesis statement." Alcott even suggests Emerson's essays can be read backward as easily as forward. For students discussing Emerson's prose style, or the compositional unity of Emerson's writing, this observation of Alcott's is a good place to start.

There is a virtuous curiosity felt by readers of remarkable books to learn something more of their authors' literary tastes, habits and dispositions than these ordinarily furnish. Yet, to gratify this is a task as difficult as delicate, requiring a diffidency akin to that with which one would accost the author himself, and without which graceful armor it were impertinent for a friend even to undertake it. We may venture but a stroke or two here.

All men love the country who love mankind with a wholesome love, and have poetry and company in them. Our essayist makes good this preference. If city bred, he has been for the best part of his life a villager and countryman. Only a traveller at times professionally, he prefers home-keeping; is a student of the landscape; is no recluse misanthrope, but a lover of his neighborhood, of mankind, of rugged strength wherever found; liking plain persons, plain ways, plain clothes; prefers earnest people, hates egotists, shuns publicity, likes solitude, and knows its uses. He courts society as a spectacle not less than a pleasure, and so carries off the spoils. Delighting in the broadest views of men and things, he seeks all accessible displays of both for draping his thoughts and works. And how is his page produced? Is it imaginable that he conceives his piece as a whole, and then sits down to execute his task at a heat? Is not this imaginable rather, and the key to the comprehension of his works? Living for composition as few authors can, and holding company, studies, sleep, exercise, affairs, subservient to thought, his products are gathered as they ripen, and stored in his commonplaces; the contents transcribed at intervals, and classified. The order of ideas, of imagination, is observed in the arrangement, not that of logical sequence. You may begin at the last paragraph and read backwards. 'Tis Iris-built. Each period is self-poised; there may be a chasm of years between the opening passage and the last written, and there is endless time in the composition. Jewels all! separate stars. You may have them in a galaxy, if you like, or view them separate and apart. But, every one knows that, if he take an essay or verses, however the writer may have pleased himself with the cunning workmanship, 'tis all cloud-fashioned, and there is no pathway for any one else. Cross as you can, or not cross, it matters not; you may climb or leap, move in circles, turn somersaults;

"In sympathetic sorrow sweep the ground,"

like his swallow in Merlin. Dissolving views, projects, vistas open wide and far,—yet earth, sky, realities all, not illusions. Here is substance, sod, sun; much fair weather in the seer as in his leaves. The whole quarternion of the seasons, the sidereal year, has been poured into these periods. Afternoon walks furnished the perspectives, rounded and melodized them. These good things have all been talked and slept over, meditated standing and sitting, read and polished in the utterance, submitted to all various tests, and, so accepted, they pass into print. Light fancies, dreams, moods, refrains, were set on foot, and sent jaunting about the fields, along wood-paths, by Walden shores, by hill and brook-sides,—to come home and claim their rank and honors too in his pages. Composed of surrounding matters, populous with thoughts, brisk with images, these books are wholesome, homelike, and could have been written only in New England, in Concord, and by our poet.

—A. Bronson Alcott,
Ralph Waldo Emerson, 1882, pp. 32–37

JAMES MARTINEAU (1882)

James Martineau, an English Unitarian minister and theologian, offers an interesting perspective on Emerson who, in 1833, was still concerned with the ritual of Communion, over which he resigned his ministry in Boston's Second Church in 1832. Since Martineau had a great influence on the course of Unitarian thought, this letter is of value to those investigating Emerson's career as a minister (and his choice to leave the ministry). Martineau's letter is a good indication that, although Emerson's resignation letter to his church shows a strong determination regarding his decision, he was still thinking about the problem of Christian ritual and the inherent conflicts he believed existed between the "evangelical pastor and the independent thinker."

Though I could never find in Emerson's effusions as a *Vates* so rich a vein of thought or so awakening a power as his most devoted readers were able to recognise, yet in his own personality he appeared to me almost all that is noble, lovely, and venerable; and in his critical and ethical writings, where he commented on the given matter of life, manners, and character, to rise to the very perfection of moral judgment, pure and keen without a trace of Cynicism, and with a selecting enthusiasm for all beauty and good, calm and passionless because full of faith in them as the permanency of the world.

I first heard of him in 1830, from Henry Ware and his wife, who visited me in my early married life in Dublin; and I have a faint impression that even then he was spoken of by the elder minister with a shade of reserve, as if the want of congeniality between the evangelical pastor and the independent thinker was already inwardly felt. Three years afterwards, in 1833, he sought me out in Liverpool, introduced by Henry Ware, and told me the story of his scruple about the Communion. He was then in a very indeterminate state of mind about questions on religion, and I was struck with the mixture of clear decision on the subject which had led to action, and of modest suspense on topics which he had not fully thought out. But I made up my mind that he would not be likely to return to the ministry.

—James Martineau, Letter to Alexander Ireland
(December 31, 1882), cited in James Drummond, *The Life and Letters of James Martineau*, 1902, Vol. 2, pp. 312–13

OLIVER WENDELL HOLMES (1884)

This selection from Oliver Wendell Holmes is an excerpt from the last chapter of his 1884 biography of Emerson. In it, Holmes details specific physical and personal characteristics of Emerson the man. These practical details of Emerson's daily life are of value to students examining Emerson's character, as well as those attempting to place Emerson in the context of his everyday existence.

Much has been written about Emerson's gentle and generous nature; Holmes offers specific details of these qualities from the perspective of one who knew Emerson intimately. When Holmes writes of Emerson that "he might have been an idol, and he broke his own pedestal to attack the idolatry which he saw all about him," he is a part of that process of demystifying the cult that cropped up around the influential thinker and writer.

Emerson's earthly existence was in the estimate of his own philosophy so slight an occurrence in his career of being that his relations to the accidents of time and space seem quite secondary matters to one who has been long living in the companionship of his thought. Still, he had to be born, to take in his share of the atmosphere in which we are all immersed, to have dealings with the world of phenomena, and at length to let them all "soar and sing" as he left his earthly half-way house. It is natural and pardonable that we should like to know the details of the daily life which the men whom we admire have shared with common mortals, ourselves among the rest. But Emerson has said truly "Great geniuses have the shortest biographies. Their cousins can tell you nothing about them. They lived in their writings, and so their home and street life was trivial and commonplace." . . .

Emerson's personal appearance was that of a scholar, the descendant of scholars. He was tall and slender, with the complexion which is bred in the alcove and not in the open air. He used to tell his son Edward that he measured six feet in his shoes, but his son thinks he could hardly have straightened himself to that height in his later years. He was very light for a man of his stature. He got on the scales at Cheyenne, on his trip to California, comparing his weight with that of a lady of the party. A little while afterwards he asked of his fellow-traveller, Professor Thayer, "How much did I weigh? A hundred and forty?" "A hundred and forty and a half," was the answer. "Yes, yes, a hundred and forty and a half! That *half* I prize; it is an index of better things."

Emerson's head was not such as Schopenhauer insists upon for a philosopher. He wore a hat measuring six and seven eighths on the *cephalometer* used by hatters, which is equivalent to twenty-one inches and a quarter of circumference. The average size is from seven to seven and an eighth, so that his head was quite small in that dimension. It was long and narrow, but lofty, almost symmetrical, and of more nearly equal breadth in its anterior and posterior regions than many or most heads.

His shoulders sloped so much as to be commented upon for this peculiarity by Mr. Gilfillan, and like "Ammon's great son," he carried one shoulder a little higher than the other. His face was thin, his nose somewhat accipitrine, casting a broad shadow; his mouth rather wide, well formed and well closed, carrying a question and an assertion in its finely finished curves; the lower lip a little prominent, the chin shapely and firm, as becomes the cornerstone of the countenance. His expression was calm, sedate, kindly, with that look of refinement, centring about the lips, which is rarely found in the male New Englander, unless the family features have been for two or three cultivated generations the battlefield and the playground of varied thoughts and complex emotions as well as the sensuous and nutritive port of entry. His whole look was irradiated by an ever active inquiring intelligence. His manner was noble and gracious. Few of our fellow-countrymen have had larger opportunities of seeing distinguished personages than our present minister at the Court of St.

James. In a recent letter to myself, which I trust Mr. Lowell will pardon my quoting, he says of Emerson: "There was a majesty about him beyond all other men I have known, and he habitually dwelt in that ampler and diviner air to which most of us, if ever, only rise in spurts."

From members of his own immediate family I have derived some particulars relating to his personality and habits which are deserving of record.

His hair was brown, quite fine, and, till he was fifty, very thick. His eyes were of the "strongest and brightest blue." The member of the family who tells me this says:—

"My sister and I have looked for many years to see whether any one else had such absolutely blue eyes, and have never found them except in sea-captains. I have seen three sea-captains who had them."

He was not insensible to music, but his gift in that direction was very limited, if we may judge from this family story. When he was in College, and the singing-master was gathering his pupils, Emerson presented himself, intending to learn to sing. The master received him, and when his turn came, said to him, "Chord!" "What?" said Emerson. "Chord! Chord! I tell you," repeated the master. "I don't know what you mean," said Emerson. "Why, sing! Sing a note." "So I made some kind of a noise, and the singing-master said, 'That will do, sir. You need not come again.'"

Emerson's mode of living was very simple: coffee in the morning, tea in the evening, animal food by choice only once a day, wine only when with others using it, but always *pie* at breakfast. "It stood before him and was the first thing eaten." Ten o'clock was his bed-time, six his hour of rising until the last ten years of his life, when he rose at seven. Work or company sometimes led him to sit up late, and this he could do night after night. He never was hungry,—could go any time from breakfast to tea without food, and not know it, but was always ready for food when it was set before him.

He always walked from about four in the afternoon till tea-time, and often longer when the day was fine, or he felt that he should work the better. . . .

He thought too much of his bodily insufficiencies, which, it will be observed, he only refers to in his private correspondence, and in that semi-nudity of self-revelation which is the privilege of poetry. His presence was fine and impressive, and his muscular strength was enough to make him a rapid and enduring walker.

Emerson's voice had a great charm in conversation, as in the lecture-room. It was never loud, never shrill, but singularly penetrating. He was apt to hesitate in the course of a sentence, so as to be sure of the exact word he wanted; picking his way through his vocabulary, to get at the best expression of his thought, as a well-dressed woman crosses the muddy pavement to reach the opposite sidewalk. It was this natural slight and not unpleasant semicolon pausing of the memory which grew upon him in his years of decline, until it rendered conversation laborious and painful to him.

He never laughed loudly. When he laughed it was under protest, as it were; with closed doors, his mouth shut, so that the explosion had to seek another respiratory channel, and found its way out quietly, while his eyebrows and nostrils and all his features betrayed the "ground swell," as Professor Thayer happily called it, of the half-suppressed convulsion. He was averse to loud laughter in others, and objected to Margaret Fuller that she made him laugh too much.

Emerson was not rich in some of those natural gifts which are considered the birthright of the New Englander. He had not the mechanical turn of the whittling Yankee. I once questioned him about his manual dexterity, and he told me he could split a shingle four ways with one nail,—which, as the intention is not to split it at all in fastening it to the roof of a house or elsewhere, I took to be a confession of inaptitude for mechanical works. He does not seem to have been very accomplished in the handling of agricultural implements either, for it is told in the family that his little son, Waldo, seeing him at work with a spade, cried out, "Take care, papa—you will dig your leg." . . .

There are stories which show that Emerson had a retentive memory in the earlier part of his life. It is hard to say from his books whether he had or not, for he jotted down such a multitude of things in his diary that this was a kind of mechanical memory which supplied him with endless materials of thought and subjects for his pen.

Lover and admirer of Plato as Emerson was, the doors of the academy, over which was the inscription . . . —Let no one unacquainted with geometry enter here,—would have been closed to him. All the exact sciences found him an unwilling learner. He says of himself that he cannot multiply seven by twelve with impunity. . . .

Emerson is reported as saying, "God has given me the seeing eye, but not the working hand." His gift was insight: he saw the germ through its envelope; the particular in the light of the universal; the fact in connection with the principle; the phenomenon as related to the law; all this not by the slow and sure process of science, but by the sudden and searching flashes of imaginative double vision. He had neither the patience nor the method of the inductive reasoner, he passed from one thought to another not by logical steps but by airy flights, which left no foot-prints. This mode of intellectual action when found united with natural sagacity becomes poetry, philosophy, wisdom, or prophecy in its various forms of manifestation. Without that gift of natural sagacity (*odoratio quaedam venatica*),—a good scent for truth and beauty,—it appears as extravagance, whimsicality, eccentricity, or insanity, according to its degree of aberration. Emerson was eminently sane for an idealist. He carried the same sagacity into the ideal world that Franklin showed in the affairs of common life.

He was constitutionally fastidious, and had to school himself to become able to put up with the terrible inflictions of uncongenial fellowships. We must go to his poems to get at his weaknesses. The clown of the first edition of "Monadnoc" "with heart of cat and eyes of bug, disappears in the afterthought of the later version of the poem, but the eye that recognized him and the nature that recoiled from him were there still. What must he not have endured from the persecutions of small-minded worshipers who fastened upon him for the interminable period between the incoming and outgoing railroad train! He was a model of patience and good temper. We might have feared that he lacked the sensibility to make such intrusions and offences an annoyance. . . .

Of Emerson's affections, his home-life and those tender poems in memory of his brothers and his son give all the evidence that could be asked or wished for. His friends were all who knew him, for none could be his enemy; and his simple graciousness of manner, with the sincerity apparent in every look and tone, hardly admitted indifference on the part of any who met him, were it but—for a single hour. Even the little children knew and loved him, and babes in arms returned his angelic smile. Of the friends who were longest and most intimately associated with him, it is needless to say much in this place. Of those who are living, it is hardly time to speak; of those who are dead, much has already been written. . . .

How nearly any friend, other than his brothers Edward and Charles, came to him, I cannot say, indeed I can hardly guess. That "majesty" Mr. Lowell speaks of always seemed to hedge him round like the divinity that doth hedge a king. What man was he who would lay his hand familiarly upon his shoulder and call him Waldo? No disciple of Father Mathew would be likely to do such a thing. There may have been such irreverent persons, but if any one had so ventured at the "Saturday Club," it would have produced a sensation like Brummel's "George, ring the bell," to the Prince Regent. His ideas of friendship, as of love, seem almost too exalted for our earthly conditions, and suggest the thought as do many others of his characteristics, that the spirit which animated his mortal frame had missed its way on the shining path to some brighter and better sphere of being.

Not so did Emerson appear among the plain working farmers of the village in which he lived. He was a good, unpretending fellow-citizen who put on no airs, who attended town-meetings, took his part in useful measures, was no great hand at farming, but was esteemed and respected, and felt to be a principal source of attraction to Concord, for strangers came flocking to the place as if it held the tomb of Washington.

What was the errand on which he visited our earth,—the message with which he came commissioned from the Infinite source of all life?

Every human soul leaves its port with sealed orders. These may be opened earlier or later on its voyage, but until they are opened no one can tell what is to be his course or to what harbor he is bound. . . .

He might have been an idol, and he broke his own pedestal to attack the idolatry which he saw all about him. He gave up a comparatively easy life for a toilsome and trying one; he accepted a precarious employment, which hardly kept him above poverty, rather than wear the golden padlock on his lips which has held fast the conscience of so many pulpit Chrysostoms. Instead of a volume or two of sermons, bridled with a text and harnessed with a confession of faith, he bequeathed us a long series of Discourses and Essays in which we know we have his honest thoughts, free from that professional bias which tends to make the pulpit teaching of the fairest-minded preacher follow a diagonal of two forces,—the promptings of his personal and his ecclesiastical opinions.

Without a church or a pulpit, he soon had a congregation. It was largely made up of young persons of both sexes, young by nature, if not in years, who, tired of routine and formulae, and full of vague aspirations, found in his utterances the oracles they sought. To them, in the words of his friend and neighbor Mr. Alcott, he

"Sang his full song of hope and lofty cheer."

Nor was it only for a few seasons that he drew his audiences of devout listeners around him. Another poet, his Concord neighbor, Mr. Sanborn, who listened to him many years after the first flush of novelty was over, felt the same enchantment, and recognized the same inspiring life in his words, which had thrilled the souls of those earlier listeners.

"His was the task and his the lordly gift
Our eyes, our hearts, bent earthward, to uplift."

This was his power,—to inspire others, to make life purer, loftier, calmer, brighter. Optimism is what the young want, and he could no more help taking the hopeful view of the universe and its future than Claude could help flooding his landscapes with sunshine.

—Oliver Wendell Holmes, *Ralph Waldo Emerson*,
1884, pp. 357–69, 372–73

LOUISA MAY ALCOTT "REMINISCENCES OF RALPH WALDO EMERSON" (1885)

Louisa May Alcott knew Emerson from the time she was born until Emerson's death in 1882. The daughter of Emerson's friend Amos Bronson Alcott, Louisa May enjoyed a close relationship with Emerson (who enjoyed the company of children). As Louisa May grew into a writer of stature, she maintained her friendship with Emerson and maintained her ties to the family through Emerson's last years.

Alcott's memories of Emerson are warm, bordering on sentimental. However, this reveals the genial nature of Emerson the father and friend, qualities Alcott was in a position to observe and experience firsthand. She gives us a unique insight into Emerson's personality apart (as much as he can be separated) from his work. These impressions are significant, because Emerson's life is so intensely connected with his essays and lectures. Alcott's essay thus emerges as an important resource, because she was not strictly a colleague of Emerson's or an immediate member of his intellectual circle. She gives us an idea of Emerson's relationship with a person who has little, or no, professional or theological ties to him. Alcott's memories stem from the close ties that existed between the Emerson and Alcott families. Students interested in the personal, as opposed to the professional, Emerson would do well to begin here.

As I count it the greatest honor and happiness of my life to have known Mr. Emerson, I gladly accede to a request for such recollections as may be of interest. My first remembrance is of the morning when I was sent to inquire for little Waldo, then lying very ill. His father came to me so worn with watching, and changed by sorrow, that I was startled, and could only stammer out my message.

"Child, he is dead," was his answer.

Then the door closed, and I ran home to tell the sad tidings. I was only eight years old, and that was my first glimpse of a great grief; but I never have forgotten the anguish that made a familiar face so tragical, and gave those few words more pathos than the sweet lamentation of the "Threnody."

Later, when we went to school with the little Emersons in their father's barn, I remember many happy times when the illustrious papa was our good playfellow. Often piling us into a bedecked hay-cart, he took us to berry, bathe, or picnic at Walden, making our day charming and memorable by showing us the places he loved, the wood-people Thoreau had introduced to him, or the wild-flowers whose hidden homes he had discovered. So that when years afterward we read of "the sweet Rhodora in the wood," and "the burly, dozing humblebee," or laughed over "The Mountain and the Squirrel," we recognized old friends, and thanked him for the delicate truth and beauty which made them immortal for us and others.

When the book-mania fell upon me at fifteen, I used to venture into Mr. Emerson's library, and ask what I should read, never conscious of the audacity of my demand, so genial was my welcome. His kind hand opened to me the riches of Shakespeare, Dante, Goethe, and Carlyle; and I gratefully recall the sweet patience with which he led me round the book-lined room till "the new and very interesting book" was found, or the indulgent smile he wore when I proposed something far above my comprehension.

"Wait a little for that," he said. "Meantime try this; and, if you like it, come again."

For many of these wise books I am waiting still, very patiently; because in his own I have found the truest delight, the best inspiration of my life. When these same precious volumes were tumbled out of the window, while his house was burning some years ago, as I stood guarding the scorched, wet pile, Mr. Emerson passed by, and, surveying the devastation with philosophic calmness, only said, in answer to my lamentations,—

"I see my library under a new aspect. Could you tell me where my good neighbors have flung my boots?"

In the tribulations of later life, this faithful house-friend was an earthly Providence, conferring favors so beautifully that they were no burden, and giving such sympathy, in joy and sorrow, that very tender ties were knit between this beneficent nature and the grateful hearts he made his own. Acquaintance with such a man is an education in itself, for "the essence of greatness is the perception that virtue is enough;" and, living what he wrote, his influence purified and brightened like sunshine.

Many a thoughtful young man and woman owe to Emerson the spark that kindled their highest aspirations, and showed them how to make the conduct of life a helpful lesson, not a blind struggle.

> For simple maids and noble youth
> Are welcome to the man of truth:
> Most welcome they who need him most;
> They feed the spring which they exhaust,
> For greater need
> Draws better deed.

He was, in truth, like his own Saadi,—a "cheerer of men's hearts."

"Friendship," "Love," "Self-Reliance," "Heroism," and "Compensation," among the essays, have become to many readers as precious as Christian's scroll; and certain poems live in the memory as sacred as hymns, so helpful and inspiring are they. No better books for earnest young people can be found. The truest words are often the simplest; and, when wisdom and virtue go hand in hand, none need fear to listen, learn, and love.

The marble walk that leads to his hospitable door has been trodden by the feet of many pilgrims from all parts of the world, drawn thither by their love and reverence for him. In that famous study, his townspeople have had the privilege of seeing many of the great and good men and women of our time, and learning of their gracious host the finest lessons of true courtesy. I have often seen him turn from distinguished guests, to say a wise or kindly word to some humble worshipper sitting modestly in a corner, content merely to look and listen, and who went away to cherish that memorable moment long and gratefully.

Here, too, in the pleasant room, with the green hills opposite, and the pines murmuring musically before the windows, Emerson wrote essays more helpful than most sermons; lectures which created the lyceum; poems full of power and sweetness; and, better than song or sermon, has lived a life so noble, true, and beautiful, that its wide-spreading influence is felt on both sides of the sea.

In all reforms he was among the foremost on the side of justice and progress. When Faneuil Hall used to be a scene of riot and danger in anti-slavery days, I remember sitting up aloft, an excited girl, among the loyal women who never failed to be there; and how they always looked for that serene face on the platform, and found fresh courage in the mere sight of the wisest man in America, standing shoulder to shoulder with the bravest.

When woman's suffrage was most unpopular, his voice and pen spoke for the just cause, undaunted by the fear of ridicule which silences so many.

His own simple, abstemious habits were his best testimony in favor of temperance in all things; while, in religion, he believed that each soul must choose its own aids, and prove the vitality of its faith by high thinking and holy living.

When travelling in various countries, I found his fame had gone before; and people were eager to hear something of the Concord poet, seer, and philosopher. In a little town upon the Rhine, where our party paused for a night, unexpectedly delayed, two young Germans, reading the word Boston on the labels of our trunks as they stood in the yard of the inn, begged to come in and see the Americans; and their first question was,—

"Tell us about Emerson." We gladly told them what they asked; and they listened as eagerly as we did to any thing we could hear concerning their great countryman, Goethe.

A letter once came to me from the Far West, in which a girl asked what she should read to build up a noble character. It was a remarkable letter; and, when I inquired what books she most desired, she answered, "All of Emerson's: he helps me most."

A prisoner just from Concord jail came to see me on his release, and proved to be an intelligent, book-loving young man, who had been led into crime by his first fit of intoxication. In talking with him, he said Emerson's books were a comfort to him, and he had spent some of the money earned in prison to buy certain volumes to take with him as guides and safeguards for the future.

In England his honored name opened many doors to us, and we felt as proud of our acquaintance with him as Englishmen feel of the medals with which their Queen decorates them; so widely was he known, so helpful was his influence, so ennobling the mere reflection of his virtue and his genius. Longfellow was beloved by children; and of Emerson it might be said, as of Plato, "He walks with his head among the stars, yet carries a blessing in his heart for every little child."

When he returned from his second visit to Europe, after his house was burned, he was welcomed by the schoolchildren, who lined his passage from the cars to the carriage, where a nosegay of blooming grandchildren awaited him; and escorted by a smiling troop of neighbors, old and young, he was conducted under green arches to his house. Here they sang "Sweet Home," gave welcoming cheers, and marched away to come again soon after to a grand house-warming in the old mansion which had been so well restored that nothing seemed changed.

Many a gay revel has been held under the pines, whole schools taking possession of the poet's premises; and many a child will gladly recall hereafter the paternal face that smiled on them, full of interest in their gambols, and of welcome for the poorest. Mrs. Emerson, from her overflowing garden, planted flowers along the roadside, and in the plot of ground before the nearest schoolhouse, to beautify the children's daily life. Sweeter and more imperishable than these will be the recollections of many kindnesses bestowed by one, who, in the truest sense of the word, was a friend to all.

As he lay dying, children stopped to ask if he were better; and all the sunshine faded out of the little faces when the sad answer came. Very willing feet roamed the woods for green garlands to decorate the old church where he would come for the last time; busy hands worked till midnight, that every house should bear some token of mourning; Spring gave him her few early flowers and budding boughs from the haunts that will know him no more; and old and young forgot, for a little while, their pride in the illustrious man, to sorrow for the beloved friend and neighbor.

Life did not sadden his cheerful philosophy; success could not spoil his exquisite simplicity; age could not dismay him, and he met death with sweet serenity.

He wrote, "Nothing can bring you peace but yourself. Nothing can bring you peace but the triumph of principles." And this well-earned peace transfigured the beautiful dead face so many eyes beheld with tender reverence, seeming to assure us that our august friend and master had passed into the larger life, for which he was ready, still to continue,—

> Without hasting, without rest,
> Lifting Better up to Best;
> Planting seeds of knowledge pure.
> Through earth to ripen, through heaven endure.

—Louisa May Alcott, "Reminiscences of
Ralph Waldo Emerson," *Some Noted Princes, Authors,
and Statesmen of Our Time,* ed. James Parton,
1885, pp. 284–88

WILLIAM JAMES "ADDRESS AT THE EMERSON CENTENARY IN CONCORD" (1903)

Philosopher and psychologist William James (brother of Henry and Alice James) served in various faculty positions at Harvard University teaching physiology, anatomy, psychology, and philosophy. James, who developed the philosophical school known as pragmatism, shared many interests with Emerson, including the phenomena of religious experience and mysticism.

James addressed an audience at Concord to commemorate the centennial of Emerson's birth. This address is notable for James's sincere affection for Emerson, but also for his explanation of the value of Emerson's thinking and its influence on America, which he correctly believed would extend far into the future.

James recognizes in Emerson the inseparable connection between the man and his work: "What gave a flavor so matchless to Emerson's individuality was, even more than his rich mental gifts, their singularly harmonious combination." And, later, "genius, as he said, is insatiate for expression, and truth had to be clad in the right verbal garment. The form of the garment was so vital with Emerson that it is impossible to separate it from the matter. . . . The style is the man . . . if we must define him in one word, we have to call him Artist." This combination of man, content, and form echoes throughout contemporary writing on Emerson. Students might especially recall the critical evaluations of Emerson's poetry. A common refrain in that analysis is that Emerson struggles with the form of his poetic expression. However, it might be said that the form is so deeply connected with expression that a conventional evaluation of the poems is too simple to thoroughly cover this issue. Emerson the artist finds the expression best suited for his work. Students exploring Emerson's poetry, or the role of form in Emerson's writing, should take note. The question of whether Emerson's expression supplants conventional notions of form is ripe for investigation.

James also notes Emerson's insistence on the primacy of the individual as central to his thinking; this quality must be understood before an informed reading of Emerson can proceed. Without understanding Emerson's idea that the individual is the conduit for the expression of God in the world, and that the individual soul will find its own unique expression in the world, Emerson becomes merely a teacher and (seemingly) a promoter of a system of belief. This is the notion James summarizes when he writes, "All God's life opens into the individual particular, and here and now, or nowhere, is reality."

James also takes pains to separate Emerson's enthusiastic optimism from mere sentimentality, which stirs emotions with no sense of direction. Emerson's optimism focused on an ever-present divinity in the world, but it was his "perception of differences" that "kept him at the opposite pole from this weakness" of mere sentimentality. James writes, "His optimism had nothing in common with that indiscriminate hurrahing for the Universe with which Walt Whitman has made us familiar." Emerson, instead, insisted that "the individual fact and moment . . . must be worthy specimens,— sincere, authentic, archetypical; they must have made connection with what he calls the Moral Sentiment, they must in some way act as symbolic mouthpieces of the Universe's meaning." Certainly Whitman and Emerson are working with different purposes and modes of expression. James wants us to remember that Emerson's love for all things, his ability to find divinity in all that exists, and his negation of evil as a force in the world is not merely a sentiment born of a flush of feeling, but requires purpose and value. Students researching these aspects of Emerson's thought—the moral requirements for an individual soul to fulfill itself in the world—will do well to consider James's excellent estimation.

⸻ ⸻ ⸻

The pathos of death is this, that when the days of one's life are ended, those days that were so crowded with business and felt so heavy in their passing, what remains of one in memory should usually be so slight a thing. The phantom of an attitude, the echo of a certain mode of thought, a few pages of print, some invention, or some victory we gained in a brief critical hour, are all that can survive the best of us. It is as if the whole of a man's significance had now shrunk into the phantom of an attitude, into a mere musical note or phrase suggestive of his singularity—happy are those whose singularity gives a note so clear as to be victorious over the inevitable pity of such a diminution and abridgement.

An ideal wraith like this, of Emerson's personality, hovers over all Concord today, taking, in the minds of those of you who were his neighbors and intimates a somewhat fuller shape, remaining more abstract in the younger generation, but bringing home to all of us the notion of a spirit indescribably precious. The form that so lately moved upon these streets and country roads, or awaited in these fields and woods the beloved Muse's visits, is now dust; but the soul's note, the spiritual voice, rises strong and clear above the uproar of the times, and seems securely destined to exert an ennobling influence over future generations.

What gave a flavor so matchless to Emerson's individuality was, even more than his rich mental gifts, their singularly harmonious combination. Rarely has a man so accurately known the limits of his genius or so unfailingly kept with them. "Stand by your order," he used to say to youthful students; and perhaps the paramount impression one gets of his life is of his loyalty to his own personal type and mission. The type was that of what he liked to call a scholar, the perceiver of pure truth; and the mission was that of the reporter in worthy form of each perception. The day is good, he said, in which we have the most perceptions. There are times when the cawing of a crow, a weed, a snowflake, or a farmer planting in his field become symbols to the intellect of truths equal to those which the most majestic phenomena can open. Let me mind my own charge, then, walk alone, consult the sky, the field and forest, sedulously waiting every morning for the news concerning the structure of the universe which the good Spirit will give me.

This was the first half of Emerson, but only half; for genius, as he said, is insatiate for expression, and truth has to be clad in the right verbal garment. The form of the garment was so vital with Emerson that it is impossible to separate it from the matter. They form a chemical combination—thoughts which would be trivially expressed otherwise, are important through the nouns and verbs to which he married them. The style is the man, and if we must define him in one word, we have to call him Artist. He was an artist whose medium was verbal and who wrought in spiritual material.

This duty of spiritual seeing and reporting determined the whole tenor of his life. It was to shield this duty from invasion and distraction that he dwelt in the country, that he consistently declined to entangle himself with associations or to encumber himself with functions which, however he might believe in them, he felt were duties for other men and not for him. Even the care of his garden, "with its stoopings and fingers in a few yards of space," he found "narrowing and poisoning," and took to long free walks and saunterings instead, without apology. "Causes" innumerable sought to enlist him as their "worker"—all got his smile and word of sympathy, but none entrapped him into service. The struggle against slavery itself, deeply as it appealed to him, found him firm: "God must govern his own world, and knows his way out of this pit without my desertion of my post, which has none to guard it but me. I have quite other slaves to face than those Negroes, to wit, imprisoned thoughts far back in the brain of man, and which have no watchman or lover or defender but me." This in reply to the possible questions of his own conscience. To hot-blooded moralists with more objective ideas of duty, such fidelity to the limits of his genius must have often made him seem provokingly remote and unavailable; but we, who can see things in moral liberal perspective, must unqualifiably approve the results. The faultless tact with which he kept his safe limits while he so dauntlessly asserted himself within them, is an example fitted to give heart to other theorists and artists the world over.

The insight and creed from which Emerson's life followed can be best summed up in his own verses:

> "So nigh is grandeur to our dust,
> So near is God to man!"

Through the individual fact there ever shone for him the effulgence of the Universal Reason. The great Cosmic Intellect terminates and houses itself in mortal men and passing hours. Each of us is an angle of its eternal vision, and the only way to be true to our Maker is to be loyal to ourselves. "O rich and various Man!" he cries, "thou palace of sight and sound, carrying in thy senses the morning and the night and the unfathomable galaxy; in thy brain the geometry of the city of God; in thy heart the power of love and the realms of right and wrong."

If the individual opens thus directly into the Absolute, it follows that there is something in each and all of us, even the lowliest, that ought not to consent to borrowed traditions and living at second hand. "If John was perfect, why are you and I alive?" Emerson writes; "As long as any man exists there is some need of him: let him fight for his own." This faith that in a life at first hand there is something sacred is perhaps the most characteristic note in Emerson's writings. The hottest side of him is this non-conformist persuasion, and if his temper could ever verge on common irascibility, it would be by reason of the passionate character of his feelings on this point. The world is still new and untried. In seeing freshly, and not in hearing of what others saw, shall a man find what truth is. "Each one of us can bask in the great morning which rises out of the Eastern Sea, and be himself one of the children of the light." "Trust thyself, every heart vibrates to that iron string. There is a time in each man's education when he must arrive at the conviction that limitation is suicide; that he must take himself for better or worse as his portion; and know that though the wide universe is full of good, no kernel of nourishing corn can come to him but through his toil bestowed on that plot of ground which it was given him to till."

The matchless eloquence with which Emerson proclaimed the sovereignty of the living individual electrified and emancipated his generation, and this bugle-blast will doubtless be regarded by future critics as the soul of his message. The present man is the aboriginal reality, the Institution is derivative, and the past man is irrelevant and obliterate for present issues. "If anyone would lay an axe to your tree with a text from I John, v, 7, or a sentence from Saint Paul, say to him," Emerson wrote, "'My tree is Yggdrasil, the tree of life.' Let him know by your security that your conviction is clear and sufficient, and, if he were Paul himself, that you also are here and with your Creator;" "Cleave ever to God," he insisted "against the name of God;"—and so, in spite of the intensely religious character of his total thought, when he began his career it seemed to many of his brethren in the clerical profession that he was little more than an iconoclast and desecrator.

Emerson's belief that the individual must in reason be adequate to the vocation for which the Spirit of the world has called him into being, is the source of those sublime pages, hearteners and sustainers of our youth, in which he urges his hearers to be incorruptibly true to their own private conscience. Nothing can harm the man who rests in his appointed place and character. Such a man is invulnerable; he balances the universe, balances it as much by keeping small when he is small, by being great and spreading when he is great. "I love and honor Epaminondas," said Emerson, "but I do not wish to be Epaminondas. I hold it more just to love the world of this hour than the world of his hour. Nor can you, if I am true, excite me to the least uneasiness by saying, 'He acted and thou sittest still.' I see action to be good when the need is, and sitting still to be also good. Epaminondas, if he was the man I take him for, would have sat still with joy and peace, if his lot had been mine. Heaven is large and affords space for all modes of love and fortitude." "The fact that I am here certainly shows me that the Soul has need of an organ here, and shall I not assume the post?"

The vanity of all superserviceableness and pretence was never more happily set forth than by Emerson in the many passages in which he develops this aspect of his philosophy. Character infallibly proclaims itself. "Hide your thoughts!—hide the sun and moon. They publish themselves to the universe. They will speak through you though you were dumb. They will flow out of your actions, your manners and your face. . . . Don't say things: What you are stands over you the while and thunders so that I cannot hear what you say to the contrary. . . . What a man *is* engraves itself upon him in letters of light. Concealment avails him nothing, boasting nothing. There is confession in the glances of our eyes; in our smiles; in salutations; and the grasp of hands. His sin bedaubs him, mars all his good impression. Men know not why they do not trust him, but they do not trust him. His vice glasses the eye, casts lines of mean expression in the cheek, pinches the nose, sets the mark of the beast upon the back of the head, and writes, O fool! fool! on the forehead of a king. If you would not be known to do a thing, never do it; a man may play the fool in the drifts of the desert, but every grain of sand shall seem to see—How can a man be concealed? How can he be concealed?"

On the other hand, never was a sincere word or a sincere thought utterly lost. "Never a magnanimity fell to the ground but there is some heart to greet and accept it unexpectedly. . . . The hero fears not that if he withstood the avowal of a just and brave act, it will go unwitnessed and unloved. One knows it,—himself—and is pledged by it to sweetness of peace and nobleness of aim, which will prove in the end a better proclamation than the relating of the incident."

The same indefeasible right to be exactly what one is, provided one only be authentic, spreads itself, in Emerson's way of thinking, from persons to things and to times and places. No date, no position is insignificant, if the life that fills it out be only genuine:

"In solitude, in a remote village, the ardent youth loiters and mourns. With inflamed eye, in this sleeping wilderness, he has read the story of the Emperor, Charles the Fifth, until his fancy has brought home to the surrounding woods the faint roar of cannonades in the Milanese, and marches in Germany. He is curious concerning that man's day. What filled it? the crowded orders, the stern decisions, the foreign despatches, the Castellan etiquette? The soul answers—Behold his day here! In the sighing of these woods, in the quiet of these gray fields, in the cool breeze that sings out of these northern mountains; in the workmen, the boys, the maidens, you meet,—in the hopes of the morning, the ennui of noon, and sauntering of the afternoon; in the disquieting comparisons; in the regrets at want of vigor; in the great idea, and the puny execution,—behold Charles the Fifth's day; another, yet the same; behold Chatham's, Hampden's, Bayard's, Alfred's, Scipio's, Pericles's day,—day of all that are born of women. The difference of circumstance is merely costume. I am tasting the self-same life,—its sweetness, its greatness, its pain, which I so admire in other men. Do not foolishly ask of the inscrutable, obliterated past, what it cannot tell,—the details of that nature, of that day, called Byron, or Burke;—but ask it of the enveloping Now . . . Be lord of a day, and you can put up your history books."

"The deep today which all men scorn" receives thus from Emerson superb revindication. "Other world! there is no other world." All God's life opens into the individual particular, and here and now, or nowhere, is reality. "The present hour is the decisive hour, and every day is doomsday."

Such a conviction that Divinity is everywhere may easily make of one an optimist of the sentimental type that refuses to speak ill of anything. Emerson's drastic perception of differences kept him at the opposite pole from this weakness. After you have seen men a few times, he could say, you find most of them as alike as their barns and pantries, and soon as musty and dreary. Never was such a fastidious lover of significance and distinction, and never an eye so keen for their discovery. His optimism had nothing in common with that indiscriminate hurrahing for the Universe with which Walt Whitman has made us familiar. For Emerson, the individual fact and moment were indeed suffused with absolute radiance, but it was upon a condition that saved the situation—they must be worthy specimens,—sincere, authentic, archetypical; they must have made connection with what he calls the Moral Sentiment, they must in some way act as symbolic mouthpieces of the Universe's meaning. To know just which thing does act in this way, and which thing fails to make the true connection, is the secret (somewhat incommunicable, it must be confessed) of seership, and doubtless we must not expect of the seer too rigorous a consistency. Emerson himself was a real seer. He could perceive the full squalor of the individual fact, but he could also see the transfiguration. He might easily have found himself saying of some present-day agitator against our Philippine conquest what he said of this or that reformer of his own time. He might have called him, as a private person, a tedious bore and canter. But he would infallibly have added what he then added: "It is strange and horrible to say this, for I feel that under him and his partiality and exclusiveness is the earth and the sea, and all that in them is, and the axis round which the Universe revolves passes through his body where he stands."

Be it how it may, then, this is Emerson's revelation: The point of any pen can be an epitome of reality; the commonest person's act, if genuinely actuated, can lay hold of eternity. This vision is the head-spring of all his outpourings; and it is for this truth, given to no previous literary artist to express in such penetratingly persuasive tones, that prosperity will reckon him a prophet, and perhaps neglecting other pages, piously turn to those that covey this message. His life was one long conversation with the invisible divine, expressing itself through individuals and particulars: "So nigh is grandeur to our dust, so near is God to man!"

I spoke of how shrunken the wraith, how thin the echo, of men is after they are departed. Emerson's wraith comes to me now as if it were but the very voice of this victorious argument. His words to this effect are certain to be quoted and extracted more and more as time goes on, and to take their place among the Scriptures of humanity. "'Gainst death and all oblivious enmity, shall you pace forth," beloved Master. As long as our English language lasts men's hearts will be cheered and their souls strengthened and liberated by the noble and musical pages with which you have enriched it.

—William James, Address at the
Emerson Centenary in Concord (May 25, 1903),
from *Memories and Studies*, 1911, pp. 19–34

GENERAL

Sampson Reed "Preface" (1838)

Sampson Reed and Emerson attended Harvard Divinity School at the same time, though Reed was the older and more self-assured student. In 1834 Emerson wrote to James Freeman Clarke, "I rejoice to be contemporary with [Reed], and cannot wholly despair of the society in which he lives." Reed first introduced Emerson to the work of Emanuel Swedenborg. The theologian and philosopher's writings had a profound impact on Emerson (as well as on the transcendentalist movement), but Emerson read and learned of Swedenborg's ideas (among them that nature is the symbol of spirit, the universe is the externalization of the soul, or the "doctrine of correspondence," that each person has a specific individual use, best developed through his or her character, and other key concepts outlined in "Nature") from Sampson Reed, who unlike Emerson was able to read and translate the Latin of Swedenborg's original texts.

This essay, Reed's preface to the 1838 edition of his book *Observations on the Growth of the Mind*, is important because he uses the opportunity to establish a clean break between the New Jerusalem Church (Swedenborg's followers) and Emersonian transcendentalism. While Emerson continued to value his friendship with Sampson Reed throughout his life (he praised Reed highly in his letters, journals, and in the essay "Swedenborg; or, The Mystic" in *Representative Men*), Reed sought to separate Swedenborg's "true" teachings from what he considered to be their misuse by Emerson. When Reed writes, "The New Church can discern, in almost every moral or religious writer of any acknowledged merit at the present day, some outbreakings of its own power. . . . It is painful to see how little willingness there is to acknowledge the source of truth; and how often a man seems to think that it has answered its legitimate purpose, when he has bedecked his own person therewith, so as to command the admiration of the multitude," he is surely referring to Emerson and his (perceived) misuse of Swedenborg's ideas.

Emerson certainly borrowed from many sources, and scholars have argued that Emerson took what he wanted and shaped ideas to his own purpose. But few writers had as significant an impact on his thinking as Swedenborg, and Sampson Reed's response suggests that misuse of the "truth" is immoral—a charge that may have wounded Emerson, who believed that the perception of truth represented a moral condition. Readers should note that *sensualism* was a loaded term in nineteenth-century theological discourse; it suggested abandoning concentration on the soul for the sake of luxury, an idea Emerson (who taught that preachers should be poets and embrace beauty and luxury) encouraged.

Nevertheless, Reed plays a significant role in Emerson's career, both
through his own writing and through his connection to Swedenborg.
Students examining the foundations of Emerson's spiritual and aesthetic
thought would do well to consider this preface as a starting point for a
critique of Emerson's borrowings from Swedenborg.

⋙— —⋙— —⋙—

"The Growth of the Mind" has now been through two editions in this
country, and one in England. It has been received with a degree of favor,
though not great, yet sufficient to make me sometimes distrustful of
its merit; and frequently apprehensive that its meaning was not fully
understood and received. That this has sometimes been the case, I have
known to be the fact.

So far as an author duly feels in whose presence he stands, it can be no
source of gratification to him to attract personal admiration or praise. He
must regard himself as only a medium of truth from the one only Source of
truth, and the forms in which he has been permitted to present it, as useful
only so far as they are suitable vessels to contain and to communicate it.
Truth itself—simple—unadorned—divine—is at the present day revealed, yet
noticed and loved by few. The King of Kings and Lord of Lords is standing in
the midst of us; "but he hath no form nor comeliness; and when we shall see
him, there is no beauty that we should desire him." The spiritual sense of the
Sacred Scripture is opened; "yet is it despised and rejected of men."

The present age is characterised by the love of pleasing, as opposed to
the love of truth. Fashionable education, as it is often pursued, may almost
be defined the cultivation of the art of pleasing. This is but too frequently
the end for which so much labor is bestowed, by which a wardrobe of
accomplishments is provided, which may be used as occasion requires. When
the disposition to please takes the first place, it is obvious that truth must be
sought only as it is subservient to this object. "How can ye believe who seek
honor one of another, and seek not that honor which cometh from God only."
The love of pleasing is opposed to the love of truth, when a person desires
to please others, in order that he may gain an influence over them, for the
sake of promoting his own private ends or personal advantage. The love of
pleasing is consistent with the love of truth, when a person desires to please,
for the sake of promoting the good of others, and the cause of truth itself.

The New Church can discern, in almost every moral or religious writer
of any acknowledged merit at the present day, some outbreakings of its own
power; while its principles are pressing into the natural sciences, like so many

gushing fountains from an inexhaustible fountain above than. It is painful to see how little willingness there is to acknowledge the source of truth; and how often a man seems to think that it has answered its legitimate purpose, when he has bedecked his own person therewith, so as to command the admiration of the multitude.

But the time is approaching when the claims of the New Church on the public attention may not be easily set aside. There is a problem to solve, to which those who reject the claims of this Church, will find it difficult to furnish a solution; and the misrepresentations and ignorance which have often prevailed in regard to it, will, before many years, be seen to be neither consistent with good manners nor good scholarship. The writings of Swedenborg are so pure in their character and influence, that the moral reuse of the community will bear testimony that there is no wilful imposture; and they are so perfect in their method and logic, that the rationality of the community will bear testimony that there is no insanity. The voice of these two witnesses cannot be silenced; and the day is approaching, when the assertion that these writings are not of sufficient importance to command the attention of the public, will not be hazarded by any one, who either is a man of intelligence or seeks to be so esteemed.

Still the natural mind is ever backward to receive *revealed truth*, both from the character of this truth itself, and from the fact of its being revealed— from the character of the truth, because it is opposed to the affections and principles of the natural mind, and calculated to reform and regenerate them—from the fact of its being revealed, because it leaves no place for the pride of discovery. "Whosoever will, let him take the water of life freely." The water of life is really as free as natural water; and this we all know is the common gift of Providence to man and beast. But the condition is, that we should *will to receive it*—that we should acknowledge it to be the water of life, and endeavor to live from it—that we should seek to be purified and regenerated by its influence. And alas! how few are disposed to comply with these conditions, and how much do these find in themselves, which requires to be subdued and put away!

From these causes it is not to be expected that the truths of the spiritual sense of the Sacred Scripture, which the Lord has now revealed through his servant Emanuel Swedenborg, will find a very ready reception. *Transcendentalism*[1] will rather be caressed. This is the product of man's own brain; and when the human mind has been compelled to relax its grasp on sensualism, and the philosophy based on the senses, it may be expected first to take refuge here. *Transcendentalism*, even now, offers indications of an approaching popularity in this country. It may be something gained, when the idolater no longer literally worships the work of its own hands; even though he be in heart an idolater still, and worship the creations of his own imagination. So it may be a step forwards from *sensualism* to *transcendentalism*. It may be a necessary step in the progress of the human mind. But they still lie near each other—almost in contact. There is among insects a class called parasites. Their instinct leads them to deposit their eggs in the bodies of other insects, where, when the young is hatched, it has only to open its mouth and eat up its brother. It would seem to be in a way analogous to this, that Providence often permits one falsity to be removed by another. *Transcendentalism* is the parasite of *sensualism*; and when it shall have done its work, it will be found to be itself a worm, and the offspring of a worm.

The Sacred Scripture is the only door through which we can enter into life, or receive living truths; and all who would climb up any other way are thieves and robbers. Imagining themselves spiritual, it is possible that they should be even the lowest of the sensual—for they may only give to their sensuality wings, by which it may gain an apparent elevation without any real change in its nature—superadding to its inherent properties that of monstrosity—becoming a winged serpent—the monstrous offspring of the infernal influence and a vain imagination. "On thy belly shalt thou go, and dust shalt thou eat, all the days of thy life," is with the serpent the law of its nature; and any attempt to *transcend* this law must rather debase than elevate it. If it presume to raise itself into the air, and live on the nectar of flowers, its real quality will become the more apparent and disgusting—it will only defile what can afford it no nutriment, and all the birds of heaven will instinctively shun its company. Let everyone know, therefore, that his real faith in the Sacred Scripture and humble dependence upon it for life and light, are the only measure of his spirituality—that whatever seems to abound more than these, is nothing, or worse than nothing. Such "sons of the morning" may be expected in these latter times—for the morning has indeed come, and, with the beginning of a brighter day than the world has yet seen, are awakened into life forms as monstrous as those of the dark ages.

In conclusion, I would dedicate this volume to the New Church and to those who are approaching it. By the approbation of that Church I shall always be strengthened, and encouraged by the approbation of those who are not of the Church, so far as it affords indications that they are drawing near to it. I have been cheered by a knowledge of the fact, that in some instances, at least, this book has been instrumental in directing the feet of the reader to the "New Jerusalem, which is descending from God out of heaven."

S. R.

Boston, Feb. 28, 1838

Note

1. By *transcendentalism*, I mean such transcendentalism as we now find, without any reference to its origin, or to the original meaning of the word.

—Sampson Reed, Preface, *Observations on
the Growth of the Mind*, 1838, pp. iiv–viii

Orestes Augustus Brownson
"Emerson's Essays" (1841)

Emerson's colleague Orestes Brownson makes the significant claim that Emerson "is no philosopher" by determining, in a general sense, what philosophy is, and how Emerson's work differs. Emerson is not a systematic thinker; his value lies in his ability to break the associations of common perception, and allow readers to see and perceive the world in a new aspect. This is important, since visual metaphors and the faculty of sight recur in Emerson's work.

Mr. Emerson, to speak scientifically, is no philosopher. He is a philosopher neither in the order of his mind, nor in his method of investigation. He explains nothing, accounts for nothing, solves no intellectual problem, and affords no practical instruction. He proposes nothing of all this, and, therefore, is not to be censured for not doing it. He is to be regarded as a Seer, who rises into the regions of the Transcendental, and reports what he sees, and in the order in which he sees it. His worth can be determined, that is, the accuracy of his reports can be properly judged of, by none except those who rise to the same regions, and behold the universe from the same point of view.

Writers like Mr. Emerson are seldom to be consulted for clear, logical, systematic expositions of any subject or doctrine, never for the purpose of taking them as teachers or guides in the formation of opinions; but for the suggestions, the incentives to thought they furnish, and the life they kindle up within us. They are thought by some to be writers without any practical value for mankind; but they have, in fact, a very high practical value; only not of the every-day sort, only not that of dogmatic teachers or scientific expositors. They present new aspects of things, or at least old familiar objects in new dresses, the various subjects of thought and inquiry in new relations, break up old associations, and excite to greater and fresher mental activity. After having read them, we cannot say that we are wiser or more learned than we were before; we cannot say that we have become acquainted with any new facts in the history of man or of the universe, or that we have any new ideas in regard to the human soul or its Creator; but we feel, that somehow or other new virtue has been imparted to us, that a change has come over us, and that we are no longer what we were, but greater and better.

These are not the only writers we need; but they have their place, and one of high trust, and of no slight influence. Their influence is not sudden, noisy, obvious to all senses, but slow, silent, subtle, permanent, entering into and becoming an integrant part of the life of the age, sometimes of the ages. They live and exert a power over the souls of men, long after their names are forgotten, and their works have ceased to be read. They are never in vogue with the multitude, but they are admired in select circles, who inhale their spirit, and breathe it into other and larger circles, who in their turn breathe it into the souls of all men. Though they may seem to have no practical aim, and no reference to every-day life, they have in the end a most important practical bearing, and exert a controlling influence over even the business concerns of the world. Let no one, then, regard them as mere idle dreamers, as mere literary toys, with whose glitter we may amuse ourselves, but without significance for the world of reality. They appear always for good or evil, and their appearance usually marks an epoch.

—Orestes Augustus Brownson, "Emerson's Essays,"
Boston Quarterly Review, July 1841, p. 292

CAROLINE FOX "JOURNAL" (1841)

J. Sterling showed me Emerson's book *(Essays)*, and drew a parallel between him and Carlyle; he was the Plato, and Carlyle the Tacitus. Emerson is the systematic thinker; Carlyle has the clearer insight, and has many deeper things than Emerson.

—Caroline Fox, *Journal* (June 8, 1841),
Memories of Old Friends,
ed. Horace N. Pym, 1882, p. 140

THOMAS CARLYLE "PREFACE BY THE ENGLISH EDITOR" (1841)

Emerson's relationship with Thomas Carlyle is among the most interesting subjects in Emerson studies. It might be said that each writer found in the other his ideal reader. Certainly in Carlyle, Emerson found a reader of like sympathies and sharp, accurate critical opinion. This makes Carlyle's writings on Emerson especially useful for students.

The purpose of Carlyle's essay is to introduce Emerson's *Essays* (1841) to an English audience. (Similarly, Emerson prepared an introduction for Carlyle's *Sartor Resartus* for American publication.) Carlyle's assessment of the book reveals much about the tastes and proclivities of the English reading public, but more importantly contextualizes Emerson's value beyond his first book of collected essays.

Carlyle qualifies Emerson as an isolationist, as "silently communing with his own soul," but students should be careful to read this description in context. Carlyle is writing for his "never-resting locomotive country"; his comment reflects Emerson's stillness, a quality Carlyle much admires. Students writing about perceptions of Emerson, though, should be careful to avoid the too-easy qualification of Emerson as a thinker in isolation, removed for the influences of his time. And, though Carlyle lists social and political concerns of the times, such as "Pleasures of Virtue, Progress of the Species, Black Emancipation, New Tarif, Eclecticism, Locofocoism, ghost of Improved-Socinianism," students should note that Emerson did not willingly remove himself from the issues of the day. Instead, Emerson, living and working in the intellectual hotbeds of Concord and Boston, was well aware of the political and social climate of his day; for example, he was an outspoken abolitionist and shared George Ripley and Bronson Alcott's interest in educational reform.

Carlyle also approaches another salient point in this essay: if we think of Emerson as a philosopher in a classical sense (meaning Emerson's work comprises an organized system), Carlyle writes, "That this little Book has no 'system,' and points or stretches far beyond all systems, is one of its merits." Indeed, Emerson might not be considered a philosopher in the strictest sense, because his body of work is difficult to reduce to an organized system of proofs. However, Emerson might be thought of as a philosopher destroying classical notions of philosophy. Students interested in the ongoing debate over Emerson's status in this regard would do well to consider Carlyle's argument here. As Carlyle suggests,

Emerson's *Essays* reaches beyond philosophy, a trait he considers a
particular strength of Emerson's unique iconoclasm.

—⁄⁄⁄— —⁄⁄⁄— —⁄⁄⁄—

To the great reading public entering Mr. Fraser's and other shops in quest
of daily provender, it may be as well to state, on the very threshold, that this
little Reprint of an American Book of Essays is in no wise the thing suited for
them; that not the great reading public, but only the small thinking public,
and perhaps only a portion of these, have any question to ask concerning it.
No Editor or Reprinter can expect such a Book ever to become popular here.
But, thank Heaven, the small thinking public has now also a visible existence
among us, is visibly enlarging itself. At the present time it can be predicted,
what some years ago it could not be, that a certain number of human creatures
will be found extant in England to whom the words of a man speaking from
the heart of him, in what fashion soever, under what obstructions soever, will
be welcome;—welcome, perhaps, as a brother's voice, to 'wanderers in the
labyrinthic Night!' For those, and not for any other class of persons, is this
little Book reprinted and recommended. Let such read, and try; ascertain
for themselves, whether this *is* a kind of articulate human voice speaking
words, or only another of the thousand thousand ventriloquisms, mimetic
echoes, hysteric shrieks, hollow laughters, and mere inarticulate mechanical
babblements, the soul-confusing din of which already fills all places? I will not
anticipate their verdict; but I reckon it safe enough, and even a kind of duty
in these circumstances, to invite them to *try.*

The name of Ralph Waldo Emerson is not entirely new in England:
distinguished Travellers bring us tidings of such a man; fractions of his
writings have found their way into the hands of the curious here; fitful hints
that there is, in New England, some spiritual Notability called Emerson,
glide through Reviews and Magazines. Whether these hints were true or not
true, readers are now to judge for themselves a little better.

Emerson's writings and speakings amount to something:—and yet
hitherto, as seems to me, this Emerson is perhaps far less notable for what
he has spoken or done, than for the many things he has not spoken and has
forborne to do. With uncommon interest I have learned that this, and in such
a never-resting locomotive country too, is one of those rare men who have
withal the invaluable talent of sitting still! That an educated man of good gifts
and opportunities, after looking at the public arena, and even trying, not with
ill success, what its tasks and its prizes might amount to, should retire for long
years into rustic obscurity; and, amid the all-pervading jingle of dollars and

loud chaffering of ambitions and promotions, should quietly, with cheerful deliberateness, sit down to spend *his* life not in Mammon-worship, or the hunt for reputation, influence, place or any outward advantage whatsoever: this, when we get notice of it, is a thing really worth noting. As Paul Louis Courrier said: "*Ce qui me distingue de tous mes contemporains c'est que je n'ai pas la pretention d'etre roi.*" 'All my contemporaries,'—poor contemporaries! It is as if the man said: Yes, ye contemporaries, be it known to you, or let it remain unknown, There is one man who does not need to be a king; king neither of nations, nor of parishes or cliques, nor even of *cent-per-annums;* nor indeed of anything at all save of himself only. 'Realities?' Yes, your dollars are real, your cotton and molasses are real; so are Presidentships, Senatorships, celebrations, reputations, and the wealth of Rothschild: but to me, on the whole, they are not the reality that will suffice. To me, without some other reality, they are mockery, and amount to *zero,* nay to a negative quantity. ETERNITIES surround this god-given Life of mine: what will all the dollars in creation do for me? Dollars, dignities, senate-addresses, review-articles, gilt coaches or cavalcades, with world-wide huzzaings and particoloured beef-eaters never so many: O Heaven, what were all these? Behold, ye shall have all these, and I will endeavour for a thing other than these. Behold, we will entirely agree to differ in this matter; I to be in your eyes nothing, you to be something, to be much, to be all things:—wherefore, adieu in God's name; go ye that way, I go this!—Pity that a man, for such cause, should be so distinguished from *all* his contemporaries! It is a misfortune partly of these our peculiar times. Times and nations of any strength have always privately held in them many such men. Times and nations that hold none or few of such, may indeed seem to themselves strong and great, but are only bulky, loud; no heart or solidity in them;—*great,* as the blown bladder is, which by and by will collapse and become small enough!

For myself I have looked over with no common feeling to this brave Emerson, seated by his rustic hearth, on the other side of the Ocean (yet not altogether parted from me either), silently communing with his own soul, and with the God's World it finds itself alive in yonder. Pleasures of Virtue, Progress of the Species, Black Emancipation, New Tarif, Eclecticism, Locofocoism, ghost of Improved-Socinianism: these with many other ghosts and substances are squeaking, jabbering, according to their capabilities, round this man; to one man among the sixteen millions their jabber is all unmusical. The silent voices of the Stars above, and of the green Earth beneath, are profitabler to him,—**tell** him gradually that these others are but ghosts, which will shortly have to vanish; that the Life-Fountain these proceeded out of does not vanish! The words of such a man, what words he finds good to speak, are worth attending to. By degrees a small circle of living souls eager to hear is gathered. The silence of this man has to become speech: may this too, in its due season, prosper for him!—Emerson has gone to lecture, various times, to special audiences, in Boston, and occasionally elsewhere. Three of those Lectures, already printed, are known to some here; as is the little Pamphlet called *Nature*, of somewhat earlier date. It may be said, a great meaning lies in these pieces, which as yet finds no adequate expression for itself. A noteworthy though very unattractive work, moreover, is that new Periodical they call *The Dial*, in which he occasionally writes; which appears indeed generally to be imbued with his way of thinking, and to proceed from the circle that learns of him. This present little Volume of *Essays*, printed in Boston a few months ago, is Emerson's first Book. An unpretending little Book, composed probably, in good part, from mere Lectures which already lay written. It affords us, on several sides, in such manner as it can, a direct glimpse into the man and that spiritual world of his.

Emerson, I understand, was bred to Theology; of which primary bent his latest way of thought still bears traces. In a very enigmatic way, we hear much of the 'universal soul,' of the &c. &c.: flickering like bright bodiless Northern Streamers, notions and half-notions of a metaphysic, theosophic, theologic kind are seldom long wanting in these Essays. I do not advise the British Public to trouble itself much with all that; still less, to take offence at it. Whether this Emerson be 'a Pantheist,' or what kind of Theist or *Ist* he may be, can perhaps as well remain undecided. If he prove a devout-minded, veritable, original man, this for the present will suffice. *Ists* and *Isms* are rather growing a weariness. Such a man does not readily range himself under *Isms*. A man to whom the 'open secret of the universe' is no longer a closed one, what can his *speech* of it be in these days? All human speech, in the best days, all human thought that can or could articulate itself in reference to such things, what is it but the eager stammering and struggling as of a wondering infant,—in view of the Unnameable! That this little Book has no 'system,' and points or stretches far beyond all systems, is one of its merits. We will call it the soliloquy of a true soul, alone under the stars, in this day. In England as elsewhere the voice of a true soul, *any* voice of such, may be welcome to some. For in England as elsewhere old dialects and formulas are mostly lying dead: some dim suspicion, or clear knowledge, indicates on all hands that they are as good as dead;—and how can the skilfullest *galvanizing* make them any more live? For they are dead: and their galvanic motions, O Heavens, are not of a pleasant sort!—That one man more, in the most modern dialect of this year 1841, recognises the oldest everlasting truths: here is a thing worth seeing, among the others. One man more who knows, and believes of very certainty, that Man's Soul is still alive, that God's Universe is still godlike, that of all Ages of Miracles ever seen, or dreamt of, by far the most miraculous is this age in this hour; and who with all these devout beliefs has dared, like a valiant man, to bid chimeras, "*Be* chimerical; disappear, and let us have an end of you!"—is not this worth something? In a word, while so many Benthamisms, Socialisms, Fourrierisms, *professing* to have no soul, go staggering and lowing like monstrous mooncalves, the product of a heavy-laden moonstruck age; and, in this same baleful 'twelfth hour of the night,' even galvanic Puseyisms, as we say, are visible, and dancings of the sheeted dead,—shall not any voice of a living man be welcome to us, even because it is alive?

For the rest, what degree of mere literary talent lies in these utterances, is but a secondary question; which every reader may gradually answer for himself. What Emerson's talent is, we will not altogether estimate by this Book. The utterance is abrupt, fitful; the great idea not yet embodied struggles towards an embodiment. Yet everywhere there is the true heart of a man; which is the parent of all talent; which without much talent cannot exist. A breath as of the green country,—all the welcomer that it is New-England country, not second-hand but first-hand country,—meets us wholesomely everywhere in these *Essays:* the authentic green Earth is there, with her mountains, rivers, with her mills and farms. Sharp gleams of insight arrest us by their pure intellectuality; here and there, in heroic rusticism, a tone of modest manfulness, of mild invincibility, low-voiced but lion-strong, makes us too thrill with a noble pride. Talent? Such ideas as dwell in this man, how can they ever speak themselves with *enough* of talent? The talent is not the chief question here. The idea, that is the chief question. Of the living acorn you do not ask first, How *large* an acorn art thou? The smallest living acorn is fit to be the parent of oaktrees without end,—could clothe all New England with oaktrees by and by. You ask it, first of all: Art thou a living acorn? Certain, now, that thou art not a dead mushroom, as the most are?—

But, on the whole, our Book is short; the Preface should not grow too long. Closing these questionable parables and intimations, let me in plain English recommend this little Book as the Book of an original veridical man, worthy the acquaintance of those who delight in such; and so: Welcome to it whom it may concern!

—Thomas Carlyle, "Preface by the English Editor"
to *Essays,* 1841, pp. v–xiii

Edgar Allan Poe
"A Chapter on Autography"
(1842)

Poe's criticism of Emerson—*cui bono?* ("Whom does it benefit?" or "For whom is it good?")—is indicative of criticism of transcendentalism from writers (notably southern and western) outside the New England transcendentalist circle. For many, Emerson's writing seemed abstract and vague. Poe's joke perhaps works on a deeper level because Emerson did not read Latin; he borrowed freely from a variety of sources and relied on English translations.

It is noticeable, though, that Poe, as serious and studied a poet as any writing in the nineteenth century, finds "beauty is apparent *by flashes*" in Emerson's poetry, which suggests that Poe does not reject all of Emerson's work. He seems instead to respond most positively to Emerson's formal poetic style. Students concerned with how Emerson was read by contemporaries who were not part of his immediate circle might consider the reasons underlying Poe's critical views.

Mr. Ralph Waldo Emerson belongs to a class of gentlemen with whom we have no patience whatever—the mystics for mysticism's sake. Quintilian mentions a pedant who taught obscurity, and who once said to a pupil "this is excellent, for I do not understand it myself." How the good man would have chuckled over Mr. E.! His present *role* seems to be the out-Carlyling Carlyle. *Lycophron Tenebrosus* is a fool to him. The best answer to his twaddle is *cui bono?*—a very little Latin phrase very generally mistranslated and misunderstood—*cui bono?*—to whom is it a benefit? If not to Mr. Emerson individually, then surely to no man living.

His love of the obscure does not prevent him, nevertheless, from the composition of occasional poems in which beauty is apparent *by flashes.* Several of his effusions appeared in the *Western Messenger*—more in the *Dial,* of which he is the soul—or the sun—or the shadow. We remember the "Sphynx," the "Problem," the "Snow Storm," and some fine old-fashioned verses entitled "Oh fair and stately maid whose eye."

—Edgar Allan Poe, "A Chapter on Autography" (1842),
Complete Works, ed. James A. Harrison,
1902, Vol. 15, p. 260

Henry David Thoreau "Journal" (1845–47)

Perhaps Emerson's most famous friendship was with fellow New England essayist and poet Henry David Thoreau. Thoreau lived with the Emerson family for several years, and the cabin he built near Walden Pond was situated on land owned by Emerson. The mutual influence between Emerson and Thoreau is impossible to overstate.

Thoreau's insight into Emerson is uniquely personal as well as highly literary in tone. For students interested in Emerson's various careers as lecturer, essayist, and poet, Thoreau's journal entry here helps tie these activities together. Emerson is, in Thoreau's accurate definition of his work, a "poetic critic, reserving the unqualified nouns for the gods." Students should note Thoreau's evaluation of Emerson's uniqueness. Emerson wrote, and created expression, unlike any writer in the nineteenth century, even among his contemporaries. This quality is hard to identify, and Thoreau chooses to do so by affirming Emerson's higher nature, his "special talents unequalled." While Thoreau's description seems highly idealized, students should note the qualities Thoreau enumerates early in this excerpt; the tone is elevated, but the qualities Thoreau identifies are commonly mentioned in other critiques of Emerson as a person and a writer.

Emerson again is a critic, poet, philosopher, with talent not so conspicuous, not so adequate to his task; but his field is still higher, his task more arduous. Lives a far more intense life; seeks to realize a divine life; his affections and intellect equally developed. Has advanced farther, and a new heaven opens to him. Love and Friendship, Religion, Poetry, the Holy are familiar to him. The life of an Artist; more variegated, more observing, finer perception; not so robust, elastic; practical enough in his own field; faithful, a judge of men. There is no such general critic of men and things, no such trustworthy and faithful man. More of the divine realized in him than in any. A poetic critic, reserving the unqualified nouns for the gods.

Emerson has special talents unequalled. The divine in man has had no more easy, methodically distinct expression. His personal influence upon young persons greater than any man's. In his world every man would be a poet, Love would reign, Beauty would take place, Man and Nature would harmonize. . . .

Emerson does not consider things in respect to their essential utility, but an important partial and relative one, as works of art perhaps. His probes pass one side of their centre of gravity. His exaggeration is of a part, not of the whole.

—Henry David Thoreau, *Journal* (1845–47),
Writings, 1906, Vol. 7, pp. 431–33

Theodore Parker "The Writings of Ralph Waldo Emerson" (1850)

Theodore Parker's influence on American theology in the nineteenth century is hard to overstate. Parker was a Unitarian minister, theologian, abolitionist and social reformer, qualities he shared with Emerson. Parker's concerns about the state of the Christian Church coincide with Emerson's own, though Parker remained within the confines of the Church, whereas Emerson chose to leave his pastoral career. There is, perhaps, no more informed commentator on Emerson in the nineteenth century than Theodore Parker.

Parker notes Emerson's writing as directed toward the interest of all of mankind, rather than the interest of any particular party or cause. As Parker notes, this does indeed separate Emerson from the intellectual trends of his time. Emerson was a writer in social context, and he was not immune to the political, social, and reform causes to which he was exposed (and often supported, such as Brook Farm, women's suffrage, the abolitionist movement, and educational reform). However, Parker's observation is that Emerson strove to avoid specific affiliations in his work, which accounts for a universal appeal, and for Emerson as a writer not merely of historical interest, but one "to write for the future." Students writing on Emerson's place in literary history should note Parker's keen observation, which indeed serves to explain Emerson's unique standing in American literary studies, past and present.

⸺⧫⧫⸻ ⸺⧫⧫⸻ ⸺⧫⧫⸻

He has not written a line which is not considered in the interest of mankind. He never writes in the interest of a section, of a party, of a church, of a man, always in the interest of mankind. Hence comes the ennobling influence of his works. Most of the literary men of America, most of the men of superior education, represent the ideas and interests of some party; in all that concerns the welfare of the Human Race, they are proportionably behind the mass who have only the common culture; so while the thought of the people is democratic, putting man before the accidents of man, the literature of the nation is aristocratic, and opposed to the welfare of mankind. Emerson belongs to the exceptional literature of the times—and while his culture joins him to the history of man, his ideas and his whole life enable him to represent also the nature of man, and so to write for the future. He is one of the rare exceptions amongst our educated men, and helps redeem American literature from the reproach of imitation, conformity, meanness of aim, and hostility to the progress of mankind. No faithful man is too low for his approval and encouragement; no faithless man too high and popular for his rebuke.

—Theodore Parker, "The Writings of Ralph Waldo Emerson,"
Massachusetts Quarterly Review, March 1850, p. 254

THOMAS BABINGTON MACAULAY "JOURNAL" (1850)

Thomas Babington Macaulay, English historian and politician, composed the five-volume *History of England*, in addition to contributing historical and literary essays to the *Edinburgh Review*. Macaulay's style is straightforward and his views uncompromising, as is reflected in this excerpt from his journal.

Macaulay's point is a noteworthy one: we should work to make literature clear, not confusing or empty, a quality he celebrates in Herodotus. But note the language Macaulay uses: *pellucid* means "more clear"; *perspicuous* means "transparent, plain to the understanding"; *coraggio* is an Italian word meaning "courage." (Clearly Macaulay expects his readers to have a broad vocabulary.) Macaulay targets Emerson as one of those confusing writers. Will Emerson be read in 2850? If so, Macaulay sees this as our failing to perceive good, clear writing, as well as the author's inability to compose it.

How little the all-important art of making meaning pellucid is studied now! Hardly any popular writer, except myself, thinks of it. Many seem to aim at being obscure. Indeed, they may be right enough in one sense; for many readers give credit for profundity to whatever is obscure, and call all that is perspicuous, shallow. But, corragio! and think of A.D. 2850. Where will your

Emersons be then? But Herodotus will still be read with delight. We must do our best to be read too.

—Thomas Babington Macaulay, *Journal* (January 12, 1850),
cited in G. Otto Trevelyan, *The Life and Letters of
Lord Macaulay*, 1876, Vol. 2, p. 234

Thomas Powell "Ralph Waldo Emerson" (1850)

Thomas Powell was born in England and moved to the United States in 1849. A playwright and essayist, he is probably best known for his books on nineteenth-century writers, such as *The Living Authors of America*, from which this essay is excerpted.

Powell's essay takes, in a sense, the opposite view of Theodore Parker's: Emerson is not a universalist, the author contends, but "is a republic, not a Universe," and this shortcoming places him in comparison to lesser writers of his times.

Powell, however, wishes not to denigrate Emerson, but to praise him. Powell clearly, and determinately, establishes the value of Emerson's work, which he considers higher than the writings of those to whom, Powell claims, no comparison is really possible. Powell's words seem to come in defense of a fairly common criticism of Emerson in his day: that he was an atheist, a pantheist, and anti-Christian; in terms of Emerson's critics, these labels generally suggest the same sense of Christian failing.

Emerson's resignation from the ministry, his stress on the primacy of individual will, his claim that all are a part of the divine whole ("man is a god in ruins"), qualified Emerson as dangerous to Christian orthodoxy and his popularity a danger to the religious and social institutions on which, it was believed by many, America rested. Powell strongly defends Emerson against these attacks, especially early in the essay. One strongly sounded note is Powell's insistence on the value of Emerson cleaving or separating American thought from its European roots.

Students investigating contemporary criticisms of Emerson's religious thought will be able to infer the nature of these attacks from Powell's defense. Those interested in Emerson's role in the creation of a uniquely American intellectual and literary identity should note Powell's observations as well.

To abuse a man because he does not write like Joseph Addison or Samuel Johnson is absurd: they may with the same reason condemn him for being himself, instead of somebody else. It is the criticism of the fool. Emerson certainly has a style more marked than most writers, but he has likewise a greater individuality of thought to accompany it. When a teacher utters profounder thought than the untaught have been accustomed to hear, the latter accuse him of being mystical or transcendental: just as boys of the lower form grumble at Euclid, and abuse their tutor. There seems something galling to an inferior mind in the confession of ignorance. It appears to wound self-love or egotism more than any other accusation. The generality would prefer to be suspected of knavery, than of boobyism. This will account for the virulence of the blockhead: to surpass him in genius or learning is to make him your deadly enemy. A warfare is always waged by the dull against the witty; they have the worst of it, and fools though they are, *they know it:* the alpha and omega of dulness is *to this extent, no more.* They are sensible of their stupidity. We admit this to be unpleasant, but it is unavoidable, and by way of consolation we recommend the old adage of—

> What can't be cured,
> Must be endured.

So there's an end of the matter, and they had better rest in silence under the misfortune. . . .

We were going to say, to any *unprejudiced* mind Emerson's writings must commend themselves; we were going to say this, when the difficulty struck us of finding *any* unprejudiced mind. We are all prejudiced, either by birth, or habit, or education, and therefore we can only hope for two classes who will appreciate Emerson—the highly cultured and the ignorant; these last, however, must be those that think for themselves. It is the middle class, the men who have a smattering of all things and know nothing entirely, to whom Emerson appears as an Atheist, a Pantheist, and an Infidel. To the first he approves himself a man—a great and worthy teacher; and to the last he is new life, new light—a spiritual sun which shines as freely, as warmly on their hearts as the sun of nature does upon their bodies. We have *felt* the truth of what we say, and therefore do not feel any diffidence in telling our experience. We belong to the lowest class; we have believed with our fathers and elders, we have doubted and thought, thought earnestly and long, and found comfort, and joy, and pleasure in the instruction Emerson has afforded us. His views have been to us a new existence, or rather have shown us the true value of the existence God has already given to us. His views have set us on our feet again, and gave us hope, and heart, and courage, when all else has proved vain, authoritative, and arbitrary. Our study of Emerson has not been exclusive; we have had time to taste of most of the poetry and philosophy written in the English language from Chaucer downwards; and we again declare that we know of no author that is so full of suggestion, speaks so directly to the heart, and is so free from the prejudices of the time, and the fashions in which we live. Bacon, the great Lord Bacon, sinks to a mere politician alongside Emerson. But we do not, nevertheless, undervalue Bacon; he was a great man in his time, and exercised a wide influence upon his age and ages after. But he was neither so deep-seeing nor so true-spoken as Emerson; for proof take any Essay these two have written on the *same* subject—'Love,' for instance— and compare them, and see how much one excels the other. Bacon's spirit, great as it was (and it was marvellous for his age), never mounted so high, never extended so wide, never descended so low as Emerson's. There is one reason, however, that is obvious why our author should greatly eclipse these luminaries, and that is, he has had all their light, all their genius to assist his own. We can trace in his writings many thoughts he has got from Chaucer, Sidney, Herbert, Shakespeare, Bacon, the Elder Dramatists, from the Greeks, from the Romans, from the Hindoos, from the Scandinavians, from the Germans, and lastly from his own experience, on which last he himself sets most value, and justly, seeing that all *his* teachers' worth was thus obtained. Truth being universal, and not anything exclusive, to those who will receive it is as common as the air we breathe, and, like the best of all things, should be most acceptable. Emerson and his philosophy are as remarkable things in this age as are the locomotive, the electric telegraph, and the daguerreotype. They are, too, exercising as deep an influence, slowly but surely winning men to look rightly at things, and with their own eyes. He is a pioneer as brave, and as indomitable in clearing away obstructions to the growth of mind, as are those of the West in clearing the soil. Many a great work and many a noble deed will yet take its date from his words, and if they have the power to produce such fruit, and we affirm that they have to a high degree, who shall say this man is an opponent to Christianity? Who, indeed, but those who make that doctrine a business, and not a rule of life! . . .

Mr. Emerson possesses so many characteristics of genius that his want of universality is the more to be regretted; the leading feature of his mind is intensity; he is deficient in heart sympathy. Full to overflowing with intellectual appreciation, he is incapable of that embracing reception of impulses which gives to Byron so large a measure of influence and fame.

Emerson is elevated, but not expansive; his flight is high, but not extensive. He has a magnificent vein of the purest gold, but it is not a mine. To vary our illustration somewhat, he is not a world, but a district; a lofty and commanding eminence we admit, but only a very small portion of the true Poet's universe. What, however, he has done is permanent, and America will always in after times be proud of Ralph Waldo Emerson, and consider him one of her noblest sons.

—Thomas Powell, "Ralph Waldo Emerson,"
The Living Authors of America,
1850, pp. 66–67, 75–77

James Russell Lowell
"Emerson the Lecturer" (1861–68)

James Russell Lowell, poet, essayist, and editor of the *Atlantic Monthly* and the *North American Review,* contributed to and helped shape the direction of American literature in the nineteenth century. While Lowell was skeptical of transcendentalism and its more eccentric writers (such as Bronson Alcott), he remained Emerson's close personal friend.

Lowell makes an important point about New Englanders of the nineteenth century: they are "reckoned a practical folk, who would rather hear about a new air-tight stove than about Plato." This is the public Emerson chiefly addresses as a speaker. Emerson, in some ways, confounded those critics such as Herman Melville who, only knowing Emerson from his seemingly mystical essays, find him to be full of Yankee practicality as a speaker. As Lowell states, "Is it not that he out-Yankees us all?" Students interested in Emerson's audience, and his public appeal as a speaker, will find valuable insight here.

Lowell makes another significant observation, "that, though he writes in prose, he is essentially a poet." Emerson's prose assumes a style that is characteristic of poetic expression; that is, it is unparaphrasable. His words are so perfectly distilled from his original observations (carefully reworked from journal and notebook entries) that separating the idea from the statement is difficult. The idea is in essence the expression itself, or, as Emerson would write, "the fact finds the form." Students examining Emerson's prose style should take note of Lowell's observations. Emerson's prose is unique among his contemporaries, and Lowell's informed insight helps us understand how this is so.

It is a singular fact, that Mr. Emerson is the most steadily attractive lecturer in America. Into that somewhat cold-waterish region adventurers of the sensational kind come down now and then with a splash, to become disregarded King Logs before the next season. But Mr. Emerson always draws. A lecturer now for something like a third of a century, one of the pioneers of the lecturing system, the charm of his voice, his manner, and his matter has never lost its power over his earlier hearers, and continually winds new ones in its enchanting meshes. What they do not fully understand they take on trust, and listen, saying to themselves, as the old poet of Sir Philip Sidney,—

> A sweet, attractive, kind of grace,
>   A full assurance given by looks,
> Continual comfort in a face,
>   The lineaments of gospel books.

We call it a singular fact, because we Yankees are thought to be fond of the spread-eagle style, and nothing can be more remote from that than his. We are reckoned a practical folk, who would rather hear about a new air-tight stove than about Plato; yet our favorite teacher's practicality is not in the least of the Poor Richard variety. If he have any Buncombe constituency, it is that unrealized commonwealth of philosophers which Plotinus proposed to establish; and if he were to make an almanac, his directions to farmers would be something like this: "OCTOBER: *Indian Summer;* now is the time to get in your early Vedas." What, then, is his secret? Is it not that he out-Yankees us all? that his range includes us all? that he is equally at home with the potato-disease and original sin, with pegging shoes and the Over-soul? that, as we try all trades, so has he tried all cultures? and above all, that his mysticism gives us a counterpoise to our super-practicality?

There is no man living to whom, as a writer, so many of us feel and thankfully acknowledge so great an indebtedness for ennobling impulses,— none whom so many cannot abide. What does he mean? ask these last. Where is his system? What is the use of it all? What the deuse have we to do with Brahma? I do not propose to write an essay on Emerson at this time. I will only say that one may find grandeur and consolation in a starlit night without caring to ask what it means, save grandeur and consolation; one may like Montaigne, as some ten generations before us have done, without thinking him so systematic as some more eminently tedious (or shall we say tediously eminent?) authors; one may think roses as good in their way as cabbages, though the latter would make a better show in the witness-box, if cross-examined as to their usefulness; and as for Brahma, why, he can take care of himself, and won't bite us at any rate.

The bother with Mr. Emerson is, that, though he writes in prose, he is essentially a poet. If you undertake to paraphrase what he says, and to reduce it to words of one syllable for infant minds, you will make as sad work of it as the good monk with his analysis of Homer in the *Epistolae Obscurorum Virorum*. We look upon him as one of the few men of genius whom our age has produced, and there needs no better proof of it than his masculine faculty of fecundating other minds. Search for his eloquence in his books and you will perchance miss it, but meanwhile you will find that it has kindled all your thoughts. For choice and pith of language he belongs to a better age than ours, and might rub shoulders with Fuller and Browne,—though he does use that abominable word *reliable*. His eye for a fine, telling phrase that will carry true is like that of a backwoodsman for a rifle; and he will dredge you up a choice word from the mud of Cotton Mather himself. A diction at once so rich and so homely as his I know not where to match in these days of writing by the page; it is like homespun cloth-of-gold. The many cannot miss his meaning, and only the few can find it. It is the open secret of all true genius. It is wholesome to angle in those profound pools, though one be rewarded with nothing more than the leap of a fish that flashes his freckled side in the sun and as suddenly absconds in the dark and dreamy waters again. There is keen excitement, though there be no ponderable acquisition. If we carry nothing home in our baskets, there is ample gain in dilated lungs and stimulated blood. What does he mean, quotha? He means inspiring hints, a divining-rod to your deeper nature. No doubt, Emerson, like all original men, has his peculiar audience, and yet I know none that can hold a promiscuous crowd in pleased attention so long as he. As in all original men, there is something for every palate. "Would you know," says Goethe, "the ripest cherries? Ask the boys and the blackbirds."

—James Russell Lowell, "Emerson the Lecturer" (1861–68),
Works, Riverside ed., Vol. 1, pp. 349–52

George Ripley "Journal" (1869)

George Ripley founded Brook Farm (1841–47), New England's most notable utopian community, based in part on Emerson's transcendental idealism. Ripley was a fellow Unitarian clergyman as well as Emerson's personal friend. Ripley felt that Emerson's direct involvement with Brook Farm was necessary for the experiment's success, and though Emerson did offer financial support, he never lived at Brook Farm or participated in the enterprise.

The following entry from Ripley's journal comes many years later, when Ripley was a literary critic for Horace Greeley's *New York Tribune*. Ripley writes as though he is offering a detached view of Emerson's essay collection *Representative Men*. While the language is almost formal, the exotic nature of the images (Emerson's "silvery rhythm," the "flavor of oriental spicery") suggests the elements Ripley found most attractive in Emerson's style. Emerson's imagery was indeed an important foundation for the transcendentalist movement.

Ripley states that the sight of Emerson's book is like "manna in the wilderness" and that Emerson is "a great master in his way," but students will want to note the qualifier in that expression. Ripley also chooses to state that Emerson's "final conclusion is that the true man has no companion." Ripley, then, demonstrates one of the problems facing readers of Emerson: his uniqueness is difficult to qualify.

Students might think of this passage as an example of the difficulty of writing about Emerson. Emerson's style depends largely on intuition, as opposed to objective observation. Ripley finds Emerson's work at odds with conventional notions of society; Emerson is thus shown to value individual perception of nature and truth, rather than finding these values through social institutions.

—⚌— —⚌— —⚌—

I discovered a copy of Emerson's *Society and Solitude,* republished in London by Sampson Low. The sight of it was like manna in the wilderness. I became the happy owner of it at once, and it afforded me a rich feast for the rest of the journey. Some portions of it, I think, are equal to anything that Emerson has ever written. Emerson is a great master in his way. His style has an incomparable charm. Its silvery rhythm captivates the ear. The affluence of his illustrations diffuses a flavor of oriental spicery over his pages. As he confesses in the essay on "Books," his learning is second-hand; but everything sticks which his mind can appropriate. He defends the use of translations, and I doubt whether he has ever read ten pages of his great authorities, Plato, Plutarch, Montaigne, or Goethe, in the original. He is certainly no friend of profound study, any more than of philosophical speculation. Give him a few brilliant and suggestive glimpses, and he is content. His catalogue of books is limited in the extreme, and presents few hints of practical value. Much of the work is devoted to the comparative influence of solitude and society, in addition to the chapter with that title. The subject is touched in several of the essays, especially in those on "Clubs" and "Domestic Life." Emerson is fond of conversation, but it always disappoints him. With him it is an experiment constantly repeated, but always without success. His final conclusion is that the true man has no companion. There may be times when two persons may hold genuine communion, but the presence of a third person is impertinent, and always breaks the charm. Such occasions, however, are rare, and must be numbered by moments, and not by hours. His remarks on Art show his want of philosophic culture. The principal point which he urges is that Nature is the foundation of Art, and that the great Artist is spontaneous, and not reflective; both good points, but by no means original. Take away the splendid language in which they are clothed, I find that but little valuable instruction remains. There are frequent hints of the grand Platonic theory of the True, the Beautiful, the Good, as the exponents of the Infinite in Humanity, which long since ripened in my mind, as the true "Intellectual System of the Universe;" but he does not appear to be aware of its fathomless significance.

In thus renewing my acquaintance with Emerson, I am struck with certain rare combinations which may serve to explain his position. His rejection of dogmas is cool and merciless; but he shows no sympathy with vulgar and destructive radicalism. He asserts an unlimited freedom of the individual, but maintains a moral tone, rigid almost to asceticism. With the wild havoc which he makes of popular opinion, he always respects the dignity of human nature. Emerson is essentially a poet. His intuitions are in the form of images. Few men have such positive tendencies toward the Ideal. But his sympathy with external nature is equally strong. He is a keen and accurate observer. His perceptions are true, so far as concerns the material world and the qualities of character that are universal in man. His judgment of individuals is often prejudiced. The practical shrewdness interwoven with his poetical nature is one of the secrets of his power. You attempt to follow his lofty flight among the purple clouds, almost believing that he has "hitched his wagon to a star," when he suddenly drops down to earth, and surprises you with an utterance of the homeliest wisdom. On this account, when they get over the novelty of his manner, plain men are apt to find themselves at home with him. His acquaintance with common things, all household ways and words, the processes of every-day life on the farm, in the kitchen and stable, as well as in the drawing-room and library, engages their attention, and produces a certain kindly warmth of fellowship, which would seem to be incompatible with the coldness of his nature. Emerson is not without a tincture of science. He often makes a happy use of its results, in the way of comparison and illustration. But I do not suppose that he could follow a demonstration of Euclid, or one of the fine analyses in physics of Tyndall or Huxley. Of such a writer as Herbert Spencer he has probably no more than a faint comprehension. Emerson has less wit than I have usually been inclined to believe; of humor only a slender trace. Perhaps the subtlety and refinement of his illustrations may sometimes have the appearance of wit, but not its real flavor or effect.

—George Ripley, *Journal* (1869), cited in Octavius Brooks Frothingham, *George Ripley*, 1882, pp. 266–68

Henry James (1879)

American novelist Henry James comes from a family steeped in New England literary tradition. His father was theologian and Swedenborgian Henry James Sr., his brother the philosopher William James, and his sister the diarist Alice James. In addition to being a novelist, James was also a critic. His introductions to his novels are required reading for students of nineteenth-century American fiction.

James notes Emerson's insistence on the individual will as key to his lasting value as a writer. This concept of the individual is fundamental to Emerson, and students working to establish the essential elements of Emerson's thought should regard this carefully. For Emerson, the individual has a distinct relation to the universe. It is the responsibility of each individual to determine the nature of that relationship and follow its natural course, even to the point of contravening comfort, doctrine, orthodoxy, or "the world's work." As James recognizes in Emerson's words "if I cannot work, at least I need not lie," the primacy of the individual is principal to all other relationships. James is especially insistent on the value of this in an age where, as he writes, "introspection . . . played almost the part of a social resource." James is writing of an American Victorian culture in which "introspection"—that is, in this usage, the examination of and adherence to social customs and appearances—supplanted the individual's realization of his or her unique relation to the self or to the world.

Emerson expressed, before all things, as was extremely natural at the hour and in the place, the value and importance of the individual, the duty of making the most of one's self, of living by one's own personal light, and carrying out one's own disposition. He reflected with beautiful irony upon the exquisite impudence of those institutions which claim to have appropriated the truth and to dole it out, in proportionate morsels, in exchange for a subscription.

He talked about the beauty and dignity of life, and about every one who is born into the world being born to the whole, having an interest and a stake in the whole. He said "all that is clearly due to-day is not to lie," and a great many other things which it would be still easier to present in a ridiculous light. He insisted upon sincerity and independence and spontaneity, upon acting in harmony with one's nature, and not comforming and compromising for the sake of being more comfortable. He urged that a man should await his call, his finding the thing to do which he should really believe in doing, and not be urged by the world's opinion to do simply the world's work. "If no call should come for years, for centuries, then I know that the want of the Universe is the attestation of faith by my abstinence. . . If I cannot work, at least I need not lie." The doctrine of the supremacy of the individual to himself, of his originality, and, as regards his own character, *unique* quality, must have had a great charm for people living in a society in which introspection—thanks to the want of other entertainment—played almost the part of a social resource.

—Henry James, Nathaniel Hawthorne, 1879, pp. 82–83

WALT WHITMAN "EMERSON'S BOOKS (THE SHADOWS OF THEM)" (1880)

Poet Walt Whitman needs little introduction to students of American literature. Whitman's career, beginning in 1855 with the publication of *Leaves of Grass*, was welcomed by Emerson, and the two remained close ever since. Emerson and Whitman shared their interest in a uniquely American literature, the democratic possibilities of America, and in the abolition of slavery.

Whitman clearly admires Emerson, but here sets himself the task of finding weaknesses in Emerson's work. Whitman notes that Emerson's diction may be "too perfect, too concentrated." Students analyzing Emerson's diction should take note. Emerson's style rests heavily on compact metaphors and dense imagery. Emerson's sentences seem to comprise complete thoughts, and lend themselves to aesthetic consideration rather than the formulaic development of an argument. As Whitman observes, there is little filler in Emerson; all the writing, is "good butter, good sugar," all the time, to the detriment of his ideas.

Whitman also notes that Emerson "is best as critic, or diagnoser." The qualification is interesting in that it answers the complaint of many critics that Emerson has no "system." However, Whitman pushes further to criticize the seeming cerebral distance Emerson's writing achieves: "cold and bloodless intellectuality dominates him." Whitman's claim is that Emerson does not people his writing with full-bodied, real Americans. Students working through Emerson's "Divinity School" address might consider the well-known "snowstorm" passage and compare it with Whitman's assertion. Whitman also contravenes another aspect elemental to Emerson's early writing, the assertion that "the United States can never produce any equal to the splendid show . . . of the principal European nations." But Emerson claims, in the opening passages of "Nature" as well as in the "American Scholar" address, to sever ties with European thinking, that America is worthy of, and demands, its own "original relation to the universe." Students writing on this aspect of Emerson's thought might consider the basis for Whitman's claims.

Whitman ends his essay with something of a paradox: "The best part of Emersonianism is, it breeds the giant that destroys itself." That is, Emerson encourages his readers to reject all systems and all doctrines, even his own. This is part of Emerson's insistence on the primacy of the individual will and the importance of intuitive experience of the world.

In the regions we call Nature, towering beyond all measurement, with infinite spread, infinite depth and height—in those regions, including Man, socially and historically, with his moral-emotional influences—how small a part, (it came in my mind to-day,) has literature really depicted—even summing up all of it, all ages. Seems at its best some little fleet of boats, hugging the shores of a boundless sea, and never venturing, exploring the unmapp'd—never, Columbus-like, sailing out for New Worlds, and to complete the orb's rondure. Emerson writes frequently in the atmosphere of this thought, and his books report one or two things from that very ocean and air, and more legibly address'd to our age and American polity than by any man yet. But I will begin by scarifying him—thus proving that I am not insensible to his deepest lessons. I will consider his books from a democratic and western point of view. I will specify the shadows on these sunny expanses. Somebody has said of heroic character that "wherever the tallest peaks are present, must inevitably be deep chasms and valleys." Mine be the ungracious task (for reasons) of leaving unmention'd both sunny expanses and sky-reaching heights, to dwell on the bare spots and darknesses. I have a theory that no artist or work of the very first class may be or can be without them.

First, then, these pages are perhaps too perfect, too concentrated. (How good, for instance, is good butter, good sugar. But to be eating nothing but sugar and butter all the time! even if ever so good.) And though the author has much to say of freedom and wildness and simplicity and spontaneity, no performance was ever more based on artificial scholarships and decorums at third or fourth removes, (he calls it culture,) and built up from them. It is always a *make,* never an unconscious *growth.* It is the porcelain figure or statuette of lion, or stag, or Indian hunter—and a very choice statuette too—appropriate for the rosewood or marble bracket of parlor or library; never the animal itself, or the hunter himself. Indeed, who wants the real animal or hunter? What would that do amid astral and bric-a-brac and tapestry, and ladies and gentlemen talking in subdued tones of Browning and Longfellow and art? The least suspicion of such actual bull, or Indian, or of Nature carrying out itself, would put all those good people to instant terror and flight.

Emerson, in my opinion, is not most eminent as poet or artist or teacher, though valuable in all those. He is best as critic, or diagnoser. Not passion or imagination or warp or weakness, or any pronounced cause or specialty, dominates him. Cold and bloodless intellectuality dominates him. (I know the fires, emotions, love, egotisms, glow deep, perennial, as in all New Englanders—but the façade hides them well—they give no sign.) He does not see or take one side, one presentation only or mainly, (as all the poets, or most of the fine writers anyhow)—he sees all sides. His final influence is to make his students cease to worship anything—almost cease to believe in anything, outside of themselves. These books will fill, and well fill, certain stretches of life, certain stages of development—are, (like the tenets or theology the author of them preach'd when a young man,) unspeakably serviceable and precious as a stage. But in old or nervous or solemnest or dying hours, when one needs the impalpably soothing and vitalizing influences of abysmic Nature, or its affinities in literature or human society, and the soul resents the keenest mere intellection, they will not be sought for.

For a philosopher, Emerson possesses a singularly dandified theory of manners. He seems to have no notion at all that manners are simply the signs by which the chemist or metallurgist knows his metals. To the profound scientist, all metals are profound, as they really are. The little one, like the conventional world, will make much of gold and silver only. Then to the real artist in humanity, what are called bad manners are often the most picturesque and significant of all. Suppose these books becoming absorb'd, the permanent chyle of American general and particular character—what a well-wash'd and grammatical, but bloodless and helpless, race we should turn out! No, no, dear friend; though the States want scholars, undoubtedly, and perhaps want ladies and gentlemen who use the bath frequently, and never laugh loud, or talk wrong, they don't want scholars, or ladies and gentlemen, at the expense of all the rest. They want good farmers, sailors, mechanics, clerks, citizens—perfect business and social relations—perfect fathers and mothers. If we could only have these, or their approximations, plenty of them, fine and large and sane and generous and patriotic, they might make their verbs disagree from their nominatives, and laugh like volleys of musketeers, if they should please. Of course these are not all America wants, but they are first of all to be provided on a large scale. And, with tremendous errors and escapades, this, substantially, is what the States seem to have an intuition of, and to be mainly aiming at. The plan of a select class, superfined, (demarcated from the rest,) the plan of Old World lands and literatures, is not so objectionable in itself, but because it chokes the true plan for us, and indeed is death to it. As to such special class, the United States can never produce any equal to the splendid show, (far, far beyond comparison or competition here,) of the principal European nations, both in the past and at the present day. But an immense and distinctive commonalty over our vast and varied area, west and east, south and north—in fact, for the first time in history, a great, aggregated, real PEOPLE, worthy the name, and made of develop'd heroic individuals, both sexes—is America's principal, perhaps only, reason for being. If ever accomplish'd, it will be at least as much, (I lately think, doubly as much,) the result of fitting and democratic sociologies, literatures and arts—if we ever get them—as of our democratic politics.

At times it has been doubtful to me if Emerson really knows or feels what Poetry is at its highest, as in the Bible, for instance, or Homer or Shakspere. I see he covertly or plainly likes best superb verbal polish, or something old or odd—Waller's "Go, lovely rose," or Lovelace's lines "to Lucasta"—the quaint conceits of the old French bards, and the like. Of *power* he seems to have a gentleman's admiration—but in his inmost heart the grandest attribute of God and Poets is always subordinate to the octaves, conceits, polite kinks, and verbs.

The reminiscence that years ago I began like most youngsters to have a touch (though it came late, and was only on the surface) of Emerson-on-the-brain—that I read his writings reverently, and address'd him in print as "Master," and for a month or so thought of him as such—I retain not only with composure, but positive satisfaction. I have noticed that most young people of eager minds pass through this stage of exercise.

The best part of Emersonianism is, it breeds the giant that destroys itself. Who wants to be any man's mere follower? lurks behind every page. No teacher ever taught, that has so provided for his pupil's setting up independently—no truer evolutionist.

—Walt Whitman, "Emerson's Books (The Shadows of Them)"
(1880), *Prose Works,* ed. Floyd Stovall,
1964, Vol. 2, pp. 515–18

Matthew Arnold "Emerson" (1883)

Matthew Arnold composed his reflection on Emerson in 1883, one year after Emerson's death. Arnold, the author of "Dover Beach," "The Scholar Gipsy," and much widely read literary and social criticism, stands as one of the foremost literary critics of his time.

Arnold's essay, organized into three distinct sections, determines what he finds to be Emerson's lasting values. To begin, however, Arnold states what is lacking in Emerson (he is not "one of the born poets," he is not a "great man of letters," he "is the propounder of a philosophy" but is not a philosophical writer, his philosophy lacks systemization). In this section, Arnold measures Emerson's work against "laws really proper to it." That is, Arnold assumes a determined set of rules by which art may be measured and qualified, and in this sense, finds Emerson's poetry unremarkable, especially compared to William Shakespeare or John Milton.

The second section of the essay begins with the reversal in paragraph 11, in which Arnold begins to reveal his purpose: "I think I have cleared the ground. I have given up to envious Time as much of Emerson as Time can fairly expect ever to obtain." Emerson, then, is less like Plato, or Immanuel Kant, or Milton, but more like Marcus Aurelius, an "aider of those who would live in the spirit." Note that Arnold sets Emerson against very high standards—Shakespeare, Milton, Thomas Gray, Plato, and Kant—not to belittle Emerson, but to reveal his more unique qualities. Students should note that the contrast Arnold determines suggests that what is unique about Emerson is the ways in which his work differs from these accepted masters.

From this point, Arnold allows Emerson to speak for himself, marking the essay's third section with insight into Emerson's unique turns of phrase and imagery. Emerson's points are "in themselves true." He is courageous in his social critique; his temper is "hopeful, serene" and marked with insight and truth "indissolubly joined." That is, Emerson cannot be qualified by the terms of the times, but has value stretching beyond his own era. As Arnold states in his conclusion, he envisions Emerson "visible upon earth still . . . in his habit as he lived, but of heightened stature and shining feature," stretching both east to England and west to the United

States. Arnold wants his readers to understand the effect Emerson has in England as well as in the United States. Emerson is often thought of as a uniquely American writer, but students can see that Arnold, an English poet, is making clear Emerson's value to English and continental European readers.

Arnold also makes extensive use of Emerson's close relationship with Thomas Carlyle (Emerson prepared *Sartor Resartus* for American publication; Carlyle prepared introductions to Wordsworth and Coleridge for Emerson). Emerson and Carlyle are often compared as literary contemporaries, and this essay provides interesting insight into these two writers; students of Emerson might make use of Arnold's well-reasoned determinations. Arnold also utilizes this contrast in order to bring out Emerson's "persistent optimism." Emerson compares unfavorably to Carlyle in the essay's first half, but Emerson's sense of hope separates him from Carlyle's abandonment of the desire for happiness.

Arnold's essay allows readers to realize that Emerson's work might not stand as the best examples of poetry or philosophy, but students can see how Emerson's uniqueness has lasting value in its own right, and by its own standards.

I was reading the other day a notice of Emerson by a serious and interesting American critic. Fifty or sixty passages in Emerson's poems, says this critic,— who had doubtless himself been nourished on Emerson's writings, and held them justly dear,—fifty or sixty passages from Emerson's poems have already entered into English speech as matter of familiar and universally current quotation. Here is a specimen of that personal sort of estimate which, for my part, even in speaking of authors dear to me, I would try to avoid. What is the kind of phrase of which we may fairly say that it has entered into English speech as matter of familiar quotation? Such a phrase, surely, as the "Patience on a monument" of Shakespeare; as the "Darkness visible" of Milton; as the "Where ignorance is bliss" of Gray. Of not one single passage in Emerson's poetry can it be truly said that it has become a familiar quotation like phrases of this kind. It is not enough that it should be familiar to his admirers, familiar in New England, familiar even throughout the United States; it must be familiar to all readers and lovers of English poetry. Of not more than one or two passages in Emerson's poetry can it, I think, be truly said, that they stand ever-present in the memory of even many lovers of English poetry. A great number of passages from his poetry are no doubt perfectly familiar to the mind and lips of the critic whom I have mentioned, and perhaps of a wide circle of American readers. But this is a very different thing from being matter of universal quotation, like the phrases of the legitimate poets.

And, in truth, one of the legitimate poets, Emerson, in my opinion, is not. His poetry is interesting, it makes one think; but it is not the poetry of one of the born poets. I say it of him with reluctance, although I am sure that he would have said it of himself; but I say it with reluctance, because I dislike giving pain to his admirers, and because all my own wish, too, is to say of him what is favourable. But I regard myself, not as speaking to please Emerson's admirers, not as speaking to please myself; but rather, I repeat, as communing with Time and Nature concerning the productions of this beautiful and rare spirit, and as resigning what of him is by their unalterable decree touched with caducity, in order the better to mark and secure that in him which is immortal.

Milton says that poetry ought to be simple, sensuous, impassioned. Well, Emerson's poetry is seldom either simple, or sensuous, or impassioned. In general it lacks directness; it lacks concreteness; it lacks energy. His grammar is often embarrassed; in particular, the want of clearly-marked distinction between the subject and the object of his sentence is a frequent cause of obscurity in him. A poem which shall be a plain, forcible, inevitable whole he hardly ever produces. Such good work as the noble lines graven on the Concord Monument is the exception with him; such ineffective work as the "Fourth of July Ode" or the "Boston Hymn" is the rule. Even passages and single lines of thorough plainness and commanding force are rare in his poetry. They exist, of course; but when we meet with them they give us a slight shock of surprise, so little has Emerson accustomed us to them. Let me have the pleasure of quoting one or two of these exceptional passages:—

> So nigh is grandeur to our dust,
>   So near is God to man,
> When Duty whispers low, *Thou must,*
>   The youth replies, *I can.*

Or again this:—

> Though love repine and reason chafe,
> There came a voice without reply:
> 'Tis man's perdition to be safe,
> When for the truth he ought to die."

Excellent! but how seldom do we get from him a strain blown so clearly and firmly! Take another passage where his strain has not only clearness, it has also grace and beauty:—

> And ever, when the happy child
> In May beholds the blooming wild,
> And hears in heaven the bluebird sing,
> "Onward," he cries, "your baskets bring!
> In the next field is air more mild,
> And o'er yon hazy crest is Eden's balmier spring."

In the style and cadence here there is a reminiscence, I think, of Gray; at any rate, the pureness grace and beauty of these lines are worthy even of Gray. But Gray holds his high rank as a poet, not merely by the beauty and grace of passages in his poems; not merely by a diction generally pure in an age of impure diction: he holds it, above all, by the power and skill with which the evolution of his poems is conducted. Here is his grand superiority to Collins, whose diction in his best poem, the "Ode to Evening," is purer than Gray's; but then the "Ode to Evening" is like a river which loses itself in the sand, whereas Gray's best poems have an evolution sure and satisfying. Emerson's "Mayday," from which I just now quoted, has no real evolution at all; it is a series of observations. And, in general, his poems have no evolution. Take for example his "Titmouse." Here he has an excellent subject; and his observation of Nature, moreover, is always marvellously close and fine. But compare what he makes of his meeting with his titmouse with what Cowper or Burns makes of the like kind of incident! One never quite arrives at learning what the titmouse actually did for him at all, though one feels a strong interest and desire to learn it; but one is reduced to guessing, and cannot be quite sure that after all one has guessed right. He is not plain and concrete enough,—in other words, not poet enough,—to be able to tell us. And a failure of this kind goes through almost all his verse, keeps him amid symbolism, and allusion, and the fringes of things, and in spite of his spiritual power deeply impairs his poetic value. Through the inestimable virtue of concreteness, a simple poem like "The Bridge" of Longfellow or the "School Days" of Mr. Whittier is of more poetic worth, perhaps, than all the verse of Emerson.

I do not, then, place Emerson among the great poets. But I go further, and say that I do not place him among the great writers, the great men of letters. Who are the great men of letters? They are men like Cicero, Plato, Bacon, Pascal, Swift, Voltaire,—writers with, in the first place, a genius and instinct for style; writers whose prose is by a kind of native necessity true and sound. Now the style of Emerson, like the style of his transcendentalist friends and of the *Dial* so continually,—the style of Emerson is capable of falling into a strain like this, which I take from the beginning of his "Essay on Love:" "Every soul is a celestial Venus to every other soul. The heart has its sabbaths and jubilees, in which the world appears as a hymeneal feast, and all natural sounds and the circle of the seasons are erotic odes and dances." Emerson altered this sentence in the later editions. Like Wordsworth, he was in later life fond of altering; and in general his later alterations, like those of Wordsworth, are not improvements. He softened the passage in question, however, though without really mending it. I quote it in its original and strongly-marked form. Arthur Stanley used to relate that, about the year 1840, being in conversation with some Americans in quarantine at Malta and thinking to please them he declared his warm admiration for Emerson's *Essays,* then recently published. However, the Americans shook their heads, and told him that for home taste Emerson was decidedly too *greeny.* We will hope, for their sakes, that the sort of thing they had in their heads was such writing as I have just quoted. Unsound it is indeed, and in a style almost impossible to a born man of letters.

It is a curious thing, that quality of style which marks the great writer, the born man of letters. It resides in the whole tissue of his work, and of his work regarded as a composition for literary purposes. Brilliant and powerful passages in a man's writings do not prove his possession of it; it lies in their whole tissue. Emerson has passages of noble and pathetic eloquence, such as those which I quoted at the beginning; he has passages of shrewd and felicitous wit; he has crisp epigrams; he has passages of exquisitely touched observation of nature. Yet he is not a great writer; his style has not the requisite wholeness of good tissue. Even Carlyle is not, in my judgment, a great writer. He has surpassingly powerful qualities of expression, far more powerful than Emerson's, and reminding one of the gifts of expression of the great poets,—of even Shakespeare himself. What Emerson so admirably says of Carlyle's "devouring eyes and portraying hand," "those thirsty eyes, those portrait-eating, portrait-painting eyes of thine, those fatal perceptions," is thoroughly true. What a description is Carlyle's of the first publisher of *Sartor Resartus,* "to whom the idea of a new edition of *Sartor* is frightful, or rather ludicrous, unimaginable"; of this poor Fraser, in whose "wonderful world of Tory pamphleteers, Conservative Younger-brothers, Regent Street Loungers, Crockford Gamblers, Irish Jesuits, drunken reporters, and miscellaneous unclean persons (whom nitre and much soap will not wash clean) not a soul has expressed the smallest wish that way!" What a portrait, again, of the well-beloved John Sterling! "One, and the best, of a small class extant here, who, nigh drowning in a black wreck of Infidelity (lighted up by some glare of Radicalism only, now growing *dim* too), and about to perish, saved themselves into a Coleridgian Shovel-Hattedness." What touches in the invitation of Emerson to London! "You shall see blockheads by the million; Pickwick himself shall be visible,—innocent young Dickens, reserved for a questionable fate. The great Wordsworth shall talk till you yourself pronounce him to be a bore. Southey's complexion is still healthy mahogany brown, with a fleece of white hair, and eyes that seem running at full gallop. Leigh Hunt, man of genius in the shape of a cockney, is my near neighbour, with good humour and no common-sense; old Rogers with his pale head, white, bare, and cold as snow, with those large blue eyes, cruel, sorrowful, and that sardonic shelf chin." How inimitable it all is! And finally, for one must not go on for ever, this version of a London Sunday, with the public-houses closed during the hours of divine service! "It is silent Sunday; the populace not yet admitted to their beershops, till the respectabilities conclude their rubric mummeries,—a much more audacious feat than beer." Yet even Carlyle is not, in my judgment, to be called a great writer; one cannot think of ranking him with men like Cicero and Plato and Swift and Voltaire. Emerson freely promises to Carlyle immortality for his histories. They will not have it. Why? Because the materials furnished to him by that devouring eye of his and that portraying hand were not wrought in and subdued by him to what his work, regarded as a composition for literary purposes, required. Occurring in conversation, breaking out in familiar correspondence, they are magnificent, inimitable; nothing more is required of them; thus thrown out anyhow, they serve their turn and fulfil their function. And therefore I should not wonder if really Carlyle lived, in the long run, by such an invaluable record as that correspondence between him and Emerson, of which we owe the publication to Mr. Charles Norton,—by this and not by his works, as Johnson lives in Boswell, not by his works. For Carlyle's sallies, as the staple of a literary work, become wearisome; and as time more and more applies to Carlyle's works its stringent test, this will be felt more and more. Shakespeare, Moliere, Swift,—they too had, like Carlyle, the devouring eye and the portraying hand. But they are great literary masters, they are supreme writers, because they knew how to work into a literary composition their materials, and to subdue them to the purposes of literary effect. Carlyle is too wilful for this, too turbid, too vehement.

You will think I deal in nothing but negatives. I have been saying that Emerson is not one of the great poets, the great writers. He has not their quality of style. He is, however, the propounder of a philosophy. The Platonic dialogues afford us the example of exquisite literary form and treatment given to philosophical ideas. Plato is at once a great literary man and a great philosopher. If we speak carefully, we cannot call Aristotle or Spinoza or Kant great literary men, or their productions great literary works. But their work is arranged with such constructive power that they build a philosophy and are justly called great philosophical writers. Emerson cannot, I think, be called with justice a great philosophical writer. He cannot build; his arrangement of philosophical ideas has no progress in it, no evolution; he does not construct a philosophy. Emerson himself knew the defects of his method, or rather want of method, very well; indeed, he and Carlyle criticise themselves and one another in a way which leaves little for any one else to do in the way of formulating their defects. Carlyle formulates perfectly the defects of his friend's poetic and literary production when he says of the *Dial:* "For me it is too ethereal, speculative, theoretic; I will have all things condense themselves, take shape and body, if they are to have my sympathy." And, speaking of Emerson's orations he says: "I long to see some concrete Thing, some Event, Man's Life, American Forest, or piece of Creation, which this Emerson loves and wonders at, well *Emersonised,*—depictured by Emerson, filled with the life of Emerson, and cast forth from him, then to live by itself. If these orations balk me of this, how profitable soever they may be for others, I will not love them." Emerson himself formulates perfectly the defect of his own philosophical productions when he speaks of his "formidable tendency to the lapidary style. I build my house of boulders." "Here I sit and read and write," he says again, "with very little system, and as far as regards composition, with the most fragmentary result; paragraphs incompressible, each sentence an infinitely repellent particle." Nothing can be truer; and the work of a Spinoza or Kant, of the men who stand as great philosophical writers, does not proceed in this wise.

Some people will tell you that Emerson's poetry indeed is too abstract, and his philosophy too vague, but that his best work is his *English Traits.* The *English Traits* are, beyond question, very pleasant reading. It is easy to praise them, easy to commend the author of them. But I insist on always trying Emerson's work by the highest standards. I esteem him too much to try his work by any other. Tried by the highest standards, and compared with the work of the excellent markers and recorders of the traits of human life,—of writers like Montaigne, La Bruyere, Addison,—the *English Traits* will not stand the comparison. Emerson's observation has not the disinterested quality of the observation of these masters. It is the observation of a man systematically benevolent, as Hawthorne's observation in *Our Old Home* is the work of a man chagrined. Hawthorne's literary talent is of the first order. His subjects are generally not to me subjects of the highest interest; but his literary talent is of the first order, the finest, I think, which America has yet produced,—finer, by much, than Emerson's. Yet *Our Old Home* is not a masterpiece any more than *English Traits*. In neither of them is the observer disinterested enough. The author's attitude in each of these cases can easily be understood and defended. Hawthorne was a sensitive man, so situated in England that he was perpetually in contact with the British Philistine; and the British Philistine is a trying personage. Emerson's systematic benevolence comes from what he himself calls somewhere his "persistent optimism"; and his persistent optimism is the root of his greatness and the source of his charm. But still let us keep our literary conscience true, and judge every kind of literary work by the laws really proper to it. The kind of work attempted in the *English Traits* and in *Our Old Home* is work which cannot be done perfectly with a bias such as that given by Emerson's optimism or by Hawthorne's chagrin. Consequently, neither *English Traits* nor *Our Old Home* is a work of perfection in its kind.

Not with the Miltons and Grays, not with the Platos and Spinozas, not with the Swifts and Voltaires, not with the Montaignes and Addisons, can we rank Emerson. His work of various kinds, when one compares it with the work done in a corresponding kind by these masters, fails to stand the comparison. No man could see this clearer than Emerson himself. It is hard not to feel despondency when we contemplate our failures and shortcomings: and Emerson, the least self-flattering and the most modest of men, saw so plainly what was lacking to him that he had his moments of despondency. "Alas, my friend," he writes in reply to Carlyle, who had exhorted him to creative work,—"Alas, my friend, I can do no such gay thing as you say. I do not belong to the poets, but only to a low department of literature,—the reporters; suburban men." He deprecates his friend's praise; praise "generous to a fault," he calls it; praise "generous to the shaming of me,—cold, fastidious, ebbing person that I am. Already in a former letter you had said too much good of my poor little arid book, which is as sand to my eyes. I can only say that I heartily wish the book were better; and I must try and deserve so much favour from the kind gods by a bolder and truer living in the months to come,—such as may perchance one day relax and invigorate this cramp hand of mine. When I see how much work is to be done; what room for a poet, for any spiritualist, in this great, intelligent, sensual and avaricious America,—I lament my fumbling fingers and stammering tongue." Again, as late as 1870, he writes to Carlyle: "There is no example of constancy like yours, and it always stings my stupor into temporary recovery and wonderful resolution to accept the noble challenge. But 'the strong hours conquer us;' and I am the victim of miscellany,—miscellany of designs, vast debility, and procrastination." The forlorn note belonging to the phrase "vast debility," recalls that saddest and most discouraged of writers, the author of *Obermann*, Senancour, with whom Emerson has in truth a certain kinship. He has in common with Senancour his pureness, his passion for nature, his single eye; and here we find him confessing, like Senancour, a sense in himself of sterility and impotence.

And now I think I have cleared the ground. I have given up to envious Time as much of Emerson as Time can fairly expect ever to obtain. We have not in Emerson a great poet, a great writer, a great philosophy-maker. His relation to us is not that of one of those personages; yet it is a relation of, I think, even superior importance. His relation to us is more like that of the Roman Emperor Marcus Aurelius. Marcus Aurelius is not a great writer, a great philosophy-maker; he is the friend and aider of those who would live in the spirit. Emerson is the same. He is the friend and aider of those who would live in the spirit. All the points in thinking which are necessary for this purpose he takes; but he does not combine them into a system, or present them as a regular philosophy. Combined in a system by a man with the requisite talent for this kind of thing, they would be less useful than as Emerson gives them to us; and the man with the talent so to systematise them would be less impressive than Emerson. They do very well as they now stand;—like "boulders," as he says;—in "paragraphs incompressible, each sentence an infinitely repellent particle." In such sentences his main points recur again and again, and become fixed in the memory.

We all know them. First and foremost, character. Character is everything. "That which all things tend to educe,—which freedom, cultivation, intercourse, revolutions, go to form and deliver,—is character." Character and self-reliance. "Trust thyself! every heart vibrates to that iron string." And yet we have our being in a *not ourselves*. "There is a power above and behind us, and we are the channels of its communications." But our lives must be pitched higher. "Life must be lived on a higher plane; we must go up to a higher platform, to which we are always invited to ascend; there the whole scene changes." The good we need is for ever close to us, though we attain it not. "On the brink of the waters of life and truth, we are miserably dying." This good is close to us, moreover, in our daily life, and in the familiar, homely places. "The unremitting retention of simple and high sentiments in obscure duties,"—that is the maxim for us. "Let us be poised and wise, and our own to-day. Let us treat the men and women well,—treat them as if they were real; perhaps they are. Men live in their fancy, like drunkards whose hands are too soft and tremulous for successful labour. I settle myself ever firmer in the creed, that we should not postpone and refer and wish, but do broad justice where we are, by whomsoever we deal with; accepting our actual companions and circumstances, however humble or odious, as the mystic officials to whom the universe has delegated its whole pleasure for us." "Massachusetts, Connecticut River, and Boston Bay, you think paltry places, and the ear loves names of foreign and classic topography. But here we are; and if we will tarry a little we may come to learn that here is best. See to it only that thyself is here." Furthermore, the good is close to us *all*. "I resist the scepticism of our education and of our educated men. I do not believe that the differences of opinion and character in men are organic. I do not recognise, beside the class of the good and the wise, a permanent class of sceptics, or a class of conservatives, or of malignants, or of materialists. I do not believe in two classes." "Every man has a call of the power to do something unique." Exclusiveness is deadly. "The exclusive in social life does not see that he excludes himself from enjoyment in the attempt to appropriate it. The exclusionist in religion does not see that he shuts the door of heaven on himself in striving to shut out others. Treat men as pawns and ninepins, and you shall suffer as well as they. If you leave out their heart you shall lose your own." "The selfish man suffers more from his selfishness than he from whom that selfishness withholds some important benefit." A sound nature will be inclined to refuse ease and self-indulgence. "To live with some rigour of temperance, or some extremes of generosity, seems to be an asceticism which common good-nature would appoint to those who are at ease and in plenty, in sign that they feel a brotherhood with the great multitude of suffering men." Compensation, finally, is the great law of life; it is everywhere, it is sure, and there is no escape from it. This is that "law alive and beautiful, which works over our heads and under our feet. Pitiless, it avails itself of our success when we obey it, and of our ruin when we contravene it. Men are all secret believers in it. It rewards actions after their nature. The reward of a thing well done is to have done it." "The thief steals from himself, the swindler swindles himself. You must pay at last your own debt."

This is tonic indeed! And let no one object that it is too general; that more practical, positive direction is what we want; that Emerson's optimism, self-reliance, and indifference to favourable conditions for our life and growth, have in them something of danger. "Trust thyself;" "what attracts my attention shall have it;" "though thou shouldst walk the world over, thou shalt not be able to find a condition inopportune or ignoble;" "what we call vulgar society is that society whose poetry is not yet written, but which you shall presently make as enviable and renowned as any." With maxims like these, we surely, it may be said, run some risk of being made too well satisfied with our own actual self and state, however crude and imperfect they may be. "Trust thyself?" It may be said that the common American or Englishman is more than enough disposed already to trust himself. I often reply, when our sectarians are praised for following conscience: Our people are very good in following their conscience; where they are not so good is in ascertaining whether their conscience tells them right. "What attracts my attention shall have it?" Well, that is our people's plea when they run after the Salvation Army, and desire Messrs. Moody and Sankey. "Thou shalt not be able to find a condition inopportune or ignoble?" But think of the turn of the good people of our race for producing a life of hideousness and immense ennui; think of that specimen of your own New England life which Mr. Howells gives us in one of his charming stories which I was reading lately; think of the life of that *lagged* New England farm in the *Lady of the Aroostook*; think of Deacon Blood, and Aunt Maria, and the straight-backed chairs with black horse-hair seats, and Ezra Perkins with perfect self-reliance depositing his travellers in the snow! I can truly say that in the little which I have seen of the life of New England, I am more struck with what has been achieved than with the crudeness and failure. But no doubt there is still a great deal of crudeness also. Your own novelists say there is, and I suppose they say true. In the New England, as in the Old, our people have to learn, I suppose, not that their modes of life are beautiful and excellent already; they have rather to learn that they must transform them.

To adopt this line of objection to Emerson's deliverances would, however, be unjust. In the first place, Emerson's points are in themselves true, if understood in a certain high sense; they are true and fruitful. And the right work to be done, at the hour when he appeared, was to affirm them generally and absolutely. Only thus could he break through the hard and fast barrier of narrow, fixed ideas which he found confronting him, and win an entrance for new ideas. Had he attempted developments which may now strike us as expedient, he would have excited fierce antagonism, and probably effected little or nothing. The time might come for doing other work later, but the work which Emerson did was the right work to be done then.

In the second place, strong as was Emerson's optimism, and unconquerable as was his belief in a good result to emerge from all which he saw going on around him, no misanthropical satirist ever saw shortcomings and absurdities more clearly than he did, or exposed them more courageously. When he sees "the meanness," as he calls it, "of American politics," he congratulates Washington on being "long already happily dead," on being "wrapt in his shroud and for ever safe." With how firm a touch he delineates the faults of your two great political parties of forty years ago! The Democrats, he says, "have not at heart the ends which give to the name of democracy what hope and virtue are in it. The spirit of our American radicalism is destructive and aimless; it is not loving; it has no ulterior and divine ends, but is destructive only out of hatred and selfishness. On the other side, the conservative party, composed of the most moderate, able, and cultivated part of the population, is timid, and merely defensive of property. It vindicates no right, it aspires to no real good, it brands no crime, it proposes no generous policy. From neither party, when in power, has the world any benefit to expect in science, art, or humanity, at all commensurate with the resources of the nation." Then with what subtle though kindly irony he follows the gradual withdrawal in New England, in the last half century, of tender consciences from the social organisations,—the bent for experiments such as that of Brook Farm and the like,—follows it in all its "dissidence of dissent and Protestantism of the Protestant religion!" He even loves to rally the New Englander on his philanthropical activity, and to find his beneficence and its institutions a bore! "Your miscellaneous popular charities, the education at college of fools, the building of meeting-houses to the vain end to which many of these now stand, alms to sots, and the thousand-fold relief societies,—though I confess with shame that I sometimes succumb and give the dollar, yet it is a wicked dollar which by and by I shall have the manhood to withhold." "Our Sunday schools and churches and pauper societies are yokes to the neck. We pain ourselves to please nobody. There are natural ways of arriving at the same ends at which these aim but do not arrive." "Nature does not like our benevolence or our learning much better than she likes our frauds and wars. When we come out of the caucus, or the bank, or the Abolition Convention, or the Temperance meeting, or the Transcendental Club, into the fields and woods, she says to us: 'So hot, my little Sir?'"

Yes, truly, his insight is admirable; his truth is precious. Yet the secret of his effect is not even in these; it is in his temper. It is in the hopeful, serene, beautiful temper wherewith these, in Emerson, are indissolubly joined; in which they work, and have their being. He says himself: "We judge of a man's wisdom by his hope, knowing that the perception of the inexhaustibleness of nature is an immortal youth." If this be so, how wise is Emerson! for never had man such a sense of the inexhaustibleness of nature, and such hope. It was the ground of his being; it never failed him. Even when he is sadly avowing the imperfection of his literary power and resources, lamenting his fumbling fingers and stammering tongue, he adds: "Yet, as I tell you, I am very easy in my mind and never dream of suicide. My whole philosophy, which is very real, teaches acquiescence and optimism. Sure I am that the right word will be spoken though I cut out my tongue." In his old age, with friends dying and life failing, his tone of cheerful, forward-looking hope is still the same: "A multitude of young men are growing up here of high promise, and I compare gladly the social poverty of my youth with the power on which these draw." His abiding word for us, the word by which being dead he yet speaks to us, is this: "That which befits us, embosomed in beauty and wonder as we are, is cheerfulness and courage, and the endeavour to realise our aspirations. Shall not the heart, which has received so much, trust the Power by which it lives?"

One can scarcely overrate the importance of thus holding fast to happiness and hope. It gives to Emerson's work an invaluable virtue. As Wordsworth's poetry is, in my judgment, the most important work done in verse, in our language, during the present century, so Emerson's *Essays* are, I think, the most important work done in prose. His work is more important than Carlyle's. Let us be just to Carlyle, provoking though he often is. Not only has he that genius of his which makes Emerson say truly of his letters, that "they savour always of eternity." More than this may be said of him. The scope and upshot of his teaching are true; "his guiding genius," to quote Emerson again, is really "his moral sense, his perception of the sole importance of truth and justice." But consider Carlyle's temper, as we have been considering Emerson's; take his own account of it: "Perhaps London is the proper place for me after all, seeing all places are improper: who knows? Meanwhile, I lead a most dyspeptic, solitary, self-shrouded life; consuming, if possible in silence, my considerable daily allotment of pain; glad when any strength is left in me for working, which is the only use I can see in myself,—too rare a case of late. The ground of my existence is black as death; too black, when all *void* too; but at times there paint themselves on it pictures of gold, and rainbow, and lightning; all the brighter for the black ground, I suppose. Withal, I am very much of a fool."—No, not a fool, but turbid and morbid, wilful and perverse. "We judge of a man's wisdom by his hope."

Carlyle's perverse attitude towards happiness cuts him off from hope. He fiercely attacks the desire for happiness; his grand point in *Sartor,* his secret in which the soul may find rest, is that one shall cease to desire happiness, that one should learn to say to oneself: "What if thou wert born and predestined not to be happy, but to be unhappy!" He is wrong; Saint Augustine is the better philosopher, who says: "Act we *must* in pursuance of what gives us most delight." Epictetus and Augustine can be severe moralists enough; but both of them know and frankly say that the desire for happiness is the root and ground of man's being. Tell him and show him that he places his happiness wrong, that he seeks for delight where delight will never be really found; then you illumine and further him. But you only confuse him by telling him to cease to desire happiness, and you will not tell him this unless you are already confused yourself.

Carlyle preached the dignity of labour, the necessity of righteousness, the love of veracity, the hatred of shams. He is said by many people to be a great teacher, a great helper for us, because he does so. But what is the due and eternal result of labour, righteousness, veracity?—Happiness. And how are we drawn to them by one who, instead of making us feel that with them is happiness, tells us that perhaps we were predestined not to be happy but to be unhappy?

You will find, in especial, many earnest preachers of our popular religion to be fervent in their praise and admiration of Carlyle. His insistence on labour, righteousness, and veracity pleases them; his contempt for happiness pleases them too. I read the other day a tract against smoking, although I do not happen to be a smoker myself. "Smoking," said the tract, "is liked because it gives agreeable sensations. Now it is a positive objection to a thing that it gives agreeable sensations. An earnest man will expressly avoid what gives agreeable sensations." Shortly afterwards I was inspecting a school, and I found the children reading a piece of poetry on the common theme that we are here to-day and gone to-morrow. I shall soon be gone, the speaker in this poem was made to say,—

> And I shall be glad to go,
> For the world at best is a weary place,
> And my pulse is getting low.

How usual a language of popular religion that is, on our side of the Atlantic at any rate! But then our popular religion, in disparaging happiness here below, knows very well what it is after. It has its eye on a happiness in a future life above the clouds, in the New Jerusalem, to be won by disliking and rejecting happiness here on earth. And so long as this ideal stands fast, it is very well. But for very many it now stands fast no longer; for Carlyle, at any rate, it had failed and vanished. Happiness in labour, righteousness and veracity,—in the life of the spirit,—here was a gospel still for Carlyle to preach, and to help others by preaching. But he baffled them and himself by preferring the paradox that we are not born for happiness at all.

Happiness in labour, righteousness and veracity; in all the life of the spirit; happiness and eternal hope;—that was Emerson's gospel. I hear it said that Emerson was too sanguine; that the actual generation in America is not turning out so well as he expected. Very likely he was too sanguine as to the near future; in this country it is difficult not to be too sanguine. Very possibly the present generation may prove unworthy of his high hopes; even several generations succeeding this may prove unworthy of them. But by his conviction that in the life of the spirit is happiness, and by his hope that this life of the spirit will come more and more to be sanely understood, and to prevail, and to work for happiness,—by this conviction and hope Emerson was great, and he will surely prove in the end to have been right in them. In this country it is difficult, as I said, not to be sanguine. Very many of your writers are over-sanguine, and on the wrong grounds. But you have two men who in what they have written show their sanguineness in a line where courage and hope are just, where they are also infinitely important, but where they are not easy. The two men are Franklin and Emerson.[1] These two are, I think, the most distinctively and honourably American of your writers; they are the most original and the most valuable. Wise men everywhere know that we must keep up our courage and hope; they know that hope is, as Wordsworth well says,—

> The paramount *duty* which Heaven lays,
> For its own honour, on man's suffering heart.

But the very word *duty* points to an effort and a struggle to maintain our hope unbroken. Franklin and Emerson maintained theirs with a convincing ease, an inspiring joy. Franklin's confidence in the happiness with which industry, honesty, and economy will crown the life of this work-day world, is such that he runs over with felicity. With a like felicity does Emerson run over, when he contemplates the happiness eternally attached to the true life in the spirit. You cannot prize him too much, nor heed him too diligently. He has lessons for both the branches of our race. I figure him to my mind as visible upon earth still, as still standing here by Boston Bay, or at his own Concord, in his habit as he lived, but of heightened stature and shining feature, with one hand stretched out towards the East, to our laden and labouring England; the other towards the ever-growing West, to his own dearly-loved America,—"great, intelligent, sensual, avaricious America." To us he shows for guidance his lucid freedom, his cheerfulness and hope; to you his dignity, delicacy, serenity, elevation.

Notes

1. I found with pleasure that this conjunction of Emerson's name with Franklin's had already occurred to an accomplished writer and delightful man, a friend of Emerson, left almost the sole survivor, alas! of the famous literary generation of Boston,—Dr. Oliver Wendell Holmes. Dr. Holmes has kindly allowed me to print here the ingenious and interesting lines, hitherto unpublished, in which he speaks of Emerson thus:—

> Where in the realm of thought, whose air is song,
> Does he, the Buddha of the West, belong?
> He seems a winged Franklin, sweetly wise,
> Born to unlock the secrets of the skies;
> And which the nobler calling—if 'tis fair
> Terrestrial with celestial to compare—
> To guide the storm-cloud's elemental flame,
> Or walk the chambers whence the lightning came
> Amidst the sources of its subtile fire,
> And steal their effluence for his lips and lyre?

—Matthew Arnold, "Emerson," (1883),
Discourses in America, 1885, pp. 150–207

W.L. COURTNEY "RALPH WALDO EMERSON" (1885)

The American essayist W.L. Courtney notes that Emerson's lasting value will lie not in his work, but in "the genial spirit of the man." (Courtney's opinions might be read as a companion to Louisa May Alcott's sentiments.) Courtney is making an insightful, but difficult, separation here. Emerson is not a philosopher, but he is more than simply a contemporary essayist. That is, Emerson's work occupies a unique place in American letters. Courtney's separation of the personal Emerson from the professional brings into question the ways in which Emerson's work might be qualified. Students discussing Emerson's place as an American writer might consider Courtney's claims.

Emerson's fame will probably be independent of any single contribution to the world's literature. For his merit does not appear to consist either in his rhetoric, or his philosophy, or his poetry, but rather in the genial spirit of the man, and in the generous and wholesome influence which he diffuses around him, like some bracing and exhilarating atmosphere. In a different sense from that of the sermon or the ethical homily, it "does one good" to read him; for he braces the sinews and sets the blood coursing more freely through the veins. In this respect he stands at the opposite pole to Carlyle, who supplies the malodorous and distasteful medicine, while Emerson gives the tonic of blithe air and happy sunshine. His spirits are so unfailing, his mental attitude is so sane and manlike, that he cannot even bear that one should mention his maladies, lest he become the querulous valetudinarian. "I beseech you by all angels to hold your peace and not pollute the morning, to which all the housemates bring serene and pleasant thoughts, by corruption and groans. Come out of the azure. Love the day." The distemper known as "blue devils" did not apparently haunt Emerson. "All my hurts my garden spade can heal," he says; albeit that his son, when he saw him digging, is reported to have told him to beware lest he should "dig his leg." There remains, however, a certain desultoriness which will probably prevent Emerson's work from becoming anything more than inspiring and suggestive. Perhaps this is the inevitable accompaniment of one who embraces a transcendental creed, like the shadow which lies across the valley even of him who walks on the heights. Perhaps it is the especial drawback of the modern American mind, which seems to rejoice in impressions and effects and symphonies as though they were the same as honest and full-blooded work. So Emerson himself thought when he asserted that the true dignity of the scholar was not realised in America. "The mark of American merit in painting, in sculpture, in poetry, in fiction, in eloquence, seems to be a certain grace without grandeur, and itself not new but derivative; a vase of fair outline, but empty, which whoso sees may fill with what wit and character is in him, but which does not, like the charged cloud, overflow with terrible beauty and emit lightning on all beholders." The grace of Emerson no one can deny, though even this is inferior to the literary finish and elegance of Hawthorne; but that he was not new but derivative, let his spiritual exemplars testify, who were Plato and Coleridge, Swedenborg and Wordsworth.

—W.L. Courtney, "Ralph Waldo Emerson,"
Fortnightly Review, September 1885, p. 331

COVENTRY PATMORE "EMERSON" (1889)

English poet and essayist Coventry Patmore registers an interesting claim here, that Emerson has limited original ideas but expresses them in fresh ways throughout his body of work. Patmore refers to this as Emerson's "tautology" (meaning that Emerson needlessly repeats the same ideas). Patmore believes this quality is the debilitating effect oratory has on Emerson's writing.

It might be said that Emerson's value as a literary artist relies on the quality Patmore dismisses; that is, Emerson's ability to re-create new expression from his observations, yielding a web of intricate, unique phrasing. In this manner, Emerson is more the literary figure than the philosopher, a claim that his lack of system (recognized by many contemporaries) supports. For students exploring Emerson's intellectual standing, this insight may help to bring Emerson into view as a literary figure, rather than as a philosopher.

***

There can be no greater misfortune for a sincere and truthful mind like Emerson's than to have to get a living by "orating." This was his predicament, however; and there can be no doubt that his mind and his writings were the worse for this necessity. His philosophy afforded him only a very narrow range of subject. In all his essays and lectures he is but ringing the changes upon three or four ideas—which are really commonplace, though his sprightly wit and imagination give them freshness; and it is impossible to read any single essay, much less several in succession, without feeling that the licence of tautology is used to its extremest limits. In a few essays—for example, "The Poet," "Character," and "Love"—the writer's heart is so much in the matter that these endless variations of one idea have the effect of music which delights us to the end with the reiteration of an exceedingly simple theme; but in many other pieces it is impossible not to detect that weariness of the task of having to coin dollars out of transcendental sentiments to which Emerson's letters and journals often bear witness. But, whether delighted with or weary of his labour, there is no progress in his thought, which resembles the spinning of a cockchafer on a pin rather than the flight of a bird on its way from one continent to another.

—Coventry Patmore, "Emerson,"
Principle in Art, 1889, pp. 130–31

Maurice Maeterlinck "Emerson" (1898)

The Belgian poet and playwright Maurice Maeterlinck is a good source for commentary on Emerson. A prolific essayist (and winner of the 1911 Nobel Prize in Literature), Maeterlinck held an interest in the operations of nature and offered mystical speculations on this account.

When Maeterlinck writes that "Man is eager for explanations," it suggests other writers and thinkers who claim that systemization is necessary for all knowledge. However, some critics considered Emerson's lack of a system to be the principal failing of his body of work. Maeterlinck sees, if not a system, then an explanation from Emerson regarding the value of each individual life, and the weight of each individual soul. Maeterlinck finds in Emerson an affirmation of the value of each soul and of each life, whether Marcus Aurelius or "a mechanic on his way to the factory." Students interested in Emerson's views on the soul (and on Emerson's definition of that term) should consider Maeterlinck's comments a noteworthy explanation of this concept.

Early in the essay, Maeterlinck writes of life having "no end other than itself," and that each life is "incomprehensible and divine." This last phrase is significant because of the implication that life is divine *because* it is incomprehensible, that the mystery of existence (or, the "common soul") is part of the divine. This is of interest to students sorting out Emerson's theories of the soul and the value of experience, especially in "Nature," "Experience," and "The Over-Soul."

He comes to many at the moment when he ought to come, and at the very instant when they were in mortal need of new interpretations. Heroic moments are less obvious, those of abnegation have not yet returned; only daily life remains to us, and yet we cannot live without grandeur. He has given to life, which had lost its traditional horizon, an almost acceptable meaning, and perhaps he has even been able to show us that it is strange enough, profound enough, great enough, to need no other end than itself. He does not know any more of it than the others do; but he affirms with more courage, and he has confidence in the mystery. You must live, all you who travel through days and years, without activities, without thought, without light, because your life, despite everything, is incomprehensible and divine. You must live because no one has a right to subtract any commonplace weeks from their spiritual sequence. You must live because there is not an hour without intimate miracles and ineffable meanings. You must live because there is not an act, not a word, not a gesture, which is free from inexplicable claims in a world "where there are many things to do, and few things to know."

Lives are neither great nor small, and the deed of Regulus or of Leonidas has no importance when I compare it with a moment of my soul's secret existence. It might do what they have done or not; these things do not reach it; and the soul of Regulus when he returned to Carthage was probably as distracted and indifferent as that of a mechanic on his way to the factory. The soul is far apart from all our deeds. It is far away from all our thoughts. It lives alone in the depth of our being a life of which it does not speak; and of the heights where it reigns, its various modes of activity can make out nothing. We walk weighed down by the weight of the soul, and there is no proportion between it and us. It perhaps never thinks of that which we are doing, and this can be read in our countenance. If one should ask an intelligence from another world what is the typical expression of the faces of men, it would reply doubtless, after having seen them in joys, in griefs, and in restless moods: "They look as if they were thinking of something else." Be great, wise, or eloquent; the soul of the beggar who holds out his hand at the corner of the bridge will not be jealous, but yours will perhaps envy him his silence. The hero needs the approbation of the ordinary man, but the ordinary man does not demand the approbation of heroes, and he pursues his course undisquieted, like one who has all his treasures in a safe place. "When Socrates speaks," says Emerson, "Lysis and Menexenus are afflicted by no shame that they do not speak. They also are good. He likewise defers to them, loves them, whilst he speaks. Because a true and natural man contains and is the same truth which an eloquent man articulates; but in the eloquent man, because he can articulate it, it seems something the less to reside, and he turns to these, silent, beautiful, with the more inclination and respect." ['Intellect.']

Man is eager for explanations. He must have his life shown to him. He rejoices to find anywhere an exact interpretation of a petty gesture he has been making for twenty-five years; yet there is no petty gesture here, but the main attitude of the common soul. You will not find the eternal quality of the soul of a Marcus Aurelius here. But Marcus Aurelius was thought itself. Who among us, moreover, leads the life of a Marcus Aurelius? One is man here, nothing more, not magnified arbitrarily, but grown nearer through habit. Here is John who is trimming his trees, Peter who is building his house; here are you who talk to me of the harvest, and I who give you my hand; yet we are made so that we draw nigh to the gods and are astonished at what we effect. We did not know that the laws of the universe attended upon us, and we turn about and stare without saying anything, like people who have seen a miracle.

Emerson comes to affirm simply this equal and secret greatness of life. He encompasses us with silence and wonder. He puts a shaft of light under the foot of the artisan coming out of his workshop. He shows us all the powers of heaven and earth busied in supporting the threshold where two neighbors speak of the falling rain or the rising wind; and above these two wayfarers accosting each other he makes us see the face of one god smiling upon another. He is nearer to us than any one in our every-day life, the most watchful and persistent of monitors, the most upright and scrupulous, perhaps the most human. He is the sage of commonplace days; and commonplace days are the sum and substance of our being.

The most of a year passes without passions, without virtues, without miracles. Let us learn to reverence the small hours of life. If I have been able to work this morning, in the spirit of Marcus Aurelius, do not find fault with what I have accomplished, for I know well enough that something has come of it. But if I think that I have wasted my day in worthless undertakings, and you can prove to me that I have lived as worthily as a hero, and that my soul has lost none of its prerogatives, you will have done more than if you had persuaded me to save my enemy; for you will have increased within me the sense, the grandeur, and the desire of life; and to-morrow perhaps I shall be able to live with reverence.

—Maurice Maeterlinck, "Emerson," trs. Charlotte Porter,
Helen A. Clarke, *Poet-Lore*, 1898, pp. 82–84

Sir Leslie Stephen "Emerson" (1901)

English writer, critic, and editor Leslie Stephen will perhaps best be remembered as the first editor of the *Dictionary of National Biography* (as well as the father of writer Virginia Woolf). Stephen's essay should remind students that Emerson was a product of his times, and his writing reflects this. More specifically, Emerson's concern with the United States results from his ideas about the strength of the individual, as well as his perception of the America of his time, a new land "flowing with freedom's honey and milk." Stephen's point that Emerson recognized the need for "a sharp intellectual shock" to awaken and realize the nation's full potential and responsibility is important for students working to place Emerson in his political and social context. Emerson realized America's lack of intellectual history, and sought to create a uniquely American approach to its intellectual definition. Stephen is very helpful in this regard; note his definition of transcendentalism.

Stephen also clarifies the significance of Emerson's relationship with Carlyle, and utilizes this explanation to suggest ways in which Emerson might be read on a fundamental level. One of the more challenging aspects of Emerson's work that students face is the dense, imagistic quality of his prose. Stephen's analysis of his own experiences encountering Emerson's prose will be useful to students wrestling with Emersonian diction.

Emerson's prose style is described by Russell Lowell as "poetic." Here, Stephen describes what this term means. Many critics find fault with Emerson's poetry, and students working on Emerson's output in that genre will encounter this. Stephen is a great help in determining the problems with Emerson's poems. He writes that Emerson's weakness is his prose: "His characteristic want of continuity made him as incapable of evolving a central idea as of expounding an argument." However, this quality lends value to his poetry. What seems a weakness commonly identified by Emerson's critics, the want of a "system," is defended, rightly, by Stephen as the writer's failure to allow for the adequate development of his style. However, this style fits more finely with poetry than with prose. When Lowell refers to Emerson as "poetic," this is what he means, in a specific sense.

Also, Stephen's analysis of Emerson's perception of evil could prove quite helpful for students. Emerson's writings on evil are difficult to untangle, since Emerson does not recognize "evil" as a force in the world in and of itself. Rather, Emerson sees evil as privation; that is, what we may think of as evil is only removal from an object's (or idea's) inherent beauty. This removal is as much a part of the perceiver's moral failing, since for Emerson, beauty is a moral condition as well as an aesthetic concern.

This is quite a complicated matter, and easily overgeneralized. Resolving Emerson's attitude regarding evil requires careful consideration. The question of evil as portrayed in Emerson's work is tantalizing and provides students with rich opportunities for research and writing. Stephen is a good source of insight on this topic.

Many years ago I had the chance of laying up an interesting reminiscence. Lowell took me to visit Emerson in his house at Concord, and, as it happened, had to leave me to perform the function of an interviewer by myself. But instead of recording an impression I have to make a confession. I was young enough at that time to believe in great authors, and to desire to offer acceptable incense. Unluckily, I had not read a word of Emerson, and on the way I had innocently confided to Lowell that I took him to be a kind of Carlyle. I did not know that Lowell had drawn an inimitably witty contrast between the two, beginning—

> There are persons mole-blind to the soul's make and style,
> Who insist on a likeness 'twixt him and Carlyle.

Though he did not accuse me of "mole-blindness," Lowell managed to intimate courteously that I was somehow in the dark. The sense of my ignorance struck me dumb. The brilliant remark which was to show at once that I appreciated Emerson, and that my appreciation was worthy having, refused to present itself. What Emerson thought of the intruder I know not, but our conversation fell hopelessly flat; and I was a happy man when Lowell relieved guard. I came away, indeed, with a certain impression of my host's personal simplicity and dignity. If I had not offered homage he had not shown the least wish that I should fall upon my knees, and had received me as at least a human being—a claim upon his courtesy which he admitted like a true democrat. Still, I was left with a problem unsolved. Emerson's ablest countrymen, I found, were never tired of expressing their gratitude to him. He had pronounced their "literary Declaration of Independence." His first lectures had made an epoch. He had removed the scales from their eyes, revealed the barrenness of the intellectual wilderness in which they had been wandering, and given them a Pisgah-sight of a new land "flowing with freedom's honey and milk." The question remained: What was the secret of his power? Then and since I have tried to answer it, partly by the obvious expedient of reading his books, and partly by reading various criticisms. I hope that I have learnt something, in spite of grave disqualifications. I was not impressed at the impressible age, and do not, I fear, belong to the class which takes most freely the impression of the Emersonian stamp. Yet it may be of some interest to more congenial disciples to know how their prophet affects one of the profane vulgar. If some rays from the luminary can pierce the opaque medium of my Philistinism it will show their intrinsic brilliance.

Matthew Arnold characteristically explained to an American audience that Emerson was not a great poet, nor a great philosopher, nor even a great man of letters. For all that, he was the friend and aider "of those who would live in the spirit." Perhaps the phrase is a little vague, though it, no doubt, indicates the truth. Emerson was the founder and leader of the American

"Transcendentalists," and Transcendentalists, I suppose, were people who meant to "live in the spirit." The name is alarming, but it represents a very harmless and a very commendable phenomenon. In Emerson's youth his countrymen were in need of a sharp intellectual shock. Their understanding, in Coleridgean phrase—this faculty which is useful in clearing forests and accumulating dollars—was thoroughly wide-awake; but their reason—the faculty which cultivates poetry and "divine philosophy"—had somehow sunk into slumber. A vague craving for better things had been roused, though by no leader with authoritative credentials. There were no trained professors profoundly learned in the past history of thought to come forward and propound new solutions of the enigma of the universe. Active but superficially educated youths were ready to take for a beacon any light, ancient or modern, of which they happened to catch a glimpse. Some enthusiasts had vague impressions that there was such a thing as German philosophy, and had heard of Schelling through Cousin or Coleridge. One swore by Pythagoras; and others took up Plotinus, or found what they wanted in Swedenborg or in Jacob Behmen, or set up some mystic doctrine of their own. "Transcendentalism" took its name from Kant, but implied no familiarity with Kant's special metaphysical system. It meant a "wave of sentiment"—a vague desire for some kind of intellectual flying machine—some impulse that would lift you above the prosaic commonplace world into the charmed regions of philosophy and poetry. Emerson had no more academical training than his followers, and, in one sense, was certainly not a "great philosopher." If "philosophy" means such a logical system as was worked out by Kant or Hegel, he was not a philosopher at all. He positively disliked such philosophies. "Who," he asked, "has not looked into a metaphysical book? And what sensible man ever looked twice?" You may collate and distil all the systems, he declared, and you will get nothing by it. We have as yet nothing but "tendency and indication." Systems are merely the outside husk, worthless except as a temporary embodiment of the essential truth. Emerson, that is, is a denizen of the region where philosophy is not differentiated from poetry. "I am," he said, "in all my theory, ethics, and politics, a poet"; and he ridicules the impression that his "transcendentalism" was, as some people fancied, "a known and fixed element, like salt or meal"—a rigid and definite creed. All the argument and all the wisdom, he declares, is not in the treatise on metaphysics, "but in the sonnet or the play." Transcendentalism, indeed, had its philosophical affinities: it represented idealism as against materialism; or, as Emerson occasionally puts it, takes the side of Plato against Locke. Lockism is the influx of "decomposition and prose," while Platonism means growth. The Platonic is the poetic tendency; the "so-called scientific" is the negative and poisonous. Spenser, Burns, Byron, and Wordsworth will be Platonists; and "the dull men will be Lockists."

The average American had fallen into such "Lockism," and Emerson, when he came to England, found the fully-blown type flourishing and triumphant. The "brilliant Macaulay," he said, represented the spirit of the governing classes, and Macaulay had explicitly declared (in his essay on Bacon) that "good" meant simply solid, sensual benefits—good food and good clothes and material comfort. Emerson does not argue with men in whom the faculty of vision is non-existent or clouded by want of use. He is content simply to see. One result is indicated in the charming correspondence with Carlyle. Each most cordially appreciated the merits of the other, and Carlyle, like Emerson, called himself a "mystic," and soared above "Lockism." But the visions of the two took a very different colouring. Emerson praises *Sartor Resartus* with a characteristic qualification. Carlyle's grim humour and daring flights of superabundant imagination cover a "simple air," he complains, with a "volley of variations." You are, he says, dispensing "that which is rarest, the simplest truths, truths which lie next to consciousness, which only the Platos and the Goethes perceive," and he hopes for the hour "when the word will be as simple and so as resistless as the thought"; for the hour, that is, when a Carlyle would be an Emerson. To find effective utterance for these "simplest truths" is, in fact, Emerson's special function. The difficulty of the task is proverbial. A simple truth is a very charming thing; but it has an uncomfortable trick of sinking into a truism. If you try to make it something more it is apt to collide with other simple truths. The function of the system-maker is to persuade the various truths to keep the peace by assigning to each its proper limits and stating it with due reserves and qualifications. But that is precisely what Emerson altogether declines to do. The most obvious peculiarity of his style corresponds. His lectures are a "mosaic" of separate sentences; each, as he put it himself, an "infinitely repellent particle." Carlyle, praising the beauty and simplicity of his sentences, complains that the paragraph is not "a beaten ingot," but "a beautiful square bag of duckshot held together by canvas." Proverbs, says Emerson, are statements of an absolute truth, and thus the sanctuary of the intuitions. They are, indeed, absolute statements of truth; and for that reason, as Sancho Panza might have pointed out, you can always quote a proverb on each side of every alternative. Solomon tells us to answer a fool and not to answer a fool according to his folly. "More haste, worse speed" is true; but it is equally true that "the early bird catches the worm." Emerson is a master of the gnomic utterances which are to the cultivated what proverbs are to the vulgar. He is well aware that they are not always reconcilable; but it is not his function to reconcile them. He cares nothing for consistency. He wishes to say what he feels to-day with "the proviso that to-morrow, perhaps, I shall contradict it all." "A foolish consistency is the hobgoblin of little minds. With consistency a great soul has nothing whatever to do. . . . Speak what you think now in hard words, and to-morrow speak what tomorrow thinks in hard words again, though it contradict everything you said to-day." The peculiarity seems to have annoyed his friends with a turn for logic. Argument was for him an absurdity. He approved as a rule for a debating society (what often enough corresponds to the practice) that no one should reply to a previous speaker. You thought that you had contradicted him; he placidly accepted both your statements and his own. He is simply playing a different tune, not denying that yours may be harmonious. The region of simple truths would seem to be altogether above the sphere in which controversy is possible. You should never conform to a church or sect, or to public opinion as to your past utterances. Leave the truths to assimilate by spontaneous affinity.

One charm of Emerson is due to this affable reception of all opinions. On his first appearance in a pulpit he is described as "the most gracious of mortals, with a face all benignity," and preached with an indefinite air of simplicity and wisdom. His lectures radiate benignity and simplicity. He had no dogmas to proclaim or heretics to denounce. He is simply uttering an inspiration which has come to him. He is not a mystagogue, affecting superinducal wisdom and in possession of the only clue to the secret. If you sympathize, well and good; if you cannot, you may translate his truth into your own. The ascent into this serene region, above all the noise of controversy, has its disadvantages. Carlyle complains gently that his friend is in danger of parting from fact and soaring into perilous altitudes. He is "soliloquizing on the mountain tops." It is easy to "screw oneself up into high and ever higher altitudes of transcendentalism," to see nothing beneath one but "the everlasting snows of the Himalaya, the earth shrinking to a planet, and the indigo firmament sowing itself with stars." Come back to the earth, he exclaims; and readers of Emerson must occasionally echo the exhortation. And yet, in his own way, Emerson was closer to the everyday world than Carlyle himself; and it is the curious union of the two generally inconsistent qualities which gives a peculiar flavour to Emersonian teaching. Lowell puts it admirably in his comparison of Emerson and Carlyle:—

> C. gives nature and God his own fits of the blues,
> And rims common-sense things with mystical hues;

> E. sits in a mystery calm and intense,
> And looks coolly round him with calm common-sense;
> C. shows you how everyday matters unite,
> With the dim trans-diurnal recesses of night;
> While E., in a plain preternatural way,
> Makes mysteries matters of mere every day.

Emerson's curious position of equilibrium between the two worlds of mystery and broad daylight comes out in his literary tastes. His reading was wide but desultory. He was entirely free from the superstition which besets the ordinary scholar and makes him unhappy till he has read a book through and got it up as a student gets up a book for an examination. Emerson looks for inspiration, not for information. He puts a book down as soon as it bores him, and does not care a straw for its authenticity or for its place assigned to it in the orthodox literary tribunals. He is content if it "makes his top spin"—as he says—if, that is, it stimulates thought or fires the imagination. "What is best in literature," he says, "is the affirming, prophesying, spermatic words of men-making poets." Shakespeare is to be valued not because he is so much greater than yourself, but because, by your receptivity of him, you become aware of the power of your own soul. To Emerson the value of a book is measured by its dynamic effect upon himself. For some great names he cared little. The list of uninteresting writers included Shelley, Aristophanes, Cervantes, Miss Austen, and Dickens. He thought Dante a prodigy, but fitter for a museum than for a welcome to your own study. In compensation he is sometimes strangely enthusiastic about very obscure people. In speaking of literature in England, his appreciation of his friend Carlyle is checked by his dislike of the Carlylian pessimism; but he finds one consolation. There is a writer whose mind has "a long Atlantic roll not known except in the deepest water"; and who is elsewhere declared to have a "vigour of understanding and imagination comparable only to Lord Bacon's." This cheering exception to British stupidity turns out, to our surprise, to be a Mr. Wilkinson. I confess that I am not acquainted with his works, which, according to Emerson, "had thrown all contemporary philosophy in England into the shade." Wilkinson (a man of real ability, as a biographical dictionary informs me) had impressed Emerson by his exposition of Swedenborg. When Emerson made Swedenborg himself one of his representative men, Carlyle had to exclaim: "*Missed* the consummate flower and divine ultimate elixir of philosophy, say you? By heaven, in clutching at it and almost getting it he has tumbled into Bedlam!" Emerson would apparently reply not by denying the truth of the remark, but by declaring it to be irrelevant. Swedenborg, like other prophets, fell into absurdities when he became a system-monger, and Emerson could condemn some of the results sharply enough. He was not the less grateful for the inspiration, because associated with absurdities, which might qualify the prophet for Bedlam. Swedenborg's leading thought, he says, is given in Milton's lines:—

> What if earth
> Be but the shadow of Heaven and things therein
> Each to the other more like than on earth is thought?

Swedenborg, he thinks, was the first to give a scientific statement of the poetical doctrine of "symbolism." He had inverted the point of view of the "poisonous" kind of science. The ideal world is the reality, and the material world should be regarded as merely a kind of "picture language." Emerson wonders that when this fruitful seed of thought was once sown men did not put by all other science to work out the results. Yet people continue to take more interest in every spider, or fossil, or fungus, than in trying to discover "the meaning and upshot of the frame of things." It may be, he thinks, but centuries will be required to elaborate so profound a conception.

The impression made upon Emerson by this doctrine appears both in his own teaching and in numerous references to Swedenborg as one of the greatest leaders of thought, to be classed with the Platos and Shakespeares; and yet Emerson is equally attracted by men to whom mysticism would be another name for nonsense. From his boyhood he had studied Montaigne, another of his "Representative men," of whom he speaks with a kind of personal affection. Montaigne appears in the *Representative Men* as the typical "sceptic"; and scepticism goes rather awkwardly with mysticism and the imperative claims of direct intuition of simple truths. Yet Emerson finds scepticism congenial so far as it implies toleration. It represents contempt for the formalism and exaggeration of "bigots and blockheads"; and every superior mind must pass through this "domain of equilibration." He delights, therefore, in Montaigne's hospitable reception of every conceivable variety of opinion. Montaigne, it is true, not only begins, but ends with doubt. *"Que sçais je?"* is his last word. But then, it is his superlative merit to admit frankly that there are doubts, instead of trying to smother them. The difference seems to be that while Montaigne remains balanced between opposite opinions, Emerson seems to hold that, though opposed, they may both be true. If we can rise to a higher sphere we shall see that they are complimentary instead of contradictory. But Montaigne has evidently another charm for Emerson. His amazing frankness, his delight in laying bare all his own weaknesses, makes the essays an incomparable text-book for the student of human nature. Montaigne has no literary affectation; he talks rather than writes. "Cut his words and they would bleed; they are vascular and alive." Montaigne plays no antics; he is "stout and solid; tastes every moment of the day; likes pain because it makes him feel himself and realize things, as we pinch ourselves to know that we are awake." If Emerson could soar into mystic regions, he is equally delighted with the broad daylight, in which you can see the actual every-day play of human nature, stripped bare of every sort of conventional disguise. The man of genius, he says, must draw strength from pure reason, and his aim from common-sense. The two poles are equally necessary, if he is not to be either too mean or too vague. That, again, is one of the merits which he sees in Plato. Plato is the "balanced soul." He combines the mystical and the practical element. He can be transcendental and yet is at home in common life. He can illustrate his philosophy from the world which philosophers despise: "from mares and puppies, from pitchers and soup-ladles; from cooks and criers; the shops of potters, horse doctors, butchers, and fishmongers." It is this synthesis or equal poise between two opposite poles of thought which stamps his genius as unique. Yet Emerson can be equally impressed by men who represent only one side of the antithesis. He makes, perhaps, more references to Napoleon than to any one, except Swedenborg. Napoleon is "the man of the world"; "the idol of common men," because he had the common qualities in a transcendent degree. He hated sentiment and despised "ideologists"; he had no moral scruples and no magnanimity. But his supreme practical ability, his "enormous self-trust," his power of seeing to the heart of things, his making readiness in every emergency and "two o'clock in the morning courage" commands our respect. "I find it easy," says Emerson, "to translate all his technics into all of mine." There is more philosophy in his despatches than in the sermons of the Academy. "We like everything to do its office, whether it be a milch-cow or a rattlesnake"; and Napoleon at least represents a stupdendous natural force. Emerson was fond of reading books upon Napoleon. They were at any rate instructive documents in the study of character. The list of authors recommended in his lecture upon "books" is characteristic. You must, of course, read the great poets. But his special favourites are, on one side, Plotinus and the Neoplatonists; and on the other, the books which give an insight into character. Plutarch, both the *Lives* and the *Morals,* should be in the smallest library; *Confessions* and autobiographies, Augustine, Benvenuto Cellini, and Rousseau; the table-talks of Luther, or Selden, or Coleridge; and books of anecdotes are invaluable. Anybody, meanwhile, will do for history: Hume and

Goldsmith, as well as Gibbon. History represents merely the background in which the great lives are set; and what you should really want is to be brought into contact with inspiring minds, not to get up dates and external facts. Emerson is weak in criticism, if the critic is to give a judicial estimate of a man's proper position in the development of poetry or philosophy; but he can say most clearly and forcibly what is the message which any great writer has delivered to him personally.

This, I think, shows how one may approach one secret of reading Emerson himself. He combines Yankee shrewdness in singular fashion with the exaltation of the mystic. The mysticism is bewildering, if not simply nonsensical, to the poor "Lockist" or the average common-sense mortal. If asked to accept it as a systematic creed, he will declare that it is mere theosophical moonshine: too vague to have any meaning, or meaning something which is palpably absurd. But, then, one may also read Emerson as Emerson read his predecessors: for stimulus or inspiration, not as a propounder of solid, substantial truths. We are not to take his philosophy for a system of truths, but for a series of vivid intuitions. His "Declaration of Independence" proclaims a truth which may be stated in many dialects. Like its political parallel, it asserts that every man has indisputable rights, to be abrogated by no human authority. But it is not aggressive or dogmatic. It does not remind us of Fourth of July celebrations, which treated George III. like a grotesque Guy Faux. The emancipation is to be effected, not by iconoclasm, but by rousing the slumbering faculties. It implies a duty to yourself, as well as a right against your rulers. The enemy to be overcome is the torpor which accepts traditions and conventions as ultimate. They benumb the soul, and make it a part of a dead mechanism, when it should be a part of the living force which moulds the world. You should be an active instead of a passive agent in that process; you must be, in his phrase, "self-reliant"; you must develop your own powers and obey your instincts, without submitting to any external rule. You then become a "ripple of the stream of tendency." "Beware," he says, "when the great God lets loose a thinker on this planet." The new thought represents a "new influx of divinity into the mind." The doctrine is sometimes expressed in language learnt from the mystics. The beautiful state of the soul is measured by its capacity for "ecstasy." Every man is capable of divine illumination, and can be elevated by intercourse with the spiritual world. The "ecstasy" corresponds to the "inner light" of the Quakers. It recalls, as he says, "the trances of Socrates, Plotinus, Porphyry, Behmen, Fox, Bunyan, Pascal, Guion, and Swedenborg." The "rapt saint," he declares, is the only logician; not exhortation, not argument, becomes our lips, but "paeans of joy and praise." He speaks of the ecstatic state with a kind of awe in the essay on self-reliance as something which cannot be fully uttered. "The soul raised over passion beholds identity and Eternal causation, perceives the self-existence of truth and right, and calms itself with knowing that all things go well."

Certainly Emerson is on the threshold of mysticism. His peculiarity is that he stops there. He does not lose his balance. He respects common-sense, and dreads to disturb his vague aspirations by translating them into a definite system. He does not wish us to swallow mystic formulas as necessary or sufficient keys to the puzzle. He is only saying with benevolent unction what corresponds to Carlyle's fierce denunciations of cants and shams; and may even be translated into the phraseology of the humble "Lockist." The Lockist, too, is aware of the evil of dead "survivals," and the importance of encouraging new intellectual variations. The difference between his prose and Emerson's poetry is great enough; but he may sympathize with the spirit, at least, of the rapture with which Emerson sets forth the blessings of intellectual independence, and the need that an individual be true to himself. Emerson's version was congenial to his audience at the time. One can understand the nature of the stimulus, even if we don't quite appreciate the merits of the "ecstatic state."

In one of its aspects Emerson's philosophy or poetry, whichever be its proper name, has scandalized his critics. His optimism, they think, is irritating. The most hopeless of all consolations is the denial that there is any need for consolation. The latter-day philosopher prefers thorough-going pessimism, and scornfully rejects Emerson's futile attempts to ignore the dark side of the world. Undoubtedly Emerson was an unequivocal optimist. "My whole philosophy, which is very real," he said to Carlyle, "teaches acquiescence and optimism." He laments his "stammering tongue and fumbling fingers," but he is not going to commit or recommend suicide. When men degrade each other, and desponding doctrines are spread, the "scholar," he said, in one of the early epoch-making lectures, "must be a bringer of hope, and must reinforce man against himself." "Power," he says elsewhere, "dwells with cheerfulness. . . . A man should make life and nature happier to us or he had better have never been born." All the talent in the world, he declares, cannot save a Schopenhauer from being odious. I confess that I do not altogether dislike this old-fashioned creed. It suited, no doubt, the time and place. America, it has been said, is the land of hope; and in Emerson's youth some symptoms which alarm modern observers were hardly perceptible. When he came to England in 1847 he was shocked by the "tragic spectacles" of misery and degradation in the streets of the great towns; and thanked God that his children were being brought up in a land where such things were unknown. The external circumstances help to explain the difference between him and Carlyle, upon whom the English pauperism and squalor had impressed the opposite lesson. But, apart from the surroundings, optimism is clearly of the essence of Emerson's temperament and philosophy. It is the teaching of the "ecstatic state." Wordsworth's nature worship lifted him to the "blessed mood" in which the

> Burthen of the mystery
> Of all this unintelligible world
> Is lightened,

and enabled him to "see into the life of things" and the harmony of the universe. With Emerson the "blessed mood" becomes normal. The greatest teachers have seen that "all nature is the rapid efflux of goodness executing and organizing itself." He frequently, as has been said, speaks as an evolutionist before Darwin. But for him evolution is rather emanation, and it does not mean a blind struggle for existence but the regular unrolling of a divine and benevolent drama, implying steady progress to perfection. Evil, he can declare, is only privation. It has no real existence, and vanishes when you can see the whole instead of dwelling upon isolated facts. Many philosophers have used similar words, and their opponents reply that such sayings are words and nothing more. To declare that this is the best or the worst of all possible worlds, as the impartial cynic is accustomed to suggest against both sides, is in reality to declare the state of your own liver. Your universe is the other side of yourself, and to give a theory which shall be valid for everyone is to claim omniscience. Emerson, at any rate, does not profess to argue; he simply asserts, and the assertion comes to this, that it is possible to take a cheerful view of things in general. That, at least, defines the point of view from which his writing may act as an inspiring source if not as revelations of fact. The essays in which he develops these doctrines most explicitly, the "Oversoul," "Compensation," "Circles," and the like, may be futile considered as philosophical dogmas; and there is not even a pretence of proving their truth. They may still be regarded as studies of the spirit in which a man may serenely front the trials of life and find comfort from forebodings. Emerson has been often compared to the great stoic moralists, and like them, he indulges in the hyperbolic and paradoxical. Macaulay, in the essay upon Bacon, in which Emerson found the typical Lockist, suggests an "amusing fiction" illustrative of the contrast. Two travellers find a village full of small-pox. The Baconian traveller vaccinates the sufferers. The stoic assures the villagers that to the wise man disease and the loss of friends is no evil. A merchant has lost his ship. The Baconian makes a diving-bell and fishes up the cargo; while the stoic exhorts him not to seek happiness in things outside himself. That is the difference, says Macaulay, between the "philosophy of words" and the "philosophy of works." When Baconians have suppressed disease and disaster the stoic will doubtless have less call for his consolations. While such things remain with us some sort of moral discipline will have its uses; and if the stoic paradoxes when taken literally are hard of acceptance by anybody who has had the toothache, they were exaggerations of principles which have formed noble characters and even had their utility in the world. The exhortations of Epictetus and Marcus Aurelius have really encouraged men who had not yet been provided with diving-bells and vaccination. The wise man of the stoics is to become independent of chance and change by identifying himself with reason; and Emerson's disciple is to perceive that in all evils there is compensation when we look upon the world as the evolution of divine ideas. He may remind us of another philosopher whom he resembled in frugality, dignity, and cheerful acceptance of life. They coincide in one significant saying. "A free man," says Spinoza, in what has been called "one of the most weighty sayings ever uttered," "thinks of death least of all things, and his wisdom is a meditation not of death but of life." So Emerson tells us that "a wise man in our time caused to be written on his tomb, 'think on living.'" We are not to waste life in doubts and fears; and one great mark of progress is that the old system of meditating upon death and surrounding the thought with terrors has gone out of fashion. That is Emerson's answer by anticipation to the charge that he has not spoken sufficiently of the terror of death.

That you should train youself to take evil bravely and cheerful is a maxim more likely to be condemned as commonplace than as paradoxical. The statement becomes paradoxical when we deny the existence of evil, and immoral if it be understood as advice to ignore instead of facing the inevitable. Emerson certainly accepts some rather startling positions. The first lesson of history, he says, is "the good of evil": "Good is a good doctor, but Bad is sometimes a better!" and he illustrates the point by some remarkable cases. The contrast of good and evil is expressed in art, and explains its powers. "What would painter do, or what would poet or saint do but for the crucifixions and hells?" But for death, as Mr. Weller remarked, what would become of the undertakers? Emerson admires great men of all classes—"scourges of God and failings of the human race." They are all parts of the general system:—

> If plague or earthquake break not Heaven's design,
> Why, then, a Borgia or a Catiline?

The knaves, he calmly observes, win in every political struggle and a change of government means delivering society from the hands of one to the hands of another set of criminals, and the march of civilization is "a train of felonies." Yet a "beneficent tendency" streams irresistibly through the centuries, even through evil agents. Once he knew a "burly Boniface" in a rural capital. This gentleman "introduced all the fiends into the town, and united in his own person the functions of bully, incendiary, bankrupt, and burglar!" And yet he was the most public-spirited citizen. The "Boss," as he would be called in modern language, was, at the same time, "a Man of Ross." The moral is that his energy was good, and only wanted to be directed to the better objects. Such illustrations of the "good of evil" are certainly rather startling, and may explain why Emerson has even been described as without a conscience. Emerson, like his mystic guides, has a tendency to what theologians call "antinomianism." The inner world is the whole real world, and a morality which takes outer consequences for a criterion becomes merely prudential. Moral goodness for him implies the harmony of the individual soul. The man approaches perfection so far as the eyes of his spirit are always open to the inner light, and his whole nature acts spontaneously in conformity with the divine will. Obedience to the moral law is equivocal or worthless so far as it depends upon any extrinsic motive. If imposed from without, it so far rather savours of evil. Virtue, to be genuine, must be the absolutely spontaneous efflux of the character, not a mere disguise for hopes of reward and fear of punishment. Emerson insists upon this aspect of the truth, till even spontaneous wickedness seems to be better than compulsory goodness. Each man, he says, should "plant himself indomitably upon his instincts." A "valued adviser" warned him against trusting his instincts against venerable traditions. Your impulses, he said, may be from below, not from above. Well, he replied, "if I am the devil's child, I will live then from the devil." No law, he adds, can be sacred to me but that of my nature. That is right which is according to my constitution, and that wrong which is against it. Emerson therefore accepts a thorough individualism. All associations impress limitation by others. Each man is "cramped and diminished" by his associates. He distrusted even the movements encouraged by transcendentalism. "Professed philanthropists, it is strange and horrible to say, are an altogether odious set of people, whom one would shun as the worst of liars and canters." Temperance and anti-slavery, and so forth, are poor things when prosecuted for themselves as an end, though appealing to generous motives. The reason is that all associations must be a product of, not dependent upon, a bond. The "union is only perfect when all the unities are isolated." When each man sees the truth for himself, all will come together. Reform, therefore, even in the case of slavery, should proceed by the gradual elevation of the human spirit, not by direct legislation and outward agitation. When you trust to external means instead of acting upon the soul you become mechanical, and take narrow and distorted views of the evil. The transcendentalists, so far so they accepted this view, were regarded as mere apostles of "culture." They were inclined to stand aside from active life, and leave things to be gradually improved by the slow infiltration of higher ideals. Emerson, says Lowell, was a truer follower of Goethe than Carlyle; his teaching tended to self-culture and the development of the individual man, till it seemed "almost Pythagorean in its voluntary seclusion from commonwealth affairs." Emerson, in his lecture upon the transcendentalists, accepts and apologizes for this tendency. They can afford to stand aside from the world where even good causes are spoilt by compromise and associated with vulgar motives. There is, he admits, a difficulty in keeping upon the higher levels of thought, in retaining the faith which reveals itself in intuition and ecstasy. Yet the world may find room for "some few persons of purer fire" to serve as "collectors of the heavenly spark, with power to convey the electricity to others." The thought which the hermit "strove to proclaim by silence" will spread till it has reorganized society.

If Emerson were to be treated as a system-maker we might suggest that he is only accentuating one aspect of a single truth. Virtue certainly is not obedience to an outward law, but the spontaneous outcome of the man's nature. It is not the less the nature which fits a man for social life. "Self-culture" does not imply retreat to a hermitage, for the most efficient culture is in the active discharge of duties. The simple truth requires to be limited by its correlatives. In any case, nothing could be really less chargeable against Emerson than an approach to ethical insensibility. It is precisely the keenness and delicacy of his moral sense which attracts us and gives point to his best sentences. He is not the man to retire to a palace of art or find in aesthetic indulgence an anodyne to dull his sympathies with human sorrow. He can indeed admire the teachers who, like Shakespeare and Montaigne, look upon morality with a certain impartiality. Shakespeare, he rather quaintly asserts, "is our city of refuge if we tire of the saints." But the critic ought to show the relation between Shakespeare and Swedenborg. Now Swedenborg's great merit is the "immolation of genius and fame at the shrine of conscience." The "atmosphere of moral sentiment opens to every wretch that has reason the doors of the universe," and "all men are commanded by the saint." If Emerson's optimism leads him to dwell upon the "good of evil," and to see the use of "scourges of God" and vulgar political scoundrels, it is because they are for him the instruments of an essentially moral force. He can condemn a vulgar exaltation over mechanical continuous railways and telegraphs; but, instead of simply denouncing them, like Ruskin, he sees their good side, and believes that in time they will become instruments of the world spirit. His "pantheism" is not belief in a power superior to or indifferent to morality, but one to which the true, the good, and the beautiful are identical. We want something beyond Shakespeare and Goethe. "We, too, must write Bibles to unite again the heavenly and the earthly worlds." The teacher who is to come will see into the ultimate laws; "see to identity of the law of gravitation with purity of heart," and show that "duty is one thing with science, with beauty, and with joy."

This, no doubt, verges upon the poetical; it is hard of acceptance for the poor "Lockist"; and can be fully appreciated only by those who have access to the "ecstatic state." Others must be content to take a lower point of view. The title of one of Emerson's books—*The Conduct of Life*—defines one less inaccessible aspect of his teaching. If he has not penetrated the secret of the universe, he can show by example what attitude and disposition of mind can make the universe tolerable. It may be suggested to the pessimist that as he cannot understand the general system of things, and certainly cannot alter it, he may as well learn how to make the best of it. Emerson may supply useful hints for such an enterprise. "The true preacher," he says, "can be known by this, that he deals out to the people his life." The phrase may explain his own secret. He had, for one thing, to depend upon popular lecturing, a trade which, it must be granted, has its drawbacks. He had, he complained, to go about "peddling with his literary pack of notions," dropping pearls before superficial hearers who would turn them into twaddle and extravagance. Still, he took his mission simply and seriously, gave what he had, and tried to indicate "the ideal and holy life," . . . to "celebrate the spiritual powers," in contrast to the mechanical philosophy of the time, and "appeal to the great optimism self-affirmed in all bosoms." His simplicity and sincerity moved congenial hearers to aspire to regions of thought higher than those of the counting-house or the market, and impressed upon them at least the beauty and dignity of Emerson's own character. His aphorism—it has, I fear, a twang of the popular lecturer about it—"hitch your waggon to a star" sums up the moral, and the power depends as much upon the sweetness of disposition as upon the mystical doctrine. The charm appears in his best poetry, in spite of its admitted shortcomings. His characteristic want of continuity made him as incapable of evolving a central idea as of expounding an argument. As in prose, he often coins exquisite phrases, but he is abrupt and fragmentary and apt to break down both in grammar and rhythm. A true inspiration comes as it came to Blake in the midst of much incoherence and stammering utterance. Few poems are more touching than the "Dirge" and the "Threnody," in which he commemorates his brothers and the son who died in infancy. The "Threnody" recalls Wordsworth in the simplicity and in the concluding meditation where he finds soothing, if not fully consoling, thought. What orthodox critics may say of it I know not, but, at any rate, few poems bring one into so close a contact with a perfectly sweet nature, or could show how a great sorrow should be met by a man equally brave and tender. In the essay upon "Experience"—in which, it must be confessed, it is not easy to put any clear interpretation—he refers again to the loss of his son. "Grief," he says, "makes us idealists. The world becomes a dream. Life is a train of moods"; the moods "are many-coloured lenses which paint the world their own hue." And yet the dream is somehow the reality. The facts, as he has learnt from Swedenborg, are only symbols. Life wears "a visionary face." It is hard, he admits, to keep ourselves at this mystical point of view. The poet who is to show us the truth under the outside world has not yet come. The prosaic person will refuse a consolation which proposes, according to him, to drop substantial facts for dreams and shadows. Yet he may allow that the emotion is in itself beautiful. If he cannot accept the optimist view of the world, he can, perhaps, learn from the optimist how to take the inevitable cheerfully. Emerson admits in one essay that Fate is a reality and has a very ugly side to it. Yet he ends by exhorting us to "build altars to the beautiful necessity"; and, without bothering us with the metaphysical puzzles, to find comfort in the thought that "all is made of one piece," and that the Law which we dread is really "Intelligence," which vivifies nature, and somehow makes Fate identical with Freedom. This is not remarkable for lucidity, and to the prosaic reasoner may seem to amount to the statement that a man of fine moral nature may protect himself against harsh truth by cultivating pleasant illusions. Yet, it shows how, without yielding to illusions, such a man can make his life beautiful. The secret is indicated in the beautiful essays upon "Love" and "Friendship." In speaking of "Friendship" Emerson becomes a little too high-flown, because he is suspicious of even cementing friendship by actual services. The stoics held that friendship was only possible for the wise man; and Emerson thinks that it requires such "rare and costly" means that it can seldom be realized. It is the product of the spontaneous affinity of soul, which must be independent of all external circumstance or reciprocity of kind actions. In the essay where he manages to give a new charm even to the ancient topic of Love, he puts a more acceptable theory. He speaks in a prose-poem, which reminds us of Mr. Meredith's "Love in a Valley," of the recollection "of the days when happiness was not happy enough, but must be drugged with the rubbish of pain and fear; for he touched the secret of the matter who said of love—

All other pleasures are not worth its pains;

and when the day was not enough but the night, too, must be consumed in keen recollections; when the head boiled all night on the pillow with the generous deed it resolved on; when the moonlight was a pleasing fever, and the stars were letters and the flowers ciphers, and the air was carved into song; when all business seemed an impertinence, and all the men and women running to and fro in the streets mere pictures." Love may generate illusions; but it makes the strong gentle and gives the coward heart. The lover becomes a "new man, with new perceptions, new and keener purposes, and a religious solemnity of character and aims." And thus love, which is "the deification of persons, becomes more impersonal every day"; and the passion of Romeo for Juliet "puts us in training for a love which knows not sex nor person nor partiality, but which seeks virtue and wisdom to the end of increasing virtue and wisdom."

I do Emerson injustice in taking a few sentences out of his fine rapture; and it would be out of place to consider the cold-blooded criticism that a Romeo sometimes fails to develop in this desirable fashion. I only refer to it to indicate the process by which, as I think, the prosaic person may get some profit even from Emerson's mysticism. It may be unintelligible or false if taken as a solid philosophy. It reveals, at any rate, the man himself, the pure, simple-minded, high-feeling man, made of the finest clay of human nature; the one man who, to Carlyle, uttered a genuine human voice, and soothed the profound glooms of dyspeptic misanthropy; a little too apt, no doubt, to fall into the illusion of taking the world to be as comfortably constituted as himself; and apt also to withdraw from the ugly drama, in which the graver passions are inextricably mixed up with the heroic and the rational, to the remote mountain-tops of mystical reflection. Yet nobody could be more fitted to communicate the "electric shock" to his disciples, because of his keen perception of the noble elements of life, in superiority to all the vulgar motives and modes of thought, which were not the less attractive because he could not see his way to any harmonious or consistent system of thought.

—Sir Leslie Stephen, "Emerson," National Review,
February 1901, pp. 882–98

George Edward Woodberry (1907)

Many scholars have commented on Emerson's unique prose style. American essayist and critic George Edward Woodberry's commentary on Emerson's diction is of interest to students examining Emerson's writing style in greater depth. Woodberry notes qualities that signify Emerson's prose style—"verbal clearness . . . and in the short sentence which he especially cultivated he achieves weight and point"—and which lead the American philosopher Stanley Cavell to remark of Emerson's prose that "every sentence is a topic sentence." Woodberry's analysis of Emerson is of note, too, in what Woodberry writes about Emerson's emerging style. Students should remember that Emerson moved from preacher to essayist, which may help to clarify Woodberry's claims about Emerson's diction.

Ranking Emerson among other literary figures is always a difficult challenge, perhaps more so in Emerson's case. Woodberry's estimation is effective, though, and softens his opening claim that Emerson will best be remembered for his personal qualities—complimentary claims, but not what a writer wants to be remembered for. Woodberry is saying that although Emerson's prose is not to the literary standards set by Francis Bacon, Miguel de Montaigne, or Blaise Pascal, his writing is infused with greatness of mind and imagination, which answers a different kind of aesthetic need. That is, Emerson's style is not classical, but it perfectly fits the expression; or, in Emerson's own terms, the thought has created its own form.

The secret of his style is his diction. It may be described as seventeenth-century diction, and is derived from his early familiarity with old English writers. It fits both the man, his profession, and the quality of his ideas. He obtains by it verbal clearness, and in the short sentence which he especially cultivated he achieves weight and point, which are both oratorical qualities. He had also in his earlier writings fluidity, not in thought but in eloquence, the flow of the orator, for comparatively brief passages; in the *Essays* this quality is almost lost, owing to the way in which these writings were composed by selection and rearrangement from more extended compositions; the method had its advantages, for condensation and brilliancy of detail, but it necessarily forfeited consecutiveness, harmony, and naturalness. The posthumous publications, made up of uncollected papers and extracts from his manuscripts, in successive editions of his complete works, add nothing to his reputation, though they afford fuller illustrations of his life and thought. In style, except in the speeches, they are inferior. He had the same defects in prose as in verse; his taste was often at fault in both word and phrase, so far as the diction is concerned, and his effort for effect in short sentences sometimes betrayed him to expressions that are grotesque and result in caricature of the thought. He was not a great writer in the sense in which Bacon, Montaigne, or Pascal are great writers; but he was a writer with greatness of mind, just as he was not a great poet, but a poet with greatness of imagination.

—George Edward Woodberry,
Ralph Waldo Emerson, 1907, pp. 186–87

RELIGIOUS VIEWS

MARY MOODY EMERSON (1831)

Emerson's aunt Mary was the intellectual matriarch of the Emerson family. Her insistence on her nephew continuing the line of ministers (he was the eighth generation of Emerson men to answer the call) placed considerable strain on Emerson. However, the bond between Waldo and Mary Emerson was close and defined by mutual personal and intellectual respect. Mary Emerson's effect on the transcendental movement has recently come into critical focus, and several current works recognize her contributions to the literary and intellectual climate of Boston and Concord.

Mary Emerson's concern in this 1831 letter is Waldo's preference for natural to revealed religion. At the time the letter was written, Waldo is still the pastor of Boston's Second Church, though we might infer from Mary's words that his thinking about nature (or "natural religion" and the attendant pantheism of which he will be accused) is in process. Mary attempts here to reestablish for Waldo the primacy of divinity revealed through "the person & ministry of Jesus." She warns Waldo that "[y]our poetic visions—your early philosophizings in a bright & particular orbit account for your wanderings from the Central sun."

Mary has reason for concern. By 1831 Waldo had been under the influence of Emanuel Swedenborg (the mystic), Plato (the idealist), and others, luring him away from the strict adherence to the scriptures that Mary encouraged. Waldo typically shared his reading and writing with his aunt, who clearly wished him to remember the nature of his calling: "'tis your high office to explore and interpret the living voices of the witnesses of Jesus—the spirit of prophecy," rather than "looking beyond the bounds of pure reason or naturalism."

⸻⸻ ⸻⸻ ⸻⸻

To RALPH WALDO EMERSON

Vale
Sep. 23 31

You wrote, some few years since, my dear Waldo you preferred nat. to revealed religion. And I do not tease to *know* your opinions—probably unfixed. In your last (welcome to the very heart) you seem still looking beyond the bounds of pure reason or naturalism so I shall write in the old loose strain—always hoping to find you beyond what mere human virtues can afford. True—if we could have but one—'twere best to adhere to the immortal principles of our own constitution—unless we were as confident of the revealed—but no Plato has been a perfect character. But in my limited notions, 'twere as hard to separate the first from the influence of the last as to separate the all surrounding electric fluid from its effects on the elements.

Your preference arises chiefly from the difficulties of nat. to revealed—for except some deductions common to all—its voice is indistinct dark & often uninterpretable—And Genius loves to stand gazing into the clouds, or like the worshipers of Baal expect to find their gods napping while the secret of the "*law of laws*" is contained in the "*mighty Compensation*," who has been typified thro' most of the earth and shadowed forth on its most ancient alters, and at length has come into the hands and mouths of men so tangibly that the supernaturalist, in faith, becomes as clear a mirror to the facts of xianity as the mind of sense is to those of the material world. They find, that, as man is said to give his idea to his age—so in the cycle of infinite existence, God may be said to give his peculiar idea (respecting so mysterious a race) in the person & ministry of Jesus to the ages w'h compose the mortal race of man. Do you want "principles" beyond what this ministry teaches? penetrate like the Newtons of nat. phi. far higher than the common traveller—and you will find the origin of the light of revelation w'h is shed so-so—like every day things—will find the curtain w'h conceals the invisible world to have been drawn enough—oh enough—to rouse the *thinker* to increasing wakefullness were there but a millioneth chance of the realities of that glorious world.

"The dead speake not"—No they rest from mortal cares—'tis your high office to explore and interpret the living voices of the wittnesses of Jesus—the spirit of prophecy.—The Angels who testified of him are still living & burning in other offices of benevolence—for their friend is risen and active—'tis yours to carry on their & his work—to apply the remedy to the poorest of the miserable—the meaner—the more respect to the Donor of all. True, the higher gifts of explaining the gospel in its advanced stages seems allotted to you & your time & place. Suffer the remembrance of Beza's caution—that "the most dangerous temptation to pride is the inventing new methods of explaining or treating a subject." This is as far from you as darkness from light. Your poetic visions—your early philsophisings in a bright & particular orbit account for your wanderings from the Central sun.

Well when I come to read over this declamatory homily I wish it otherwise—but I cannot write a better now—And I've been reading again & again yours of 30 of Au. and if you could see it with my eyes—you would pardon all my faded truisms.

And now how many rich & happy thoughts crowd to my idea of you—and as the long benefactor of many a weary hour—of your own hopes & prospects how fully I share. And sympathise in the illness of your Mother & Sister. It is hard for you—very hard to trace the same dark way which left you bereft of one of the loveliest beings that ever graced our world. My love to M. and tell I hope she will live. Tell me more of where you go & what you feel. I've just read J. Adams' bio. What a noble career! Yet of all the contests he endured what real advantage to his Country? Could we be worse if we had remained? The *Country* surely made a few heroes—but what they did for *that* seems a problem. The German writers never meddle with politicks—Monarchies have given Homers & Archimedes & Newtons & Isaiahs & Pauls!

My love to C C E & will do just as he says when I can send the papers—He is my patron of patrons in sending me some pens. One failed of any use—& the 2$^\text{d}$ in two or 3 days—but I hope by keeping this 3$^\text{d}$ out of ink to preserve it? Love to my Sister. Write to your most truly

MME

Sad disapp$^\text{t}$ last eve to hear W.H. is not coming with letters & books. I don't know how to send R. E—'s pamphlets to Andover.

I referred to a few expressions in yours which are not of the grave stern cast that even occasional speculations require from a man of your cast.

—Mary Moody Emerson, letter to
Ralph Waldo Emerson (September 23, 1831)

MARY MOODY EMERSON (1832)

It is obvious from Mary Emerson's letter that her nephew had shared with her his intention to leave the ministry. (He resigned his pastorate at Boston's Second Church in September 1832, approximately seven months following this letter.) It is also plain, by her first few sentences, how she feels about the direction of Waldo's thinking.

Students interested in Emerson's religious life (and his pastoral career) should note in Mary's response the ideas Waldo has contemplated: "'a great truth whose authority you would feel is its own,'" and "whether the heart were not the Creator." Certainly Mary wishes Waldo would realign himself with "your Creator if you have one."

Resigning the ministry was a difficult decision for Emerson. As this letter makes clear, there were familial as well as spiritual concerns. Students may detect the germinating seeds of ideas Emerson would develop and work out in "Nature" four years later. Students might also note the hostility Mary feels toward "this withering Lucifer doctrine of pantheism," of which Emerson will be accused. No doubt Mary Emerson knew the Latin source for the term *lucifer* ("shining," "light"), but since she argues that Christ is the center of religious truth (the "Central sun" of the 1831 letter), and since she chooses to capitalize Lucifer (suggesting a reference to the devil), her point cannot be missed.

———————————

To RALPH WALDO EMERSON

Vale
Feb [1832]

And is it possible that one nurtured by the happiest institutions whose rich seeds have been bedewed by them—should be parrisidical! Or is it only the great one w'h lies at the root you reject? You most beloved of ministers, who seemed formed by face manner & pen to copy & illustrate the noblest of all institutions, are you at war with that angelic office? What a problem your existence. Love of truth (& practice of it w'h has always commanded my uncommon respect) leads you to sin against what is believed by the highest men to be truth in its origin to man & leading to all others. It was at that fountain your infant mind imbibed the development of your moral nature! Oh why not seek it again with simplicity & intense exclusion. If truth can't be found as your preaching demands, then the sacrifice to it of all comfort & fame demands your attention. For the relation between your Creator if you have one, remains paramount. On what footing you are to treat with Him excites the deepest curiosity. But I take not the liberty to inquire. What you commit to me is enough. And I may ask—what you mean by speaking of "a great truth whose authority you would feel is its own"? In the letter of Dec 25 you [ask] "whether the heart were not the Creator." Now if this withering Lucifer doctrine of pantheism be true, what moral truth can you preach or by what authority should you feel it? Without a personal God you are on an ocean mast^n unrigged for any port or object. Then why not continue to preach—& pray too? Where is the truth, so infinitely weighty with the true theist, injured? Some body must keep up these idle institutions & they may keep men from jail and gallows. What better scope for the intellectual reservoir? And such has been your integrity, whenever I have been indulged with hearing or reading, that St Paul, who had the fullest convictions of

Jesus being the only medium of communication with the Incomprehensible, would not tax your sincerity, tho' he would regret the different character you assigned. Pardon me if I declaim with the garrulity of age. But it was you—so constituted—& placed with the benevolence of these institutions, without the bustle & detail whom I expected would rise to an eminence from w'h you would have as strong convictions of the only true phi.—the divine personal agency as of your own consciousness—God within the heart but not the heart. And how was your correspondence to brighten & renew my wrinkled mind! Another, & perhaps childish antisapation. That an old venerable pastor in the most delightfull spot, you could point to your grand children that within a few miles reposed the ashes of your pious ancestors—who preached the gospel—and that the very place w'h gave you birth & contains your father should witness your last aspirations after the sovereign Good. It may be that the short lives of those most dear to me have given couler to the hopes of one minister remaining to be enrolled with the Mathers & Sewells of that venerable City. But it is rather idle to name hopes. It is, however, images of virtue, truth, & success w'h cheers the patriotic heart at it's own dissolution. As a man, were you a stranger, the unique trait in your history of having "no intimate friend" would excite interest. If it has disadvantages they are infinitely surpassed by the preservation of one's own magnanimity—one of the greatest in this weary wasting world of effort. Charles 5th's motto is good in all cases "*not yet.*" Time enough when your faith shall be decided and your opinions vital with it's warmth.

Your study of nat. his. & phi. I suspect has been among the "senses" writers. Decartes, Malbra. & Clarke studied the *Cause.* Fixed there the student resembles the noble Abdiel while the mechanists & rationals the busy & dainty Ariel. 23. I wrote on having yours to send by a neighbour—he dont go for some time. This is too much to burn—too little to send—to lie bye is unsafe—The Spectre, clothed with beauty at my curtain by night & table by day, forbids. I venture not on argument—& you can't be offended with *me* poor me. The hope of learning your process is tempting to my wish for excitement. The intellectual diseases of the day I cannot otherwise find. Do tell me of EBE. CC did not name the other members of your own le doute most noble *institution.* Did you ever read Foster's sermon on the nullity of friendship to perfection of character? I used to exult in that when young. Did I understand rightly Coleridge leaning to pantheism when he talks of human nature being subsumed in the divine? Perhaps Channing got disturbed by his adherence to the complications of this mystic, who is taxed I believe with the disease. Farewell

Your obliged & affectionate

MME

I've learnt to speake of you as Mr E. It is proper to youth & strangers. I've a mania for talking today.

—Mary Moody Emerson,
letter to Ralph Waldo Emerson (February 1832)

George Gilfillan "Emerson" (1854)

George Gilfillan was a Scottish author and secessionist pastor whose analysis of Emerson's work centers on one note: that "Emerson is *one* of the *few sceptics* who has *personally*, and by *name*, insulted the Lord Jesus Christ," and has in some ways supplanted God. From this initial observation comes Gilfillan's other accusations: Emerson is a materialist; his theory is "a gospel of despair, which in reality he teaches, of the most fixed despair"; his poetry is overly mystical and vague. The tone of Gilfillan's entry seems harsh. However, Gilfillan's accusations should be carefully weighed, especially by those students interested in Emerson's religious thought.

Gilfillan is correct in arguing that Emerson rejected the divinity of Christ, wrote of the divinity of nature, and the elevation of man to the position of a god (at least, "a god in ruins"). However, Gilfillan seems, like Joseph O'Connor in the excerpt that follows this one, to be looking for a system by which Emerson might justify these views.

Gilfillan considers Emerson's lack of a system a weakness; he writes that "Emerson, while striking hard, and often, and openly, at the divinity of Jesus . . . has never yet propounded or sought to propound any probable or intelligible theory of Christ." Other readers see Emerson's purpose as not specifically the denigration of Christ, but the elevation of the soul in order for the individual to experience his or her full potential (which Emerson sees as divine).

Gilfillan's take on Emerson seems in almost complete opposition to the praise heaped on Emerson by his admirers. Gilfillan considers him negative, inaccurate, and a materialist. Considering Gilfillan's point of view, these charges are accurate enough. Gilfillan's essay is valuable in order to consider specific opposition to Emerson levied by orthodox Christians of his time.

— —

The fame of Emerson has had a singular cycle of history, within the last thirteen years, in Britain. His first Essays, re-published in 1841, with a preface by Carlyle, were, on the whole, coldly welcomed by the public; with the exceptions of the *Eclectic Review,* which praised their genius while condemning their opinions, and *Tait's Magazine,* the monthly and quarterly press either ignored or abused them. Their admirers, indeed, were very ardent, but they were very few, and principally young men, whose enthusiasm was slightly shaded with a sceptical tendency. Between this period and his visit to Britain, in 1848, a great revolution in his favour had taken place. The publication of a second volume of Essays, still more peculiar and daring than the first, the re-appearance of his tractate, entitled *Nature*—the most complete and polished of all his works—the deepening enthusiasm of his admirers, and the exertions of one or two of them, who had gained the ear of the public, and were determined to fill it with his fame, as well as the real merit of his writings, had amply prepared the country for his approach, when, among the last days of 1847, he set the impress of his foot upon our shores. Then his name and influence came to a culminating point, and ever since they seem to us to have declined. For this, various causes may be assigned.

In the first place, his appearance disappointed many; they did not meet the rapt, simple, dreaming enthusiast of whom they had been dreaming.

Secondly, his Lectures were chiefly *double entendres.* There were alike commissions and omissions in them, which proved this to a certainty. We have seen him scanning an audience ere he resolved which of two lectures he should give. Think of Paul on Mars Hill, balancing between two Greek variations of his immortal speech, or, on consideration, choosing another text than "Ye men of Athens, I perceive that in all things ye worship DEMONS too much." We have heard of him, too, sacrificing, to suit an audience, the principal pith, marrow, and meaning of a whole lecture; as if, in quoting the words, "thou shalt worship the Lord thy God," he had slily and *sub voce* substituted the little word "not." Nay, even when there was no such disingenuous concealment or subtraction, there was a game of "hide-and-seek" continually going on—a use of Scripture phrases in an unscriptural sense, a trimming, and turning, and terror at the prejudices of his audience, altogether unworthy of his genius. Indeed, we wonder that the tribe of expectant materialists in England and Scotland, with Holyoake, MacAll, and

George Combe at their head, had not, disgusted at the doubledealing of their American champion, met at Berwick-upon-Tweed, and burned him in effigy. *They,* at least, are direct, and honest, and thoroughgoing men, we mean animals, for they are perpetually boasting of their lineal descent from brutes, and reptiles, and fishes, and slime, and everything but God, and we are not disposed to deny *their* far-come *and dearly-won honours,* or to quarrel, so far as *they* are concerned, with this mud heraldry.

Thirdly, the better portion of the age is fast becoming sick of all systems of mere negation. And what else is Emerson's? Any man who has ever thought for himself is competent to deny, and even to make his system of denial almost impregnable. A child of six or seven is quite able to trace the syllable No. To use again the allusion of the prophet, "it is a populous city—No;" and assuredly Emerson keeps one of its principal gates. But, with the exception of a mangled Platonism, although he seldom if ever quotes the Greek of Plato, there is not a trace of system, of consistent intuition, of progressive advancement in thought, in all his writings. In one part of them he makes man's soul all; in a second, he makes nature all; and, in a third, he magnifies some shadowy abstraction which he calls the "Oversoul," a sort of sublime overhead negro-driver, compelling men to hell or heaven, as seems good in his own blind eyes. In one place he declares that society never advances, and in another he gives a chart of a Millennium in society which love is by "pushing" to produce. Contradictory intuitions, as he would call them, abound in almost every page, and the question naturally arises, which are we to believe? which of the deliverances of this Paul-Pyrrho, this oracular sceptic, this captive to the "Oversoul," are we to receive as *his?* To refute them were difficult, because, in the first place, it is not easy to see what they are; because, secondly, he often saves us the trouble, by contradicting them next page or volume himself; and because, thirdly, while it is the simplest matter in the world to rear or to dwell in the "City No," it is the most difficult matter to overturn it. It is like hunting a dream, or trampling on a shade, or fitting out an expedition to overset Aladdin's palace.

Such are some of the reasons why Emerson's influence over the young, sincere, and liberal minds of the age must rapidly go down—like an October sun, very bright, but which is too late for ripening anything, and which, after a brief meridian, and a briefer afternoon, sinks, as if in haste and confusion, below the horizon. Another reason we are reluctantly, and in deep sorrow, compelled to add—Emerson is *one* of the *few sceptics* who has *personally,* and by *name,* insulted the Lord Jesus Christ, and, through him, that Humanity of which Jesus is the Hope, the Glory, the Ideal, and the Crown. This extreme

Carlyle has always avoided, and he has never spoken of Christ, or of the Divine Mystery implied in him, but with deep reverence. Many other of the sublimer order of doubters have been equally guarded. But Emerson, with Julian the Apostate, Voltaire, Paine, and Francis Newman, must bear the brand of using language to Christ which no man of culture would now apply to a Caesar, a Danton, or a Napoleon. He says, "this *shoves* Jesus and Judas both aside." He speaks, again, of Christ's "tropes," as if the man who died on Calvary because he *would* not lie, was an exaggerator and a rhetorician, when he said, "I and my Father are one," or, "he that has seen me, has seen the Father."

We have heard a dog baying at the moon—we have heard of a maniac spitting foam at the stars—we have watched the writhings of crushed mediocrity as it gazed on the bright pages of genius—and we have understood, excused, pitied, and forgiven all such in their morbid or mistaken feelings. But how one calling himself a man, and reputed really a man of genius, could, in his most unhappy hour, have uttered a word against our Brother—God—the Eternal Child—the Babe in the Manger—the Boy in the Temple—the Carpenter in the Shed—the Weeper at the Grave—the Sufferer on the Cross—the Risen from the Tomb—the Exalted to the Heavens—the Friend by eminence of our fallen Family—the Expected from the Clouds—The Type and Test of whatever is holy, and charitable, and lovely, and lofty in the race of man—passes our conceptions, and has strained to its utmost *our* power of forgiveness.

Why, we must also inquire, has he said such things, and yet not said more of Jesus? "What thinkest thou of Christ?" If he was an impostor, say so. If he was a madman, say so. If he was God in human shape, say so. If he is merely the conventional ideal of human nature, say so more distinctly. If he is neither, nor all of these, then *what is he?* whence has he come? Emerson, while striking hard, and often, and openly, at the divinity of Jesus, and not sparing quiet *sotto voce* insinuations against his character and his power over the minds of men, has never yet propounded or sought to propound any probable or intelligible theory of Christ. He has simply, with muttered, or more than muttered, sneers or sighs over his unacknowledged claims, turned away, refusing to look at or to worship this "great sight."

Man seems the Christ of Emerson. And a sorry Christ he is. "Man," says Bacon, "is the god of the dog;" but were a dog fancying himself a man, it were a supposition less monstrous than the universal Immanuelism of Emerson. If man be the Christ, where are the works which prove him so? If every man has the divinity within him, why are the majority of men so corrupt and malignant? If the history of man be the history of God in human nature, why is it little else than one tissue of blood, falsehood, and low sin? We think he might far more plausibly start and defend the hypothesis that man *is* the devil; and that his history has hitherto been but a long development of diabolism. And, in proving this, he might avail himself to great advantage of Quetelet's tables, which demonstrate the significant fact, that certain works of a rather infernal character, such as murder, arson, and rape, re-appear in steady and mathematical succession, and no more than summer and winter, seed-time and harvest, are ever to cease. The presence of such an eternal law would go far to prove that man was an immutable and hopeless child of hell.

Many strange deductions seem to follow from Emerson's theory, nay, are more or less decidedly admitted by him. If man be the Christ or God incarnate, then there can be no such thing as guilt, and there ought to be no such thing as punishment. Whatever is done, is done, not by God's permission or command, but by God himself. God is at once the judge and the offender. If man be God incarnate, it follows that he is the creator of all things. This Emerson repeatedly intimates. The sun is but a splendid mote in man's eye; the moon is but his produced and prolonged smile; the earth is the shadow of his shape; the stars are lustres in the room of his soul; the universe is the bright precipitate of his thought. He is the Alpha and Omega, the beginning of the Creation of God, and its ending too. "The simplest person," he says, "who, in his integrity, worships God, *becomes* God." It follows, again, that no supernaturalism ever did or ever could exist. It was, according to Emerson, Moses, not Jehovah, who spoke on Sinai. It was Isaiah's own human soul which saw the fate of empires as distinctly as we see stars falling through the midnight. It was the mere man Christ Jesus who taught, and worked, and died in Judea. The possibility, in like manner, of any future revelation from heaven is ignored—ignored by the denial of any heaven save the mind of man. This is the dunghill-Olympus on which Emerson seats his shadowy gods. And whatever strange and aerial-seeming shapes may hereafter appear upon its summit, are to be in reality only sublimated mud—the beauty and the strength of—dirt. "Man," to use Foster's language, is to produce an "apotheosis of himself, by the hopeful process of exhausting his own corruptions," or sublimating them into a putrid holiness.

It follows, again, that, whatever he may say in particular passages, there can be no advancing or steady progress in humanity. The laws which develop it are unchangeable, the climate in which it lives is subject to very slight variations; its "Oversoul" is a stern demon, with, perhaps, as he says, "a secret kindness in its heart," but outwardly a very Moloch of equal calm and cruelty; and under his eye, society and man must work, and bleed, and suffer on, upon this rolling earth, as on an eternal treadmill in a mist. 'Tis a gospel of despair, which in reality he teaches, of the deepest and the most fixed despair. The dungeon into which he introduces his captives is cold and low; it has no outlet: no key called Promise is to be found therein; the sky, indeed, is seen above through the dome, but it is distant—dark—with strange and melancholy stars, and but one hope, like a cup of prison-water, is handed round among the dwellers in this dreary abode—that of Death. And yet, but of late thousands of our young, rising, and gifted minds were, and many are still, forsaking the free atmosphere, the strait but onward way, and the high-hung star of hope, and Christianity, for this dismal insulated and under-ground abyss, where the very light is as darkness. It follows, again, that humility and all its cognate virtues are mere mistakes. "Trust thyself—every heart vibrates to that iron string." A greater than Emerson said, two thousand years ago, "Blessed are the poor in spirit, for theirs is the kingdom of heaven;" and another of the same school said, "When ye are weak, then are ye strong." We are not defending a false or voluntary humility. But surely, unless you can prove that all strength, and purity, and peace, are enclosed in yourself, to bow before the higher—to draw strength from the stronger—to worship the divine—is the dictate of cultured instinct, as well as of common sense. Almost all the powers and elements of nature combine in teaching man the one great simple word, "bend." "Bend," the winds say it to the tall pines, and they gain the curve of their magnificence by obeying. "Bend," gravitation says it to the earth, as she sweeps in her course round the sun; and she knows the whisper of her ruler, and stoops and bows before the skiey blaze. "Bend," the proud portals of human knowledge say it to all aspirants, and were it the brow of a Bacon or a Newton, it must in reverence bow. "Bend," the doors, the ancient doors of heaven, say it, in the music of their golden hinges, to all who would pass therein; and the Son of Man himself, although he could have prayed to his Father, and presently obtained twelve legions of angels, had to learn obedience, to suffer, to bow the head, ere as a King of Glory he entered in. "Trust thyself." No; Christianity says, "Mistrust thyself—trust God. Do thy humble duty, and call the while on the lofty help that is above thee." Even Shelley, a far more gifted mind than Emerson, tells us, borrowing the thought from Burke, to "*fear* ourselves, and love all human-kind."

It follows, finally, that there seems no hope to us from the exclusive and idolatrous devotion to nature which Emerson has practised and recommends. He, appearing to believe that nature is his *own* work, has conned its pages with all the fondness which a young author feels for his first poems. And yet he has learned from it, or at least taught us, extremely little. If he has, as he says, met "God in the bush," why no particulars of the interview? Why no intelligible precept, no new law, from that "burning bush" of the West? Why does nature, in his hands, remain as cold, silent, enigmatic, and repulsive—we mean as a moral teacher—as ever it was? Why does its "old silence" remain silent still, or only insult us with fragments of mysticism and echoes of blasphemy? Alas! Emerson's Essays are another proof of what Hazlitt, from bitter experience, said long ago, "Neither poetry nor nature are sufficient for the soul of man." And although Emerson has, with more severe self-purgation, if not with a truer heart, approached the shrine, he has derived, or at least circulated, quite as little of real knowledge, or of real satisfaction and peace, as the honest but hapless author of *The Spirit of the Age*.

The fact is (and we are grieved to announce it), this writer, with all his talk about spiritualism and idealism, seems to us, in essence, if anything at all, a mere materialist—believing not, however, in the wide matter of suns and stars, but in the sublimated matter of his proper brain. He has brought the controversy of ages to a point—the point of his own head. This he claps and clasps, and says, "Talk of God, Heaven, Jesus, Shakspere, the earth, the stars—it's *all here*." Even as, not long ago, we heard a poor woman, in fever, declaring that there was "more sense in her head than in all the world besides!" And into what wilds have some of his followers, both in America and here, wandered, till, in search of their master, they have lost themselves. One of them will make an earth-heap among the woods, and show his companions how God *should* make a world. Others take to living on acorns and water; and one lady, of some abilities, has lately written a small volume of poems, in which, amid many other symptoms of the most rabid Emersonianism, such as sneering at the power and influence of the Bible, magnifying the soul, &c, she, in one little copy of verses, avows herself a *worshipper of the Sun*—it being the epic, we suppose, of *her* transcendent spirit!

It is high time that all such egregious nonsense should be exposed; and we only regret that our space does not permit us more fully at present to expose it. We "bide our time." And we can speak the more freely, that *we* have passed through a section of the Emersonian shadow ourselves—never into its deepest gloom, but along the outskirts of its cold and hopeless darkness. We, however, never lost our faith in Jesus, nor regarded Emerson's notions of Him with any other feelings but disgust and sorrow. *We* never "kissed our hands" to the sun. But we at one time regarded Emerson as a sincere man, astray on one of the by-paths from the road leading up to the "City." We have seen reason to change our mind, and to say of him, and of all such, "Beware of the Flatterer." His system, to our knowledge, has shaken belief, has injured morality, has poisoned the purest natures, has embittered the sweetest tempers, has all but maddened the strongest minds, has been for years a thick cosmical cloud between lofty souls and the God of their childhood and their fathers, has not even led to that poor, beggarly, outwardly clean life, in which he seems to believe all morality to consist (as if the plagues of the *soul* were not infinitely worse than the diseases of the body), and has led to life "without hope and without God in the world." And without laying all the blame of this—and it has been the experience of hundreds—upon Emerson himself, we do advisedly lay it upon the back of his heartless and hopeless creed.

After all this, to speak of Emerson's genius seems mere impertinence. It is little to the point, and, besides, has often been largely descanted on by us and others. It is undoubtedly of a high order. If he cannot interpret, he can paint, nature as few else can. He has watched and followed all her motions like a friendly spy. He has the deepest egotistic interest in her. He appropriates her to himself, and because he loves and clasps, imagines that he has made her. His better writings seem shaken, sifted, and cooled in the winds of the American autumn. The flush on his style is like the red hue of the Indian summer inscribed upon the leaf. One of the most inconsistent and hopelessly wrong of American thinkers, he is the greatest of American poets. We refer not to his verse—which is, in general, woven mist, involving little—but to the beautiful and abrupt utterances about nature in his prose. No finer things about the outward features, and the transient meanings of creation, have been said, since the Hebrews, than are to be found in some of his books. But he has never, like them, pierced to the grand doctrine of the Divine Personality and Fatherhood.

—George Gilfillan, "Emerson,"
A Third Gallery of Portraits 1854, pp. 328–36

JOSEPH O'CONNOR "RALPH WALDO EMERSON" (1878)

Catholic theologian Joseph O'Connor's criticism of Emerson is that he has no system, and that "systemization is necessary to all knowledge." According to O'Connor, this lack of systematic expression is debilitating to the Church, which is O'Connor's primary concern. O'Connor attempts to explain why Emerson's ideas are beyond serious consideration: a lack of systematic organization, vagueness of expression, and a lack of reverence for religious institutions and rituals. These concerns, in O'Connor's view, make Emerson's work invalid for serious spiritual consideration.

Students investigating Emerson's religious views should take note of O'Connor's concerns. It comes as no surprise that O'Connor criticizes Emerson's lack of systemization (a common refrain among contemporary critics). However, O'Connor's concern is for the Church, and for Emerson's effect on Christians and on the legacy of Christian theology. O'Connor's unstated assumption is that Emerson is propounding a philosophy, a body of views directed at spiritual philosophy. However, O'Connor's views might be read in contrast to those critics who identify Emerson not as a philosopher but as an artist, concerned more with expression than creating a sustainable philosophical system.

⚹⚹⚹   ⚹⚹⚹   ⚹⚹⚹

It may be Emerson's boast that he has no system. This restlessness under any, even nominal, *regime* is a characteristic of contemporaneous philosophy outside the church. There is liberty enough in the church; and, in fact, beyond it we see nothing but imprisonment, for nothing so practically chains the intellect of man as irresponsible freedom. It is like the liberty of the ocean enjoyed (?) by a mariner without sails or compass. A Catholic philosopher can speculate as much as he pleases. The security of the faith gives him a delightful sense of safe freedom. Like O'Connell's driving a coach and four through an act of Parliament, he may go to the outermost verge of speculation. St. Thomas moves the most outrageous fallacies, speculations, and objections, and discusses them, too, with all the boldness of intellectual freedom. It is Dr. Marshall, we think, who shows that all intellectual activity and freedom are enjoyed within the spacious bounds of Catholic truth. Even in theology there are wide differences. The Catholic intellect is supposed to be completely bridled. We once read a powerful arraignment of our Scriptural proofs for purgatory, written by an eminent Protestant theologian. He must have been surprised to learn that Catholic theologians do not attach all importance to the Scriptural argument for purgatory. The different schools of Catholic theology argue *pro* and *con.* as keenly as old Dr. Johnson himself would have desired, but without the slightest detriment to the unity of the faith. Nothing can be falser than the received Protestant notion that we are helplessly bound by a network of petty definitions and regulations. There are, however, great and immovable principles which are understood to guide and vivify the Catholic intellect. And such systemization is necessary to all knowledge. Without it a man's mind, like Emerson's, wanders comet-like, attracting attention by its vagaries, but is of no intelligible use to the universe, and gives no light, except of a nebulous and perplexing nature.

Nathaniel Hawthorne, who, of all American writers, had the true transcendental mind, ridicules it unsparingly. His doleful experience upon Brook Farm, when he attempted to milk a cow, may have had a practical awakening effect upon his dreams. In a little sketch entitled "The Celestial Railroad," in which he whimsically carries out Bunyan's *Pilgrim's Progress,* he introduces Giant Transcendentalism, who has taken the place of Giant Pope, and Giant Despair, that interrupted Christian's progress to the Delectable Mountains. Giant Transcendentalism is a huge, amorphous monster, utterly indescribable, and speaking an unintelligible language. This language, which Emerson strives to make articulate, we read with mingled amusement and astonishment in the German writers. Emerson is not a member of the *Kulturkampf,* like Carlyle. His mind does not take in their wild rhapsodies. His essay on Goethe (in *Representative Men*) is cold and unappreciative when compared with the Scotchman's eulogies. We firmly believe that no healthy intellect can feed upon Fichte, Schelling, Hegel, or even Kant, who was the most luminous intellect of the group. Emerson has not the stolid pertinacity of Herr Teufelsdrockh. His genius is French. He delights in paradox and verbal gymnastics. Carlyle works with a sort of furious patience at such a prosaic career as Frederick the Great's. He gets up a factitious enthusiasm about German *Herzhogs* and *Erstfursts.* Emerson would look with dainty disdain upon his Cyclopean work among big, dusty, musty folios and the hammering out of shining sentences from such pig-iron.

Whence his transcendentalism? We believe that it has two elements, nature-worship and Swedenborgianism. Of nature-worship we have very little. Like Thomson, the author of the *Seasons,* who wrote the finest descriptions of scenery in bed at ten o'clock in the morning, we are frightfully indifferent to the glories of earth, sea, and sky, whilst theoretically capable of intense rapture. This tendency to adore nature, and this intense modern cultivation of the natural sciences, we take as indicative of the husks of religion given by Protestantism. Man's intellect seeks the certain, and where he cannot find it in the supernatural he will have recourse to the natural. The profound attention paid to all the mechanical and natural sciences, to the exclusion, if not denial, of supernatural religion, is the logical result of the absurdity of Protestantism. Perhaps Emerson's poetic feeling has much to do with his profound veneration for fate, nature, and necessity, which are his true god, with a very little Swedenborgianism to modify them.

And here we meet him on his philosophy of words. A word, according to St. Thomas, should be the *adæquatio rei et intellectus,* for a word is really the symbol and articulation of truth. Where words convey no clear or precise idea to the mind they are virtually false. The terminology of Emerson falls even below Carlyle's in obscurity. What does he mean by the one-soul? What by compensation? What by fate and necessity? *Explica terminos* is the command of logic and reason; yet he maunders on in vague and extravagant speech, using terms which it is very probable he himself only partly or arbitrarily understands. He is not master of his own style. His own words hurry him along. This fatal bondage to style spoils his best thoughts. He seems to aim at striking phrases and ends in paradox. His very attempt to strengthen and compress his sentences weakens and obscures his meaning. The oracular style does not carry well. He is happiest where he does not don the prophetic or poetical mantle. When we get a glimpse of his shrewd character, he is as gay as a lark and sharp as a fox. He muffles himself in transcendentalism, but fails to hide his clear sense, which he cannot entirely bury or obfuscate. It seems strange to us that such a mind could be permanently influenced by the fantasies of Swedenborg, whom he calls a mystic, but who, very probably, was a madman. The pure mysticism of the Catholic Church is not devoid of what to those who have not the light to read it may seem to wear a certain air of extravagance, which, apparently, would be no objection to Emerson; but it is kept within strict rational bounds by the doctrinal authority of the church. We do not suppose that Emerson ever thought it worth his while to study the mystic or ascetic theology of the church, though here and there in his writings he refers to the example of saints, and quotes their sayings and doings. But it must be a strange mental state that passively admits the wild speculations of Swedenborgianism with its gross ideas of heaven and its fanciful interpretations of Scripture. Besides, Emerson clearly rejects the divinity of Jesus Christ, which is extravagantly (if we may use the expression) set forth in Swedenborgianism, to the exclusion of the Father and the Holy Ghost. He is, or was, a Unitarian, and his allusions to our Blessed Lord have not even the reverence of Carlyle.

Naturalism, as used in the sense of the Vatican decrees, is the proper word to apply to the Emersonian teaching. He has the Yankee boastfulness, materialistic spirit, and general laudation of the natural powers. His transcendentalism has few of the spiritual elements of German thought. He does not believe in contemplation, but stimulates to activity. In his earlier essays he seemed pantheistic, but his last book *(Society and Solitude)* affirmed his doubt and implicit denial of immortality. He appears to be a powerful personality, for he has certainly influenced many of the finer minds of New England, and, no doubt, he leads a noble and intellectual life. His exquisite aestheticism takes away the grossness of the results to which his naturalistic philosophy leads, and it is with regret that we note in him that intellectual pride which effectually shuts his mind even to the gentlest admonitions and enlightenments of divine grace.

It is a compliment to our rather sparse American authorship and scholarship that England regards him as the typical American thinker and writer. We do not so regard him ourselves, for his genius lacks the sturdy American originality and reverent spirit. But Emerson made a very favorable impression upon Englishmen when he visited their island, and he wrote the best book on England *(English Traits)* that, perhaps, any American ever produced. The quiet dignity and native independence of the book charmed John Bull, who was tired of our snobbish eulogiums of himself and institutions. Emerson met many literary men, who afterward read his books and praised his style. He has the air of boldness and the courage of his opinions. Now and then he invents a striking phrase which sets one a-thinking. He has also in perfection the art of quoting, and his whole composition betokens the artist and scholar.

There is a high, supersensual region, imagination, fantasy, or soul-life, in which he loves to disport, and to which he gives the strangest names. One grows a little ashamed of what he deems his own unimaginativeness when he encounters our philosopher "bestriding these lazy-pacing clouds." He wonders at the "immensities, eternities, and fates" that seem to exert such wondrous powers. When Emerson gets into this strain he quickly disappears either in the clouds or in a burrow, according to the taste and judgment of different readers. There is often a fine feeling in these passages which we can understand yet not express. Sublime they are not, though obscurity may be considered one of the elements of sublimity. They are emotional. Emerson belongs rather to the sensualistic school; at least, he ascribes abounding power to the feelings, and, in fact, he is too heated and enthusiastic for the coldness and calmness exacted by philosophical speculation. Many of his essays read like violent sermons; and his worst ones are those in which he attempts to carry out a ratiocination. He is dictatorial. He announces but does not prove. He appears at times to be in a Pythonic fury, and proclaims his oracles with much excitement and contortion. It is impossible to analyze an essay, or hold on to the filmy threads by which his thoughts hang together. It is absurd to call him a philosopher who has neither system, clearness of statement, nor accuracy of thought.

—Joseph O'Connor, "Ralph Waldo Emerson,"
Catholic World, April 1878, pp. 92–95

HENRY JAMES SR. "MR. EMERSON" (1884)

Henry James Sr., father of Henry, William, and Alice James, was a literary figure in his own right. James was a Swedenborgian minister and lecturer who found popularity among the transcendentalists. He also wrote essays and literary criticism. His work was compiled by William James as *The Literary Remains of Henry James* (1885).

James opens with a series of statements regarding conscience: defining it and qualifying it, in order to demonstrate Emerson's *lack* of it. James will claim that Emerson's value is that he has no sense of conscience, if conscience represents separation from God, the result of a fall from grace. James paints Emerson as a liaison between God and man; thus, James's referral to Emerson as "like Christ," "virgin-born," "divinely begotten," and "vestal virgin." Of course James does not believe Emerson to be divine in the accepted sense but in the sense that he is not *aware* of his lack of conscience.

Students should be aware of the comic rhetoric in James's entry. However, his claims about Emerson—James very nicely crystallizes Emerson's spiritual attributes—are serious and well founded. When James remarks that Emerson is "without conscience," he employs a comic tone to satirize Emerson, but he is correct in noting Emerson's lack of allegiance to any specific cause or orthodoxy. If Emerson is "devoid of spiritual understanding," we can be sure that James is commenting on Emerson's lack of interest in orthodoxy, and his focus on the connection between the human and the divine. If Emerson is "unconscious of himself as either good or evil," we understand James's comment because we know that Emerson did not recognize evil, and thought of it as mere privation.

James becomes more serious in the final paragraph, and students should note that it is there that James states his true feelings about Emerson. The notion of Emerson as a liaison between the divine and human lies at the heart of his earliest writings (students writing about "Nature" or the "Divinity School" address may find this relationship of particular interest). James finally draws Emerson back to Christ at the excerpt's conclusion, not in a comic sense, but in the real sense of Emerson's thought. Students writing about Emerson's views on evil, his theology, or his thoughts about Christ should especially note this passage as a good evaluation from a valuable source.

———————

At all events, if we are still to go on cherishing any such luxury as a private conscience towards God, I greatly prefer for my own part that it should be an evil conscience. Conscience was always intended as a rebuke and never as an exhilaration to the private citizen; and so let it flourish till the end of our wearisome civilization. There are many signs, however, that this end is near. My recently deceased friend Mr. Emerson, for example, was all his days an arch traitor to our existing civilized regimen, inasmuch as he unconsciously managed to set aside its fundamental principle in doing without conscience, which was the entire secret of his very exceptional interest to men's speculation. He betrayed it to be sure without being at all aware of what he was doing; but this was really all that he distinctively did to my observation. His nature had always been so innocent, so unaffectedly innocent, that when in later life he began to cultivate a club consciousness, and to sip a glass of wine or smoke a cigar, I felt very much outraged by it. I felt very much as if some renowned Boston belle had suddenly collapsed and undertaken to sell newspapers at a street corner. "Why, Emerson, is this *you* doing such things?" I exclaimed. "What profanation! Do throw the unclean things behind your back!" But, no; he was actually proud of his accomplishments! This came from his never knowing (intellectually) what he stood for in the evolution of New England life. He was lineally descended to begin with, from a half-score of comatose New England clergymen, in whose behalf probably the religious instinct had been used up. Or, what to their experience had been religion, became in that of their descendant *life*. The actual truth, at any rate, was that he never felt a movement of the life of conscience from the day of his birth till that of his death. I could never see any signs of such a life in him. I remember, to be sure, that he had a great gift of friendship, and that he was very plucky in behalf of his friends whenever they felt themselves assailed—as plucky as a woman. For instance, whenever Wendell Phillips ventilated his not untimely wit at the expense of our club-house politicians, Emerson, hearing his friends among these latter complain, grew indignant, and for several days you would hear nothing from his lips but excessive eulogies of Mr. Garrison, which sounded like nothing else in the world but revilings of Mr. Phillips. But, bless your heart! there was not a bit of conscience in a bushel of such experiences, but only wounded friendship, which is a totally different and much lower thing.

The infallible mark of conscience is that it is always a subjective judgment couched in some such language as this: "God be merciful to *me* a sinner!" and never an objective judgment such as this: God *damn Wendell Phillips, or some other of my friends!* This latter judgment is always an outbreak of ungovernable temper on our part, and was never known to reach the ear of God save in this guise: *God* BLESS *W.P. or any other friend implicated!* Now Emerson was seriously incapable of a subjective judgment upon himself; he did not know the inward difference between good and evil, so far as he was himself concerned. No doubt he perfectly comprehended the outward or moral difference between these things; but I insist upon it that he never so much as dreamed of any inward or spiritual difference between them. For this difference is vitally seen only when oneself seems unchangeably evil to his own sight, and one's neighbor unchangeably good in the comparison. How could Emerson ever have known this difference? I am satisfied that he never in his life had felt a temptation *to bear false-witness* against his neighbor, *to steal, to commit adultery,* or *to murder;* how then should he have ever experienced what is technically called a conviction of sin?—that is, a conviction of himself as *evil* before God, and all other men as *good.* One gets a conviction of the evil that attaches to the natural selfhood in man in no other way than—as I can myself attest—by this growing acquaintance with his own moral infirmity, and the consequent gradual decline of his self-respect. For I myself had known all these temptations—in forms of course more or less modified—by the time I was fourteen or fifteen years old; so that by the time I had got to be twenty-five or thirty (which was the date of my first acquaintance with Emerson) I was saturated with a sense of spiritual evil—no man ever more so possibly, since I felt thoroughly *self-condemned* before God. Good heavens! how soothed and comforted I was by the innocent lovely look of my new acquaintance, by his tender courtesy, his generous laudatory appreciation of my crude literary ventures! and how I used to lock myself up with him in his bed-room, swearing that before the door was opened I would arrive at the secret of his immense superiority to the common herd of literary men! I might just as well have locked myself up with a handful of diamonds, so far as any capacity of self-cognizance existed in him. I found in fact, before I had been with him a week, that the immense superiority I ascribed to him was altogether personal or practical—by no means intellectual; that it came to him by birth or genius like a woman's beauty or charm of manners; that no other account was to be given of it in truth than that Emerson himself was an unsexed woman, a veritable fruit of almighty power in the sphere of our *nature.*

This after a while grew to be a great discovery to me; but I was always more or less provoked to think that Emerson himself should take no intellectual stock in it. On the whole I may say that at first I was greatly disappointed in him, because his intellect never kept the promise which his lovely face and manners held out to me. He was to my senses a literal divine presence in the house with me; and we cannot recognize literal divine presences in our houses without feeling sure that they will be able to say something of critical importance to one's intellect. It turned out that any average old dame in a horse-car would have satisfied my intellectual rapacity just as well as Emerson. My standing intellectual embarrassment for years had been to get at the bottom of the difference between law and gospel in humanity—between the head and the heart of things—between the great God almighty, in short, and the intensely wooden and ridiculous gods of the nations. Emerson, I discovered immediately, had never been the least of an expert in this sort of knowledge; and though his immense personal fascination always kept up, he at once lost all intellectual prestige to my regard. I even thought that I had never seen a man more profoundly devoid of spiritual understanding. This prejudice grew, of course, out of my having inherited an altogether narrow ecclesiastical notion of what spiritual understanding was. I supposed it consisted unmistakably in some doctrinal lore concerning man's regeneration, to which, however, my new friend was plainly and signally incompetent. Emerson, in fact, derided this doctrine, smiling benignly whenever it was mentioned. I could make neither head nor tail of him according to men's ordinary standards—the only thing that I was sure of being that he, like Christ, was somehow divinely begotten. He seemed to me unmistakably virgin-born whenever I looked at him, and reminded me of nothing so much as of those persons dear to Christ's heart who should come after him professing no allegiance to him—having never heard his name pronounced, and yet perfectly fulfilling his will. He never seemed for a moment to antagonize the church of his own consent, but only out of condescension to his interlocutor's weakness. In fact he was to all appearance entirely ignorant of the church's existence until you recalled it to his imagination; and even then I never knew anything so implacably and uniformly mild as his judgments of it were. He had apparently lived all his life in a world where it was only subterraneously known; and, try as you would, you could never persuade him that any the least living power attached to it. The same profound incredulity characterized him in regard to the State; and it was only in his enfeebled later years that he ever lent himself to the idea of society as its destined divine form. I am not sure indeed that the lending was ever very serious. But he was always greedy, with all a Yankee's greediness, after facts, and would at least appear to listen to you with earnest respect and sympathy whenever you plead for society as the redeemed form of our nature.

In short he was, as I have said before, fundamentally treacherous to civilization, without being at all aware himself of the fact. He himself, I venture to say, was peculiarly unaware of the fact. He appeared to me utterly unconscious of himself as either good or evil. He had no conscience, in fact, and lived by perception, which is an altogether lower or less spiritual faculty. The more universalized a man is by genius or natural birth, the less is he spiritually individualized, making up in breadth of endowment what he lacks in depth. This was remarkably the case with Emerson. In his books or public capacity he was constantly electrifying you by sayings full of divine inspiration. In his talk or private capacity he was one of the least remunerative men I ever encountered. No man could look at him speaking (or when he was silent either, for that matter) without having a vision of the divinest beauty. But when you went to him to hold discourse about the wondrous phenomenon, you found him absolutely destitute of reflective power. He had apparently no private personality; and if any visitor thought he discerned traces of such a thing, you may take for granted that the visitor himself was a man of large imaginative resources. He was nothing else than a show-figure of almighty power in our nature; and that he was destitute of all the apparatus of humbuggery that goes to eke out more or less the private pretension in humanity, only completed and confirmed the extraordinary fascination that belonged to him. He was full of living inspiration to me whenever I saw him; and yet I could find in him no trivial sign of the selfhood which I found in other men. He was like a vestal virgin, indeed, always in ministry upon the altar; but the vestal virgin had doubtless a prosaic side also, which related her to commonplace people. Now Emerson was so far *unlike* the virgin: he had no prosaic side relating him to ordinary people. Judge Hoar and Mr. John Forbes constituted his spontaneous political conscience; and his domestic one (equally spontaneous) was supplied by loving members of his own family—so that he only connected with the race at second-hand, and found all the material business of life such as voting and the payment of taxes transacted for *him* with marvellous lack of friction.

Incontestably the main thing about him, however, as I have already said, was that he unconsciously brought you face to face with the infinite in humanity. When I looked upon myself, or upon the ordinary rabble of ecclesiastics and politicians, everything in us seemed ridiculously undivine. When I looked upon Emerson, these same undivine things were what gave *him* his manifest divine charm. The reason was that in him everything seemed innocent by the transparent absence of selfhood, and in us everything seemed foul and false by its preternatural activity. The difference between us was made by innocence altogether. I never thought it was a real or spiritual difference, but only a natural or apparent one. But such as it was, it gave me my first living impression of the great God almighty who alone is at work in human affairs, avouching his awful and adorable spiritual infinitude only through the death and hell wrapped up in our finite experience. This was Emerson's incontestable virtue to every one who appreciated him, that he recognized no God outside of himself and his interlocutor, and recognized him there only as the *liaison* between the two, taking care that all their intercourse should be holy with a holiness undreamed of before by man or angel. For it is not a holiness taught by books or the example of tiresome, diseased, self-conscious saints, but simply by one's own redeemed flesh and blood. In short, the only holiness which Emerson recognized, and for which he consistently lived, was innocence. And innocence—glory be to God's spiritual incarnation in our nature!—has no other root in us than our unconscious flesh and bones. That is to say, it attaches only to what is definitively universal or natural in our experience, and hence appropriates itself to individuals only in so far as they learn to denude themselves of personality or self-consciousness; which reminds one of Christ's mystical saying: *He that findeth his life (in himself) shall lose it, and he that loseth his life for my sake shall find it.*

—Henry James Sr., "Mr. Emerson,"
Literary Remains, 1884, pp. 293–302

Elizabeth Palmer Peabody
"Emerson as Preacher" (1885)

Elizabeth Palmer Peabody was a central figure in New England literary circles. She assisted Bronson Alcott with his Temple School, published the *Dial* from 1841–43, was a member of the Transcendental Club, and hosted several of Margaret Fuller's famous "Conversations" at her bookstore. She also published several early works of Nathaniel Hawthorne, who was also her brother-in-law.

Peabody's close friendship with Emerson, combined with her authorial sense of propriety, results in some of the best contemporary writing on Emerson. This essay was offered first as a lecture in 1885 on the subject "Emerson as Preacher." Students investigating this phase of Emerson's career will want to take note of how Peabody qualifies her terms ("Emerson as Preacher" rather than "Emerson in the Pulpit"), as well as her knowledge of Emerson's pastoral life. Peabody was a friend of Emerson's aunt Mary Moody Emerson and so knew the family's proclivities for entering the ministry and the strain this placed on Emerson.

Students should also pay attention to Peabody's estimation of the ministerial effect of Emerson's life after resigning his pastorate. She writes, "[It] was Mr. Emerson's conscious life-purpose to minister the Living Spirit." She goes on to note that Emerson realized this spirit in art, poetry, literature, and nature. Students should pay heed to Peabody's use of the term *minister* as "teacher" or "guide." Emerson sought to illuminate his hearers, not to speak to them and lead them from a position of authority.

Finally, for students researching Emerson the man, Peabody reinforces the idea that the man and the work are inseparable. As difficult as it might be to imagine, Emerson seems to have embodied the idealism expressed in his work.

When Mr. Sanborn wrote to me that I was appointed to this lecture, he told me that the subject assigned to me was "Mr. Emerson as Preacher"—not "Mr. Emerson in the Pulpit," as it stands in the printed programme. But I hold on to what I had immediately agreed to do, for I think Mr. Emerson was always pre-eminently the preacher to his own generation and future ones, but as much—if not more—out of the pulpit as in it; faithful unto the end to his early chosen profession and the vows of his youth. Whether he spoke in the pulpit or lyceum chair, or to friends in his hospitable parlor, or *tête-à-tête* in his study, or in his favorite walks in the woods with chosen companions, or at the festive gatherings of scholars, or in the conventions of philanthropists, or in the popular assemblies of patriots in times and on occasions that try men's souls,—always and everywhere it was his conscious purpose to utter a "Thus saith the Lord." It was, we may say, a fact of his pre-existence. Looking back through eight generations of Mr. Emerson's paternal ancestry, we find there were preachers in every one of them. . . . Considering these antecedents, it is not surprising that [Emerson and his] brothers all naturally gravitated to the profession of preacher. The outlook at the time, however, was not alluring. . . . Although William Emerson, the eldest brother, went to Germany to study for the Christian ministry, he had not the nerve of his great ancestor[s]; and, on his return, shrank from the battle that he had discernment enough to see was impending, and took up what he deemed the kindred profession of law. Edward and Charles also entered the latter profession, with the most serious conceptions of its ideal, and neither for fame nor fortune,—both being strong Christians of the heroic old type. Our Mr. Emerson always spoke of these brothers as his spiritual and intellectual superiors; but I was told, by one who knew them all intimately, that both of them regarded him as the high-priest of their Holy of Holies, reverencing his every intuition as a sacred oracle. Mr. Emerson's poem, entitled "The Dirge," is the memorial of this rare fraternal relation.

My own acquaintance with Mr. Emerson dated from 1822, when I took a few private lessons from him in Greek,—a study that he was at the time immersed in, having just graduated from Harvard University, and being an assistant in the young ladies' school, kept in his mother's house in Federal Street by his brother William. Mr. Conway mentions this circumstance in his very beautiful apotheosis of Mr. Emerson; and, as usual, entirely transforms, by his imaginative memory, something I probably did tell him, which I will take leave to repeat here, as I have often told it myself. It is true that both of us were very shy (Mr. Emerson then nineteen and I eighteen years old), and we did not get into a chatting acquaintance, but sat opposite each other at the study table, not lifting our eyes from our books,—I reciting the poems of the "Graeca Majora," and he commenting and elucidating in the most instructive manner; and we were quite too much afraid of each other to venture any other conversation. When about to leave the city for what proved a two years' sojourn on the Kennebec, I sent for his bill, through his cousin George B. Emerson, who had introduced him to me. He came with that gentleman to say that he had no bill to render, for he found he could teach me nothing. It was then that, protected by his cousin's presence, he ventured to speak freely; and he poured out quite a stream of eloquence in praise of Mr. Edward Everett's oratory, of which I happened to express my admiration, and was delighted to find hum as great an admirer of it as I was. . . . After this our acquaintance lapsed for ten years, comprehending all the time Mr. Emerson was studying divinity and preaching at the Second Church in Boston. Then he resumed it (in 1839) on occasion of reading a little paper of mine which his aunt, Miss Mary Emerson,—who was my great friend, and bent on bringing us into intimate acquaintance,—had found among some loose papers of a journal of thoughts I fitfully kept, on the same principle that Mr. Emerson kept a journal all his life. This paper was a very free paraphrase of the first chapter of the Gospel of Saint John. . . .

He was on the eve of his first voyage to Europe, soon after the death of his first wife and the relinquishment of his Boston pulpit. He was at the time too feeble in health to make visits, and sent to me to come to his house in Chardon Street, where I found him quite absorbed in Goethe and Carlyle; but he immediately turned his attention to Saint John's grand peroration; and we discussed every phrase of it. It was one of those conversations which "make the soul," to use a favorite expression of his aunt Mary's. It was, therefore, on the highest plane of human thought that we first met, our theme being the Eternal Relations of God, Nature, and Man; beginning an intercourse that continued there with more or less interval during his lifetime. . . .

In 1835 or 1836, when he was still supplying the pulpit at East Lexington, it was my privilege to make frequent visits to his house in Concord, and he would always invite me to go down with him in his chaise on Sundays. In one of these precious seasons for conversation, as we were returning to Concord, I repeated to him the reply of an unconsciously wise and pious woman of the congregation, with whom I had walked to the afternoon meeting, and had asked her why the society did not call to settle over them an eminent preacher that Mr. Emerson had sent in his stead on a previous Sunday. . . . "Oh, Miss Peabody" her words were, "we are a very simple people here; we cannot understand anybody but Mr. Emerson." "There is a 'tell' for a Transcendentalist," said I to him playfully, thinking he would laugh in contrasting it with the current cant in Boston among the Philistines, who said they "could not understand Mr. Emerson." But he did not laugh. On the contrary, with an accent that was almost pathetic, he replied, "If I had not been cut off untimely in the pulpit, perhaps I might have made something of the sermon." "It is evident from this attentive Lexington audience," I said, "that you have already made something of the sermon." "Did you observe, he replied, "that row of venerable, earnest faces of old men who sit just in front of the platform? It would be rather difficult to be frivolous when speaking to them. But in the back part of the hall there were some young men cunning over the leaves of a hymn-book. No preacher can be satisfied with himself when he leaves any of his audience at leisure to turn over the leaves of a book." "That is a high standard, I replied. And soon he added, in a livelier tone, "Henceforth the lyceum chair must be my pulpit. The word of moral truth makes one of any place." . . .

[It] was Mr. Emerson's conscious life-purpose to minister the Living Spirit, whom he sought alike in the material universe and in human history, in literature and in ethics, in art, and, above all, in his own heart and imagination. In every form of his utterance he touched the profound depth of poetry, whether he sung in verse or spoke in prose. Much of his prose is as melodious as his verse,—witness his first publication on "Nature," his lecture on the "Method of Nature," and the opening, and indeed the whole, of his Address at Divinity Hall, . . . which was not to me alone the apocalypse of our Transcendental era in Boston. For, if the lifeless understanding of the day mistook it for a denial of Christ, we now see that upon those whose hearts "the forms of young imagination had kept pure," and whom the pulpit entirely ignored or seldom addressed, it flashed the first light of the revelation of "the friend of man," whom he then affirmed that an effete ecclesiasticism had made "the enemy of man." . . .

And here I take leave to introduce another personal reminiscence. I had the happiness of listening to this truly prophetic discourse; and when, soon after, he was correcting the proof-sheets of it for the press, I was visiting at his house. One day he came from his study into the room where his wife and myself were sitting at our needle-work, and said, "How does this strike your Hebrew souls?" proceeding to read the paragraph containing the above expression, which begins with the words, "This Eastern monarchy of a Christianity," etc. I said, "You will put a capital 'F' to the word 'friend'?" He seemed to reflect a few moments, and then deliberately replied, "No; directly I put that capital 'F' my readers go to sleep!"

He then went on to read another paragraph, which he remarked he had omitted to deliver because he thought he "was getting too long." It came immediately after the paragraph in which he accused the "historical Christianity" of corrupting all attempts to communicate living religion, "making Christianity a mythus, and founding the Church not on Jesus' principles, but on his tropes." . . .

I can recall only one word of this omitted paragraph, but remember perfectly the sense. It was a caveat anticipating the development of a new party, only half understanding him, which would fall into what he called the "puppyism" of a criticism irreverent of the person of Jesus. And this party did soon appear, and has not entirely passed away yet; some of our free religionists being guilty of this lack of just conception of "the one man who, alone in all history," as Mr. Emerson says, "estimated the greatness of man!" . . . I said, interrogatively, "You will certainly print that passage, for it will convict Mr. Ware of misunderstanding and so misrepresenting you in his sermon." . . . This was an unlucky suggestion of mine; for, after a moment's silence, he replied: "No, it would be shabby to spring upon Mr. Ware this passage now. I must abide by what I delivered, whatever was its lack of full expression." I was struck silent at the moment by this exhibition of an exquisite gentlemanly loyalty, the very poetry of self-respect and politeness. But some months later, irritated by many exhibitions of the "puppyism" he had predicted, and which stupidly professed itself to be Emersonian, I said to him, "Are you quite sure you did not sacrifice a greater duty to a less, when you decided not to publish that paragraph which defined your exact meaning, lest it should put Mr. Ware in the awkward predicament of having fought a shadow?" He replied, deliberately but emphatically, "No." . . . [He] expressed that gentlemanly courtesy was simply social justice, and that anxiety to be personally understood, rather than to have the truth understood, was the special weakness of the hour. Apology, and even explanation, were the blunders of egotism. . . .

Mr. Emerson said that it was the duty of the individual to affirm all that his experience had proved to be true, and never to be satisfied short of a generalization covering a principle. He had the faith that our growing experience would contain the solution of all questions, the consummation of all hopes, the satisfaction of all unselfish desires, inasmuch as the social law was intercommunication of experiences forevermore. His humility was a quickening hope, not a weak agnosticism,—the humility of a son of God who feels that all that his Father has will duly become his. He never presumes to call the Unknown unknowable. . . .

Mr. Emerson in his use of the words Brahm, Pan, Apollo, the Greek Bacchus, Uriel, and other burning personifications of the Persian Muse, revivifies the Pentecostal Muse and brings home to the imagination of this duller modern time the various attributes of the Eternal Spirit; making a language of his own, that creates unity of understanding in all who speak the differing and therefore imperfect languages of man in their partial creeds. Do we not hear this in [his] great lyric utterances? . . .

I will not attempt to read the whole of what is to me the most profoundly touching of all Emerson's divine songs, the "deep Heart's" reply in the "Threnody," when he himself came up from the most transforming personal experience of his life, expressed in that wild wad over the child lost to him for "the forever of this world," that for a long time plunged him into a deep of sorrow of which the first part of the poem is the all but unequalled expression. But at length he found what fully developed the human tenderness, that gave the last divine touch to the decline of his life. . . . [This] rich strain of poetry was of all his utterances the most touching to me. For several years before this season of his personal experience he was struggling to bear the loss of his brother Charles with the dignity of a man. To the question I had put to him, "Is there not something in God corresponding to and justifying this human sensibility?" he had replied, "No!" And at that period of his life he seemed to measure spiritual strength by a man's stoical denial of the fact of pain. His intellectual fin could not smelt the ore of human suffering. A gentleman who stood with him at his brother Charles's grave, said he turned away from it with the words, "Death is an absurdity!" . . .

Not only do all his great apocalyptic chants, but nearly all his smaller pieces,—such as, "Rhea," "Each and All," "The Rhodora," "Hamatreya," "Lines to J. W." . . . seem a true preaching, . . . sometimes catching up our spirits into the vision of principles, sometimes kindling private virtue and patriotic heroism, and sometimes plunging the soul into the unfound infinite. In one of his lectures he defined prayer as, "a plunge into the unfound infinite." It seems to me, therefore, that I am not irreverent, but reverent, when . . . I say of him, more and more "the multitude hears him gladly," for, like Jesus, he preaches "with authority," and not as the Scribes.

Postscript

There was no time for a conversation after I closed my reading, . . . but to a question that was asked just as we broke up, "What was Mr. Emerson's attitude towards religious institutions?" I will here take leave to reply. It was an essentially temporary one, like that he held to the technics of the pulpit of his day. His attitude towards the Lord's Supper naturally brought him into sympathy with the Quakers on the point of stated times for public prayer, and he actually ceased to go to meeting on Sundays because church-going also had at that time become merely perfunctory. But I heard him say, at that very date, that to meet together to consider all our duties in the light of the Divine Omnipresence was by far the most legitimate of human assemblies; and he considered it a great misfortune to society that it had become such a routine that "a devout person" (he meant his own ardently Christian wife) said, "It seems wicked to go to church."

At the time he ceased to go to church he was making a pulpit of the study-table where he composed his lectures. He never abandoned his office of preacher. I heard him say, in the last half of his life, "My special parish is young men inquiring their way of life." . . .

In the last of his life, when the infirmities of old age tied his tongue, and he could no longer minister the word of moral truth to others, he resumed his early habit of going to church himself on Sundays; and his wife told me he thanked her for bringing up his children to do so.

—Elizabeth Palmer Peabody, "Emerson as Preacher," 1885,
from *The Genius and Character of Emerson: Lectures at the
Concord School of Philosophy*, ed. F.B. Sanborn, 1885,
pp. 146–47, 149, 152, 156–62, 167–68, 169–72

EDWIN P. WHIPPLE
"AMERICAN LITERATURE" (1886)

American literary essayist and critic Edwin Whipple shared Emerson's desire for an American literature free of continental European influence. Whipple considered Emerson the ideal American essayist and critic. The following excerpt is especially helpful for students examining the ways Emerson connected beauty and moral truth. This can be a complicated

relationship to untangle, but Whipple helps to clarify the key aspects of
Emerson's thinking in this regard.

Emerson recognized beauty in terms of "moral righteousness," but
his definition of "moral" is perhaps new to students working through
Emerson's terminology. Whipple is particularly insightful when addressing
this matter. He is also helpful in defining what the term *soul* implies in
Emerson's work, especially the term *over soul*. Whipple establishes this as
elementary, by which he means fundamental, to Emerson's thinking.

Students should note that Whipple recognizes Emerson as a radical.
Readers may not understand this today, but Whipple helps us realize
that, in a contemporary context, Emerson was unorthodox (to the point
of threatening) to established religious and social systems (see Joseph
O'Connor's entry in this volume). Emerson's "radicalism penetrated to
the very root of dissent," Whipple writes, and Emerson's emphasis on the
primacy of the individual challenged the accepted orthodoxies of the
day. To a culture that encounters Emerson largely through aphorisms and
self-help catchphrases, this may seem a peculiar claim. But for students
interested in Emerson's views on the religious, social, and cultural mores
of his time, this perception of Emerson as a dangerous, even threatening
intellect is important because Emerson's radicalism helped determine
the condition of the American intellectual landscape.

—◊◊◊—   —◊◊◊—   —◊◊◊—

He came from a race of clergymen; doubtless much of his elevation of character
and austere sense of the grandeur of the moral sentiment is his by inheritance;
but after entering the ministry he soon found that even Unitarianism was a
limitation of his intellectual independence to which he could not submit;
and, in the homely New England phrase, "he set up on his own account,"
responsible *for* nobody, and not responsible *to* anybody. His radicalism
penetrated to the very root of dissent, for it was founded on the idea that in
all organizations, social, political, and religious, there must be an element
which checks the free exercise of individual thought; and the free exercise
of his individual thinking he determined should be controlled by nothing
instituted and authoritative on the planet. Descartes himself did not begin his
philosophizing with a more complete self-emancipation from all the opinions
generally accepted by mankind. But Descartes was a reasoner; Emerson is a
seer and a poet; and he was the last man to attempt to overthrow accredited
systems in order to substitute for them a dogmatic system of his own. In his
view of the duty of "man thinking," this course would have been to violate
his fundamental principle, which was that nobody "could lay copyright on

the world;" that no theory could include Nature; that the greatest thinker and discoverer could only add a few items of information to what the human mind had previously won from "the vast and formless infinite;" and that the true work of a scholar was not to inclose the field of matter and mind by a system which encircled it, but to extend our knowledge in straight lines, leading from the vanishing points of positive knowledge into the illimitable unknown spaces beyond. Emerson's peculiar sphere was psychology. By a certain felicity of his nature he was a non-combatant; indifferent to logic, he suppressed all the processes of his thinking, and announced its results in affirmations; and none of the asperities which commonly afflict the apostles of dissent ever ruffled the serene spirit of this universal dissenter. He could never be seduced into controversy. He was assailed both as an atheist and as a pantheist; as a writer so obscure that nobody could understand what he meant, and also as a mere verbal trickster, whose only talent consisted in vivifying commonplaces, or in converting, by inversion, stale truisms into brilliant paradoxes; and all these varying charges had only the effect of lighting up his face with that queer, quizzical, inscrutable smile, that amused surprise at the misconceptions of the people who attacked him, which is noticeable in all portraits and photographs of his somewhat enigmatical countenance. His method was very simple and very hard. It consisted in growing up to a level with the spiritual objects he perceived, and his elevation of thought was thus the sign and accompaniment of a corresponding elevation of character. In his case, as in the case of Channing, there was an unconscious return to Jonathan Edwards, and to all the great divines whose "souls had sight" of eternal verities. What the orthodox saints called the Holy Ghost, he, without endowing it with personality, called the Over Soul. He believed with them that in God we live and move and have our being; that only by communicating with this Being can we have any vital individuality; and that the record of a communication with Him or It was the most valuable of all contributions to literature, whether theological or human. The noblest passages in his writings are those in which he celebrates this august and gracious communion of the Spirit of God with the soul of man; and they are the most serious, solemn, and uplifting passages which can perhaps be found in our literature. Here was a man who had earned the right to utter these noble truths by patient meditation and clear insight. Carlyle exclaimed, in a preface to an English edition of one of Emerson's later volumes: "Here comes our brave Emerson, with *news* from the empyrean!" That phrase exactly hits Emerson as a transcendental thinker. His insights were, in some sense, revelations; he could "gossip on the eternal politics;" and just at the time when science, relieved from the pressure of theology, announced materialistic hypotheses with more than the confidence with which the bigots of theological creeds had heretofore announced their dogmas, this serene American thinker had won his way into all the centres of European intelligence, and delivered his quiet protest against every hypothesis which put in peril the spiritual interests of humanity. It is curious to witness the process by which this heresiarch has ended in giving his evidence, or rather his experience, that God is not the Unknowable of Herbert Spencer, but that, however infinitely distant He may be from the human understanding, He is still intimately near to the human soul. And Emerson knows by experience what the word *soul* really means!

> Were she a body, how could she remain
>   Within the body which is less than she?
> Or how could she the world's great shape contain,
>   And in our narrow breasts contained be?
> All bodies are confined within some place,
>   But she all place within herself confines;
> All bodies have their measure and their space,
>   *But who can draw the souls dimensive lines?*

In an unpublished speech at a celebration of Shakspeare's birthday, he spoke of Shakspeare as proving to us that "the soul of man is deeper, wider, higher than the spaces of astronomy;" and in another connection he says that "a man of thought must feel that thought is the parent of the universe," that "the world is *saturated* with deity and with law."

It is this depth of spiritual experience and subtilty of spiritual insight which distinguish Emerson from all other American authors, and make him an elementary power as well as an elementary thinker. The singular attractiveness, however, of his writings comes from his intense perception of Beauty, both in its abstract quality as the "awful loveliness" which such poets as Shelley celebrated, and in the more concrete expression by which it fascinates ordinary minds. His imaginative faculty, both in the conception and creation of beauty, is uncorrupted by any morbid sentiment. His vision reaches to the very sources of beauty,—the beauty that cheers. The great majority even of eminent poets are "saddest when they sing." They contrast life with the beautiful possibilities of life which their imaginations suggest, and though their discontent with the actual may inspire by the energy of its utterance, it tends also to depress by emphasizing the impossibility of realizing the ideals it depicts. But the perception of beauty in nature or in human nature, whether it be the beauty of a flower or of a soul, makes Emerson joyous and glad; he exults in celebrating it, and he communicates to his readers his own ecstatic mood. He has been a diligent student of many literatures and many religions; but all his quotations from them show that he rejects everything in his manifold readings which does not tend to cheer, invigorate, and elevate, which is not nutritious food for the healthy human soul. If he is morbid in anything, it is in his comical hatred of all forms of physical, mental, and moral disease. He agrees with Dr. Johnson in declaring that "every man is a rascal as soon as he is sick." "I once asked," he says, "a clergyman in a retired town who were his companions—what men of ability he saw. He replied that he spent his time with the sick and the dying. I said he seemed to me to need quite other company, and all the more that he had this; for if people were sick and dying to any purpose, we should leave all and go to them, but, as far as I had observed, they were as frivolous as the rest, and sometimes much more frivolous." Indeed, Emerson, glorying in his own grand physical and moral health, and fundamentally brave, is impatient of all the weaknesses of humanity, especially those of men of genius. He never could be made to recognize the genius of Shelley, except in a few poems, because he was disgusted with the wail that persistently runs through Shelley's wonderfully imaginative poetry. In his taste, as in his own practice as a writer, he is a stout believer in the desirableness and efficacy of mental tonics, and a severe critic of the literature of discontent and desperation. He looks curiously on while a poet rages against destiny and his own miseries, and puts the ironical query, "Why so hot, my little man?" His ideal of manhood was originally derived from the consciousness of his own somewhat haughty individuality, and it has been fed by his study of the poetic and historic records of persons who have dared to do heroic acts and dared to utter heroic thoughts. Beauty is never absent from his celebration of these, but it is a beauty that never enfeebles, but always braces and cheers.

—Edwin P. Whipple, "American Literature" (1886),
American Literature and Other Papers, 1887, pp. 59–65

GEORGE SANTAYANA "EMERSON" (1900)

The Spanish-American philosopher George Santayana made valuable contributions to the fields of aesthetics and literary criticism while serving on the philosophy faculty, with William James, at Harvard University. His books include *The Sense of Beauty* (1896) and *Interpretations of Poetry and Religion* (1900), both of which inform his views on Emerson.

Santayana recognizes that an initial requirement for Emerson is his "insurrection," his "shaking loose from convention," his "revolutionary thinking." This departure or severance was necessary for Emerson to work out his own thinking, which Santayana believes centers on imagination, Emerson's "single theme." All of Emerson's recurring ideas—"compensation, continuity, the self-expression of the Soul in the forms of Nature and of society"—spring from "the omnipotence of imaginative thought; its power first to make the world, then to understand it, and finally to rise above it."

It is important for students to understand that in order to, as Santayana writes, "stand aside from the life of the world," Emerson first had to rearrange the world he inherited from his forbearers, from his religious training, and from his education. This was a difficult step for Emerson, since the process was fraught with challenges from family and colleagues alike. Santayana's analysis of Emerson's understanding is a close one; for Emerson to be "open to all philosophic influences, from whatever quarter they might blow," he first had the task of removing himself from conventional Unitarian thinking. Only then was he able to foment "a fresh subject on a fresh subject."

Santayana's other significant point has to do with common sense and mysticism. Those students examining the structure of Emerson's thought or writing on Emerson's views regarding the individual should consider Santayana's definition of some key terms: *mysticism, common sense, philosophy* (and its corollary Emersonian term *moral energy*).

Readers should also take special note of Santayana's conclusion: "[Emerson is] not an independent philosopher, in spite of his belief in independence." To qualify Emerson as a "Puritan mystic" may seem a simplistic categorization, but Santayana is careful throughout his essay to point out exactly those qualities that form Emerson's intellectual context and the significance mysticism played in his imaginative reconstruction of the world. Emerson is not without his environment; that is, he exists within his culture. However, Emerson's imagination, his rebuilding of the human connection to the divine, makes him "belong very little to the past, very little to the present," and "a Puritan whose religion was all poetry."

—*∽∿∽— —∽∿∽— —∽∿∽—

Those who knew Emerson, or who stood so near to his time and to his circle that they caught some echo of his personal influence, did not judge him merely as a poet or philosopher, nor identify his efficacy with that of his writings. His friends and neighbours, the congregations he preached to in his younger days, the audiences that afterward listened to his lectures, all agreed in a veneration for his person which had nothing to do with their understanding or acceptance of his opinions. They flocked to him and listened to his word, not so much for the sake of its absolute meaning as for the atmosphere of candour, purity, and serenity that hung about it, as about a sort of sacred music. They felt themselves in the presence of a rare and beautiful spirit, who was in communion with a higher world. More than the truth his teaching might express, they valued the sense it gave them of a truth that was inexpressible. They became aware, if we may say so, of the ultra-violet rays of his spectrum, of the inaudible highest notes of his gamut, too pure and thin for common ears.

This effect was by no means due to the possession on the part of Emerson of the secret of the universe, or even of a definite conception of ultimate truth. He was not a prophet who had once for all climbed his Sinai or his Tabor, and having there beheld the transfigured reality, descended again to make authoritative report of it to the world. Far from it. At bottom he had no doctrine at all. The deeper he went and the more he tried to grapple with fundamental conceptions, the vaguer and more elusive they became in his hands. Did he know what he meant by Spirit or the "Over-Soul"? Could he say what he understood by the terms, so constantly on his lips, Nature, Law, God, Benefit, or Beauty? He could not, and the consciousness of that incapacity was so lively within him that he never attempted to give articulation to his philosophy. His finer instinct kept him from doing that violence to his inspiration.

The source of his power lay not in his doctrine, but in his temperament, and the rare quality of his wisdom was due less to his reason than to his imagination. Reality eluded him; he had neither diligence nor constancy enough to master and possess it; but his mind was open to all philosophic influences, from whatever quarter they might blow; the lessons of science and the hints of poetry worked themselves out in him to a free and personal religion. He differed from the plodding many, not in knowing things better, but in having more ways of knowing them. His grasp was not particularly firm, he was far from being, like a Plato or an Aristotle, past master in the art and the science of life. But his mind was endowed with unusual plasticity, with unusual spontaneity and liberty of movement—it was a fairyland of thoughts and fancies. He was like a young god making experiments in creation: he blotched the work, and always began again on a new and better plan. Every day he said, "Let there be light," and every day the light was new. His sun, like that of Heraclitus, was different every morning.

What seemed, then, to the more earnest and less critical of his hearers a revelation from above was in truth rather an insurrection from beneath, a shaking loose from convention, a disintegration of the normal categories of reason in favour of various imaginative principles, on which the world might have been built, if it had been built differently. This gift of revolutionary thinking allowed new aspects, hints of wider laws, premonitions of unthought-of fundamental unities to spring constantly into view. But such visions were necessarily fleeting, because the human mind had long before settled its grammar, and discovered, after much grouping and many defeats, the general forms in which experience will allow itself to be stated. These general forms are the principles of common sense and positive science, no less imaginative in their origin than those notions which we now call transcendental, but grown prosaic, like the metaphors of common speech, by dint of repetition.

Yet authority, even of this rational kind, sat lightly upon Emerson. To reject tradition and think as one might have thought if no man had ever existed before was indeed the aspiration of the Transcendentalists, and although Emerson hardly regarded himself as a member of that school, he largely shared its tendency and passed for its spokesman. Without protesting against tradition, he smilingly eluded it in his thoughts, untamable in their quiet irresponsibility. He fled to his woods or to his "pleached garden," to be the creator of his own worlds in solitude and freedom. No wonder that he brought thence to the tightly conventional minds of his contemporaries a breath as if from paradise. His simplicity in novelty his profundity, his ingenuous ardour must have seemed to them something heavenly, and they may be excused if they thought they detected inspiration even in his occasional thin paradoxes and guileless whims. They were stifled with conscience and he brought them a breath of Nature; they were surfeited with shallow controversies and he gave them poetic truth.

Imagination, indeed, is his single theme. As a preacher might under every text enforce the same lessons of the gospel, so Emerson traces in every sphere the same spiritual laws of experience—compensation, continuity, the self-expression of the Soul in the forms of Nature and of society, until she finally recognizes herself in her own work and sees its beneficence and beauty. His constant refrain is the omnipotence of imaginative thought; its power first to make the world, then to understand it, and finally to rise above it. All Nature is an embodiment of our native fancy, all history a drama in which the innate possibilities of the spirit are enacted and realized. While the conflict of life and the shocks of experience seem to bring us face to face with an alien and overwhelming power, reflection can humanize and rationalize that power by conceiving its laws; and with this recognition of the rationality of all things comes the sense of their beauty and order. The destruction which Nature seems to prepare for our special hopes is thus seen to be the victory of our impersonal interests. To awaken in us this spiritual insight, an elevation of mind which is at once an act of comprehension and of worship, to substitute it for lower passions and more servile forms of intelligence—that is Emerson's constant effort. All his resources of illustration, observation, and rhetoric are used to deepen and clarify this sort of wisdom.

Such thought is essentially the same that is found in the German romantic or idealistic philosophers, with whom Emerson's affinity is remarkable, all the more as he seems to have borrowed little or nothing from their works. The critics of human nature, in the eighteenth century, had shown how much men's ideas depend on their predispositions, on the character of their senses and the habits of their intelligence. Seizing upon this thought and exaggerating it, the romantic philosophers attributed to the spirit of man the omnipotence which had belonged to God, and felt that in this way they were reasserting the supremacy of mind over matter and establishing it upon a safe and rational basis.

The Germans were great system-makers, and Emerson cannot rival them in the sustained effort of thought by which they sought to reinterpret every sphere of being according to their chosen principles. But he surpassed them in an instinctive sense of what he was doing. He never represented his poetry as science, nor countenanced the formation of a new sect that should nurse the sense of a private and mysterious illumination, and relight the fagots of passion and prejudice. He never tried to seek out and defend the universal implications of his ideas, and never wrote the book he had once planned on the law of compensation, foreseeing, we may well believe, the sophistries in which he would have been directly involved. He fortunately preferred a fresh statement on a fresh subject. A suggestion once given, the spirit once aroused to speculation, a glimpse once gained of some ideal harmony, he chose to descend again to common sense and to touch the earth for a moment before another flight. The faculty of idealization was itself what he valued. Philosophy for him was rather a moral energy flowering into sprightliness of thought than a body of serious and defensible doctrines. In practising transcendental speculation only in this poetic and sporadic fashion, Emerson retained its true value and avoided its greatest danger. He secured the freedom and fertility of his thought and did not allow one conception of law or one hint of harmony to sterilize the mind and prevent the subsequent birth within it of other ideas, no less just and imposing than their predecessors. For we are not dealing at all in such a philosophy with matters of fact or with such verifiable truths as exclude their opposites. We are dealing only with imagination, with the art of conception, and with the various forms in which reflection, like a poet, may compose and recompose human experience.

A certain disquiet mingled, however, in the minds of Emerson's contemporaries with the admiration they felt for his purity and genius. They saw that he had forsaken the doctrines of the Church; and they were not sure whether he held quite unequivocally any doctrine whatever. We may not all of us share the concern for orthodoxy which usually caused this puzzled alarm: we may understand that it was not Emerson's vocation to be definite and dogmatic in religion any more than in philosophy. Yet that disquiet will not, even for us, wholly disappear. It is produced by a defect which naturally accompanies imagination in all but the greatest minds. I mean disorganization. Emerson not only conceived things in new ways, but he seemed to think the new ways might cancel and supersede the old. His imagination was to invalidate the understanding. That inspiration which should come to fulfil seemed too often to come to destroy. If he was able so constantly to stimulate us to fresh thoughts, was it not because he demolished the labour of long ages of reflection? Was not the startling effect of much of his writing due to its contradiction to tradition and to common sense?

So long as he is a poet and in the enjoyment of his poetic license, we can blame this play of mind only by a misunderstanding. It is possible to think otherwise than as common sense thinks; there are other categories beside those of science. When we employ them we enlarge our lives. We add to the world of fact any number of worlds of the imagination in which human nature and the eternal relations of ideas may be nobly expressed. So far our imaginative fertility is only a benefit: it surrounds us with the congenial and necessary radiation of art and religion. It manifests our moral vitality in the bosom of Nature.

But sometimes imagination invades the sphere of understanding and seems to discredit its indispensable work. Common sense, we are allowed to infer, is a shallow affair: true insight changes all that. When so applied, poetic activity is not an unmixed good. It loosens our hold on fact and confuses our intelligence, so that we forget that intelligence has itself every prerogative of imagination, and has besides the sanction of practical validity. We are made to believe that since the understanding is something human and

conditioned, something which might have been different, as the senses might have been different, and which we may yet, so to speak, get behind— therefore the understanding ought to be abandoned. We long for higher faculties, neglecting those we have, we yearn for intuition, closing our eyes upon experience. We become mystical.

Mysticism, as we have said, is the surrender of a category of thought because we divine its relativity. As every new category, however, must share this reproach, the mystic is obliged in the end to give them all up, the poetic and moral categories no less than the physical, so that the end of his purification is the atrophy of his whole nature, the emptying of his whole heart and mind to make room, as he thinks, for God. By attacking the authority of the understanding as the organon of knowledge, by substituting itself for it as the herald of a deeper truth, the imagination thus prepares its own destruction. For if the understanding is rejected because it cannot grasp the absolute, the imagination and all its works—art, dogma, worship—must presently be rejected for the same reason. Common sense and poetry must both go by the board, and conscience must follow after: for all these are human and relative. Mysticism will be satisfied only with the absolute, and as the absolute, by its very definition, is not representable by any specific faculty, it must be approached through the abandonment of all. The lights of life must be extinguished that the light of the absolute may shine, and the possession of everything in general must be secured by the surrender of everything in particular.

The same diffidence, however, the same constant renewal of sincerity which kept Emerson's flights of imagination near to experience, kept his mysticism also within bounds. A certain mystical tendency is pervasive with him, but there are only one or two subjects on which he dwells with enough constancy and energy of attention to make his mystical treatment of them pronounced. One of these is the question of the unity of all minds in the single soul of the universe, which is the same in all creatures; another is the question of evil and of its evaporation in the universal harmony of things. Both these ideas suggest themselves at certain turns in every man's experience, and might receive a rational formulation. But they are intricate subjects, obscured by many emotional prejudices, so that the labour, impartiality, and precision which would be needed to elucidate them are to be looked for in scholastic rather than in inspired thinkers, and in Emerson least of all. Before these problems he is alternately ingenuous and rhapsodical and in both moods equally helpless. Individuals no doubt exist, he says to himself. But, ah! Napoleon is in every schoolboy. In every squatter in the western prairies we shall find an owner—

Of Caesar's hand and Plato's brain,
Of Lord Christ's heart, and Shakespeare's strain.

But how? we may ask. Potentially? Is it because any mind, were it given the right body and the right experience, were it made over, in a word, into another mind, would resemble that other mind to the point of identity? Or is it that our souls are already so largely similar that we are subject to many kindred promptings and share many ideals unrealizable in our particular circumstances? But then we should simply be saying that if what makes men different were removed, men would be indistinguishable, or that, in so far as they are now alike, they can understand one another by summoning up their respective experiences in the fancy. There would be no mysticism in that, but at the same time, alas, no eloquence, no paradox, and, if we must say the word, no nonsense.

On the question of evil, Emerson's position is of the same kind. There is evil, of course, he tells us. Experience is sad. There is a crack in everything that God has made. But, ah! the laws of the universe are sacred and beneficent. Without them nothing good could arise. All things, then, are in their right places and the universe is perfect above our querulous tears. Perfect? we may ask. But perfect from what point of view, in reference to what ideal? To its own? To that of a man who renouncing himself and all naturally dear to him, ignoring the injustice, suffering, and impotence in the world, allows his will and his conscience to be hypnotized by the spectacle of a necessary evolution, and lulled into cruelty by the pomp and music of a tragic show? In that case the evil is not explained, it is forgotten; it is not cured, but condoned. We have surrendered the category of the better and the worse, the deepest foundation of life and reason; we have become mystics on the one subject on which, above all others, we ought to be men.

Two forces may be said to have carried Emerson in this mystical direction; one, that freedom of his imagination which we have already noted, and which kept him from the fear of self-contradiction; the other the habit of worship inherited from his clerical ancestors and enforced by his religious education. The spirit of conformity, the unction, the loyalty even unto death inspired by the religion of Jehovah, were dispositions acquired by too long a discipline and rooted in too many forms of speech, of thought, and of worship for a man like Emerson, who had felt their full force, ever to be able to lose them. The evolutions of his abstract opinions left that habit unchanged. Unless we keep this circumstance in mind, we shall not be able to understand the kind of elation and sacred joy, so characteristic of his eloquence, with which he propounds

laws of Nature and aspects of experience which, viewed in themselves, afford but an equivocal support to moral enthusiasm. An optimism so persistent and unclouded as his will seem at variance with the description he himself gives of human life, a description coloured by a poetic idealism, but hardly by an optimistic bias.

We must remember, therefore, that this optimism is a pious tradition, originally justified by the belief in a personal God and in a providential government of affairs for the ultimate and positive good of the elect, and that the habit of worship survived in Emerson as an instinct after those positive beliefs had faded into a recognition of "spiritual laws." We must remember that Calvinism had known how to combine an awestruck devotion to the Supreme Being with no very roseate picture of the destinies of mankind, and for more than two hundred years had been breeding in the stock from which Emerson came a willingness to be, as the phrase is, "damned for the glory of God."

What wonder, then, that when, for the former inexorable dispensation of Providence, Emerson substituted his general spiritual and natural laws, he should not have felt the spirit of worship fail within him? On the contrary, his thought moved in the presence of moral harmonies which seemed to him truer, more beautiful, and more beneficent than those of the old theology. An independent philosopher would not have seen in those harmonies an object of worship or a sufficient basis for optimism. But he was not an independent philosopher, in spite of his belief in independence. He inherited the problems and the preoccupations of the theology from which he started, being in this respect like the German idealists, who, with all their pretence of absolute metaphysics, were in reality only giving elusive and abstract forms to traditional theology. Emerson, too, was not primarily a philosopher, but a Puritan mystic with a poetic fancy and a gift for observation and epigram, and he saw in the laws of Nature, idealized by his imagination, only a more intelligible form of the divinity he had always recognized and adored. His was not a philosophy passing into a religion, but a religion expressing itself as a philosophy and veiled, as at its setting it descended the heavens, in various tints of poetry and science.

If we ask ourselves what was Emerson's relation to the scientific and religious movements of his time, and what place he may claim in the history of opinion, we must answer that he belong very little to the past, very little to the present, and almost wholly to that abstract sphere into which mystical or philosophic aspiration has carried a few men in all ages. The religious tradition in which he was reared was that of Puritanism, but of a Puritanism

which, retaining its moral intensity and metaphysical abstraction, had minimized its doctrinal expression and become Unitarian. Emerson was indeed the Psyche of Puritanism, "the latest-born and fairest vision far" of all that "faded hierarchy." A Puritan whose religion was all poetry, a poet whose only pleasure was thought, he showed in his life and personality the meagreness, the constraint, the frigid and conscious consecration which belonged to his clerical ancestors, while his inmost impersonal spirit ranged abroad over the fields of history and Nature, gathering what ideas it might, and singing its little snatches of inspired song.

The traditional element was thus rather an external and unessential contribution to Emerson's mind; he had the professional tinge, the decorum, the distinction of an old-fashioned divine; he had also the habit of writing sermons, and he had the national pride and hope of a religious people that felt itself providentially chosen to establish a free and godly commonwealth in a new world. For the rest, he separated himself from the ancient creed of the community with a sense rather of relief than of regret. A literal belief in Christian doctrines repelled him as unspiritual, as manifesting no understanding of the meaning which, as allegories, those doctrines might have to a philosophic and poetical spirit. Although as a clergyman he was at first in the habit of referring to the Bible and its lessons as to a supreme authority, he had no instinctive sympathy with the inspiration of either the Old or the New Testament; in Hafiz or Plutarch, in Plato or Shakespeare, he found more congenial stuff.

While he thus preferred to withdraw, without rancour and without contempt, from the ancient fellowship of the church, he assumed an attitude hardly less cool and deprecatory toward the enthusiasms of the new era. The national ideal of democracy and freedom had his entire sympathy; he allowed himself to be drawn into the movement against slavery; he took a curious and smiling interest in the discoveries of natural science and in the material progress of the age. But he could go no farther. His contemplative nature, his religious training, his dispersed reading, made him stand aside from the life of the world, even while he studied it with benevolent attention. His heart was fixed on eternal things, and he was in no sense a prophet for his age or country. He belonged by nature to that mystical company of devout souls that recognize no particular home and are dispersed throughout history, although not without intercommunication. He felt his affinity to the Hindoos and the Persians, to the Platonists and the Stoics. Like them he remains "a friend and aider of those who would live in the spirit." If not a star of the first magnitude, he is certainly a fixed star in the firmament of philosophy.

Alone as yet among Americans, he may be said to have won a place there, if not by the originality of his thought, at least by the originality and beauty of the expression he gave to thoughts that are old and imperishable.

—George Santayana, "Emerson,"
Interpretations of Poetry and Religion,
1900, pp. 217–33

WORKS

LECTURES

WALTER WHITMAN (1842)

This brief review of Emerson's lecture "Poetry of the Times," by Walter (soon to be Walt) Whitman, provides a valuable description of the types of people who commonly attended Emerson's lectures. Students delving into the reaction to, and popularity of, transcendentalism (this lecture was delivered in 1842, at the height of the transcendentalist movement), may take note of Whitman's bemused descriptions. Students should also note that the "Greeley" Whitman refers to is Horace Greeley, publisher of the *New York Daily Tribune.*

Regarding the lecture Whitman has surprisingly little to say. He is impressed with Emerson's address (and the comment that "the first man who called another an ass was a poet"), though Whitman, certainly skilled with words, makes no attempt to summarize the content of the lecture. Since this is a newspaper review (for the *New York Aurora*), he might simply have run out of the limited space afforded him. However, it seems as though he is more interested in the crowd of attendees, since he devotes a majority of his text to describing it.

<hr />

The transcendentalist had a very full house on Saturday evening. There were a few beautiful maids—but more ugly women, mostly blue stockings; several interesting young men with Byron collars, doctors, and parsons; Grahamites and abolitionists; sage editors, a few of whom were taking notes; and all the other species of literati. Greeley was in ecstasies whenever any thing particularly good was said, which seemed to be once in about five minutes— he would flounce about like a fish out of water, or a tickled girl—look around, to see those behind him and at his side; all of which very plainly told to those both far and near, that he knew a thing or two more about these matters than other men.

This lecture was on the "Poetry of the Times." He said that the first man who called another an ass was a poet. Because the business of the poet is expression—the giving utterance to the emotions and sentiments of the soul; and metaphors. But it would do the lecturer great injustice to attempt anything like a sketch of his ideas. Suffice it to say, the lecture was one of the richest and most beautiful compositions, both for its matter and style, we have ever heard anywhere, at any time.

—Walter Whitman, *New York Aurora* (March 7, 1842)

Maria Mitchell "Journal" (1855)

American astronomer Maria Mitchell, professor of astronomy at Vassar College, was a revolutionary in terms of the scientific and social positions afforded women in the nineteenth century. She knew many of the literary personages in New England (she traveled in Europe with Nathaniel Hawthorne and his family), and heard Emerson lecture in November 1855, details of which she recounts below.

Mitchell notes Emerson's characteristics as a speaker, communicating through obscure quotations and unique expressions, which is a quality of Emerson's essays as well. Students interested in Emerson as lecturer should note Mitchell's description. The significance of this entry is Mitchell's detailing of the Emerson persona; Mitchell states that "every heart in the house admitted to the truth of his words." The key word here is *heart*. Emerson, like his predecessor and model William Ellery Channing, was a captivating speaker able to capture an audience and convey his ideas to them through his manner and expressiveness.

Last night I heard Emerson give a lecture. I pity the reporter who attempts to give it to the world. I began to listen with a determination to remember it in order, but it was without method, or order, or system. It was like a beam of light moving in the undulatory waves, meeting with occasional meteors in its path; it was exceedingly captivating. It surprised me that there was not only no commonplace thought, but there was no commonplace expression. If he quoted, he quoted from what we had not read; if he told an anecdote, it was one that had not reached us. At the outset he was very severe upon the science of the age. He said that inventors and discoverers helped themselves very much, but they did not help the rest of the world; that a great man was felt to the centre of the Copernican system; that a botanist dried his plants, but the plants had their revenge and dried the botanist; that a naturalist bottled up reptiles, but in return the man was bottled up.

There was a pitiful truth in all this, but there are glorious exceptions. Professor Peirce is anything but a formula, though he deals in formulae.

The lecture turned at length upon beauty, and it was evident that personal beauty had made Emerson its slave many a time, and I suppose every heart in the house admitted the truth of his words.

It was evident that Mr. Emerson was not at ease, for he declared that good manners were more than beauty of face, and good expression better than good features. He mentioned that Sir Philip Sydney was not handsome, though the boast of English society; and he spoke of the astonishing beauty of the Duchess of Hamilton, to see whom hundreds collected when she took a ride. I think in these cases there is something besides beauty; there was rank in that of the Duchess, in the case of Sydney there was no need of beauty at all.

—Maria Mitchell, *Journal* (November 14, 1855),
Life, Letters, and Journals of Maria Mitchell, ed.
Phebe Mitchell Kendall, 1896, pp. 45–47

Franklin Benjamin Sanborn (1864)

Journalist, reformer, and teacher Franklin Benjamin Sanborn recorded the events and personages that collectively made up the transcendental movement, as well as writing biographies of Emerson, Henry David Thoreau, and Bronson Alcott. Sanborn's rather personalized view of history, however, leaves his reputation and legacy in doubt. In the following excerpt, though, he offers an accurate report on an 1864 lecture on "American Life" delivered by Emerson in Boston.

Sanborn offers an interesting description of the lecture environment and circuit of the nineteenth century, which Emerson helped popularize. Sanborn's description is at once lightly comic and informative. His portrait of Emerson contrasts his characterization of the scene by virtue of Emerson's rare qualities as a speaker, able to make "the most ideal themes familiar and admired." Students drawn to this aspect of Emerson's career should note Sanborn's description of the audience and of Emerson as an accurate portrait of the Athenaeum lecture circuit.

Students should also note Sanborn's claim that Emerson has "directed his attention to Life rather than to Art." This seems to echo a distinction made by other critics and observers between Emerson the speaker and Emerson the essayist (note Herman Melville's entry in this volume). Emerson knows the temper of his audience, and while he "has few of the graces of an orator," he seems to engender an enthusiastic response from many of his critics as recorded here by Sanborn.

The course of lectures on "American Life" which Mr. Emerson is now reading in this city deserves a notice more adequate than we have yet given. We have become so acclimated and inured to lectures and courses of lectures, here in Boston, that we are in some danger of losing our interest in everything called by that name. Do we read the report of a lecture in the *Advertiser* with any more zest than wait upon the daily doings of the "State Valuation Committee," or the unctuous chronicle of "Whalers" on the fourth page?

This indifference ought to be dispelled by the announcement of a new lecture by Mr. Emerson, and so it always is in the minds of the earnest and the thoughtful. On the evening announced, the benches are filled by an audience which in itself is a pleasure and a study. There sit the gray-haired couple, who have listened to every one of his lectures since the music of the young scholar's voice first enchanted them thirty years ago. There, too, are their children and their grandchildren, . . . who can scarcely remember when they first heard what is yet constantly new to them, and nevertheless recalls to mind some gracious memory of earlier lessons from the same lips. There is the saintly woman, the adored beauty, the polished gentleman, and beside them the brown-faced farmer, the rustic maiden, and the shy stripling from the Maine woods, to whom a single evening at one of these lectures is the event of the year, perhaps impossible to be repeated. There are always just so many students from Cambridge, and so many fair-faced girls from Boston parlors. And scattered among the audience are always a few strangers, a foreigner or two, a great many clergymen, and reformers.

Of this audience, so various, yet so select and so appreciative, about one-third disappears every two years, . . . and their places are filled by new hearers. And so, while they meet like old friends from one course of lectures to another, there is constantly a band of novices, in whom the elders of the company see with joy their own emotions of years ago reproduced and perpetuated. So much that is exalted in character and ardent in aspiration,— so much serene gravity and so much rosy enthusiasm,—assembles nowhere else and on no other occasion in Boston.

If this were a tribute to the lecturer, . . . it could not be better deserved. This grave and melodious voice, which has now been heard in Boston for more than a generation . . . never uttered an ignoble word, or failed to appeal to high sentiments. It has advocated opinions which were for the moment unpopular, and others about which men will always contend, but all who listened to it were forced to recognize the lofty key which it struck, and to which the moral sentiment in the hearer was sure to respond. Amid a people slow to appreciate what is purely ideal, Mr. Emerson has made the most ideal themes familiar and admired. He, better than any American, verifies his own definition of the Scholar, who "is to resist the vulgar prosperity that retrogrades ever to barbarism, by preserving and communicating heroic sentiments, noble biographies, melodious verse, and the conclusions of history." . . .

The charm and the power of Mr. Emerson's lectures is not merely that they "preserve and communicate" the words and thoughts of other men, though for this they are remarkable. His quotations are numerous and apt, and they seem to adorn not only his own subject, but the name of his authority. To be quoted by him is a stamp of renown, and though he will not transmit to memory so many forgotten sayings as Montaigne, they will be sweeter and more enduring. But the secret of his profound influence on the minds of his hearers and the literature of his time, lies in his creative and inspiring genius, combined as it is with a rectitude and simplicity of the moral sense which makes his criticism as decisive as it is searching. "If you are to live near Mr. Emerson," said one of his neighbors, "you might as well be made of glass as any other way." His piercing eye detects every sham and makes disguise useless, whether he is dealing with a person or a form of thought or of society. In many men this would be a dangerous quality; but here it is lodged where it is scarcely susceptible of misuse.

It may seem strange to some of our readers that we speak of the "creative" genius of a man who has produced no great work of the imagination or of the philosophic intellect,—who has founded no system of thought, and organized no institution or association of men. It is true that Mr. Emerson has done none of these things, but none the less is he to be styled original and creative. He has directed his attention to Life rather than to Art, and has presented to his own age with irresistible force and persuasion the problems which it must meet, and the method to be pursued. He has thus acted directly upon the hearts of his hearers and readers, not as the artist works, by representation, or as the man of science by observation and deduction; but rather as Love or Conscience dart their suggestions into the soul. We are not conscious how we were convinced or inspired; it seems, rather, as if we had always cherished the sentiment which glows so warm at the kindling breath of the speaker.

Nothing less than this will account for Mr. Emerson's power over his hearers. Except the tones of his voice, (nor are these greatly varied,) he has few of the graces of an orator. He is neither fluent nor passionate, nor excellent in action. It is the quality of what he says, not its volume, or its manner of expression, which fascinates and is remembered. His style is admirable, to be sure, but no more so than that of many men of far inferior powers. The purity of his English, the salt of his wit, the simple grandeur of his periods, are agreeable accidents of his oratory; but they are only accidents. Its substance is the moral certitude which it expresses, and the immediate flight which it makes to the listener's spirit, like an unseen arrow cleaving the white of the target.

It should be the pride of Boston that she gave this wise poet a birthplace, and for so many years a hearing. She has not always known how to receive what he delivered, and has pouted, or chattered, or shuddered, at some of his winged words. . . .

But now the city is happily more in accord with the words of the speaker. The *Advertiser* and the *Post* vie in their reports of his lectures, and the voice of censure seems to be hushed at last. We are almost sorry to find it so, for as Socrates called himself the gadfly of the Athenians, so has Mr. Emerson performed the same office for his native town. With all the virtues of Boston, she cherishes such vices and prejudices as call for the stern reprehension of the philosopher whose theme is American life. Without bitterness and without complaisance he will surely speak of these things, and we shall not believe the city hears him if she does not give some sign of dissent.

We have heard it intimated that these may be the last lectures which Mr. Emerson will read in Boston. He has long cherished the hope of withdrawing from the active duties of an American scholar, and exchanging the platform for the study. It will he hard to excuse him from the burden of public speaking, which, like the Athenian *liturgy*, is imposed on every man according to his ability. Few have done their part so well as Mr. Emerson.

—Franklin Benjamin Sanborn,
Boston Commonwealth (December 10, 1864), p. 2

Oliver Wendell Holmes (1884)

Dr. Holmes's famous statement—that Emerson's address is "our Intellectual Declaration of Independence"—is notable for the strength of the comparison with America's founding document. Just as the original Declaration of Independence created a demarcation from European influence, Emerson's address also calls for a separation from the dominance of European intellectual and spiritual thinking. Emerson recognizes that the United States requires its own national literature in order to fulfill its democratic destiny intellectually, politically, and spiritually.

In the "American Scholar" address, Emerson writes, "Perhaps the time has already come . . . when the sluggard intellect of this continent will look from under its iron lids and fill the postponed expectation of the world with something better than the exertions of mechanical skill. Our day of independence, our long apprenticeship to the learning of other lands, draws to a close. . . ."

Certainly, as biographer Robert Richardson notes, Emerson was in a rebellious mood, but fifty years later, the address stands as one of America's founding intellectual statements. Holmes's comments, written in 1884 (two years after Emerson's death), reflect the power and radical nature of Emerson's original assertion. Students reading the "American Scholar" address should keep this passage in mind, as it supports the idea that American literature has its origins, in a sense, in this groundbreaking address. Students exploring the more radical nature of Emerson's thinking might look to this address, and to Holmes's commentary, as support for the claim that Emerson is not entirely the genial, sentimental figure recalled in personal remembrances, but also added a sharp, uncompromising tone to his more radical ideas, such as those expressed in the "American Scholar."

———

"We will walk on our own feet; we will work with on own hands; we will speak our own minds. . . . A nation of men will for the first time exist, because each believes himself inspired by the Divine Soul which also inspires all men."

This grand oration was our intellectual Declaration of Independence. Nothing like it had been heard in the halls of Harvard since Samuel Adams supported the affirmative of the question, "Whether it be lawful to resist the chief magistrate, if the commonwealth cannot otherwise be preserved." It was easy to find fault with an expression here and there. The dignity, not to say the formality, of an Academic assembly was startled by the realism that looked for the infinite in "the meal in the firkin, the milk in the pan." They could understand the deep thoughts suggested by "the meanest flower that blows," but these domestic illustrations had a kind of nursery homeliness about them which the grave professors and sedate clergymen were unused to expect on so stately an occasion. But the young men went out from it as if a prophet had been proclaiming to them "Thus saith the Lord." No listener ever forgot that address, and among all the noble utterances of the speaker it may be questioned if one ever contained more truth in language more like that of immediate inspiration.

—Oliver Wendell Holmes,
Ralph Waldo Emerson, 1884, p. 88

PROSE: NATURE

Elizabeth Palmer Peabody
"Nature—A Prose Poem" (1838)

Elizabeth Palmer Peabody's review of Emerson's "Nature" begins by offering a brief summary of the book's purpose. With that accomplished, she provides the most useful information for the student: elucidating the role of the literary critic. The term *critic* is used so casually, and so often, that it runs the risk of losing its sense of specific purpose. Peabody suggests that "criticism, in its worthiest meaning, is not, as is too often supposed, fault-finding, but interpretation of the oracles of genius. Critics are the priests of literature." This last statement has fallen into disrepute, but her earlier contention—the distinction between interpretation and cynicism—is still the basis of literary criticism. It is in this manner that Peabody proceeds, and this is part of the great significance of her essay. Students should note the process involved in her evaluation of "Nature" as a demonstration of the office of the critic.

Peabody goes on to consider the sections of Emerson's book, and offers an interface for the reader wrestling with the text. Peabody seems to agree that the lack of a "system" reveals the need for interpretation: "As to his own solution, some say he is unintelligible, talks darkly. They do not seem to have observed that he says nothing in the way of solution, so that nothing can be darkly said." This is a problem often encountered by students reading Emerson. Rather than look for the clear statement of a problem and the resulting formulation of a solution, readers are encouraged to take Emerson at his own purpose: "if he does not give his own solution to the enigma, he does what is next best, he tells us the condition of solving it ourselves."

Peabody's explication of the sections of "Nature" are an excellent guide for students reading or writing about the book; she is particularly helpful with the section on (and the concept of) idealism. Students interested in the book can benefit not only from her commentary, but also from noting the manner of her interpretation.

Perhaps the most intriguing aspect of her evaluation, though, is her claim early on that "We have said that 'Nature' is a poem; but it is written in prose." Also, "we would call those together who have feared that the spirit of poetry was dead, to rejoice that such a poem as 'Nature' is written." Peabody refers to the sections of the book as cantos, and considers the book a prose poem. This, too, is a term too often used without specificity (the reader will come across it in other essays in this volume), but Peabody effectively demonstrates what she means by this usage, through her interpretation of specific passages. Certainly Emerson's prose style is "poetic" in terms of image and metaphor, but Peabody casts the entire work as a poem. Students writing on the structure of the book, or on Emerson's prose style, will benefit from Peabody's determination, and defense, of the work as poetry.

—⁓⁓— —⁓⁓— —⁓⁓—

Minds of the highest order of genius draw their thoughts most immediately from the Supreme Mind, which is the fountain of all finite natures. And hence they clothe the truths they see and feel, in those forms of nature which are generally intelligible to all ages of the world. With this poetic instinct, they have a natural tendency to withdraw from the conventions of their own day; and strive to forget, as much as possible, the arbitrary associations created by temporary institutions and local peculiarities. Since the higher laws of suggestion operate in proportion as the lower laws are made subordinate, suggestions of thought by mere proximity of time and place must be subtracted from the habits of the mind that would cultivate the principle of analogy; and this principle of suggestion, in its turn, must be made to give place to the higher law of cause and effect; and at times even this must be set aside, and Reason, from the top of the being, look into the higher nature of original truth, by Intuition,—no unreal function of our nature:

> Nor less I deem that there are powers,
>   Which, of themselves, our minds impress;
> That we can feed these minds of ours,
>   In a wise passiveness.

But if it is precisely because the most creative minds take the symbols of their thoughts and feelings from the venerable imagery of external nature, or from that condition of society which is most transparent in its simplicity, that, when they utter themselves, they speak to all ages, it is also no less true, that this is the reason why the greatest men, those of the highest order of intellect, often do not appear very great to their contemporaries. Their most precious sayings are naked, if not invisible, to the eyes of the conventional, precisely because they are free of the thousand circumstances and fashions which interest the acting and unthinking many. The greatest minds take no cognizance of the local interests, the party spirit, and the pet subjects of the literary coteries of particular times and places. Their phraseology is pure from the ornament which is the passing fashion of the day. As, however, they do not think and speak for their own order only, as they desire to address and receive a response from the great majority of minds—even from those that doubt their own power of going into the holy of holies of thought for themselves—there is needed the office of an intermediate class of minds, which are the natural critics of the human race. For criticism, in its worthiest meaning, is not, as is too often supposed, fault-finding, but interpretation of the oracles of genius. Critics are the priests of literature. How often, like other priests, they abuse their place and privilege, is but too obvious. They receive into their ranks the self-interested, the partisan, the lover of power, besides the stupid and frivolous; and thus the periodical literature of the day is in the rear, rather than in advance of the public mind.

After this preamble, which we trust has suitably impressed the minds of our readers with the dignity of the critical office, we would call all those together who have feared that the spirit of poetry was dead, to rejoice that such a poem as "Nature" is written. It grows upon us as we reperuse it. It proves to us, that the only true and perfect mind is the poetic. Other minds are not to be despised, indeed; they are germs of humanity; but the poet alone is the man—meaning by the poet, not the versifier, nor the painter of outward nature merely, but the total soul, grasping truth, and expressing it melodiously, equally to the eye and heart.

The want of apprehension with which this poem has been received, speaks ill for the taste of our literary priesthood. Its title seems to have suggested to many persons the notion of some elementary treatise on physics, as physics; and when it has been found that it treats of the metaphysics of nature—in other words, of the highest designs of God, in forming nature and man in relations with each other—it seems to have been laid down with a kind of disgust, as if it were a cheat; and some reviewers have spoken of it with a stupidity that is disgraceful alike to their sense, taste, and feeling.

It has, however, found its readers and lovers, and those not a few; the highest intellectual culture and the simplest instinctive innocence have alike received it, and felt it to be a divine Thought, borne on a stream of English undefiled, such as we had almost despaired could flow in this our world of grist and saw mills, whose utilitarian din has all but drowned the melodies of nature. The time will come, when it will be more universally seen to be a gem of purest ray serene, and be dived after, into the dark unfathomed caves of that ocean of frivolity, which the literary productions of the present age spread out to the eyes of despair.

We have said that "Nature" is a poem; but it is written in prose. The author, though wanting the accomplishment of verse, is a devoted child of the great Mother; and comes forward bravely in the midst of the dust of business and the din of machinery; and naming her venerable name, believes that there is a reverence for it left, in the bottom of every heart, of power to check the innumerable wheels for a short Sabbath, that all may listen to her praises.

In his introduction, he expresses his purpose. He tells us, that we concede too much to the sceptic, when we allow every thing venerable in religion to belong to history. He tells us that were there no past, yet nature would tell us great truths; and, rightly read, would prove the prophecies of revelation to be "a very present God"; and also, that the past itself, involving its prophets, divine lawgivers, and the human life of Him of Nazareth, is comparatively a dead letter to us, if we do not freshen these traditions in our souls, by opening our ears to the living nature which forevermore prepares for, and reechoes, their sublime teachings.

> "The foregoing generations," he says, "beheld God face to face: we, through their eyes. Why should not *we* also enjoy an original relation to the Universe?"

Why should we not indeed? for we not only have the Universe, which the foregoing generations had, but *themselves* also. Why are we less wise than they? Why has our wisdom less of the certainty of intuition than theirs? Is it because we have more channels of truth? It may be so. The garden of Eden, before the fall of man, and when God walked in its midst, was found to be a less effective school of virtue, than the workshop of a carpenter, in a miserable town of Judea, of which an Israelite without guile could ask, "*Can* any good come out of Nazareth?" And is not this, by the way, a grave warning to the happily circumstanced of all time to tremble—lest they grow morally passive, just in proportion to their means of an effective activity? With the religion of history must always be combined the religion of experience, in order to a true apprehension of God. The poet of "Nature" is a preacher of the latter. Let us hear him gladly, for such are rare.

The first Canto of this song respects the outward form of Nature. He sketches it in bold strokes. The stars of Heaven above—the landscape below— the breathing atmosphere around—and the living forms and sounds—are brought up to us, by the loving spirit of the singer; who recognizes in this drapery of the world without, the same Disposer that arranged the elements of his own conscious soul. Thus, in his first recognition of Nature's superficies, he brings us to Theism. There is a God. Our Father is the author of Nature. The brotherly nod of companionship assures us of it.

But wherefore is Nature? The next Canto of our Poem answers this question in the most obvious relation. It is an answer that all men apprehend. Nature's superficies is for the well-being of man's body, and the advantage of his material interests. This part of the book requires no interpretation from the critic. Men are active enough concerning commodity, to understand whatever is addressed to them on this head. At least there is no exception but in the case of the savage of the tropics. *His* mind has not explored his wants even to the extent of his body. He does not comprehend the necessities of the narrowest civilization. But whoever reads Reviews, whoever can understand our diluted English, can understand still better this concentrated and severely correct expression of what every child of civilization experiences every day. There is but one sentence here, that the veriest materialist can mistake. He may not measure all that the poet means when he says, man is thus conveniently waited upon in order "that he may work." He may possibly think that "work" relates to the physical operations of manufacture or agriculture. But what is really meant is no less than this; man is fed that he may work with his mind; add to the treasures of thought; elaborate the substantial life of the spiritual world. This is a beautiful doctrine, and worthy to be sung to the harp, with a song of thanksgiving. Undoubtedly Nature, by working for man with all her elements, is adequate to supply him with so much "commodity" that the time may be anticipated when all men will have leisure to be artists, poets, philosophers,—in short, to live through life in the exercise of their proper humanity. God speed to the machinery and application of science to the arts which is to bring this about!

The third Song is of Nature's Beauty, and we only wonder why it was not sung first; for surely the singer found out that Nature was beautiful, before he discovered that it was convenient. Some children, we know, have asked what was the use of flowers, and, like little monkeys, endeavouring to imitate the grown-up, the bearings of whose movements they could not appreciate, have planted their gardens with potatoes and beans, instead of sweet-briar and cupid's delights. But the poet never made this mistake. In the fullness of his first love for his "beautiful mother," and his "gentle nest," he did not even find out those wants, which the commodity of Nature supplies.

> "Give me health and a day," he says, "and I will make the pomp of emperors ridiculous. The dawn is my Assyria; the sunset and moonrise my Paphos and unimaginable realms of faerie; broad

noon shall be my England of the senses and understanding; the night shall be my Germany of mystic philosophy and dreams."

If this subjection of all nature to himself does not prove intimate acquaintance, the following severe truth of fact must do so:

> "The shows of day, the dewy morning, the rainbow, mountains, orchards in blossom, stars, moonlight shadows in the still water, and the like, if too eagerly hunted, become shows merely, and mock us with their unreality. Go out of the house to see the moon and ['tis] mere tinsel," &c.

The second passage on Beauty, is one of those which recalls the critic to the office of interpreter, for it is one which the world has called mystical. To say the same thing in worse English, the oracle here tells us, that if we look on Nature with pleasurable emotions only, and without, at the same time, exerting our moral powers, the mind grows effeminate, and thus becomes incapable of perceiving the highest beauty of whose original type the external forms are but the varied reflections or shadows. When man's moral power is in action, the mind spontaneously traces relations between itself and surrounding things, and there forms with Nature one whole, combining the moral delight which human excellence inspires, with that suggested by Nature's forms.

The next passage rises a step higher in the praise of Beauty. It recognizes the cherishing influence of Nature's forms upon the faculties. Nature not only calls out taste, not only glorifies virtue, and is in its turn by virtue glorified, but it awakens the creative impulse—God's image in man. Hence Art, or Nature in miniature. And the works of Art lead back to Nature again. Thus Beauty circulates, and becomes an aspect of Eternity.

The next chapter, showing that Language is founded on material Nature, is quite didactic. But even here one critic [*Christian Examiner*] quotes a sentence, of which he says, he cannot understand "what it means."

> This relation between the mind and matter is not fancied by some poet, but stands in the will of God, and so is free to be known by all men. It appears to men, or it does not appear.

Where lies the obscurity? We have heard some men say that they did not believe that the forms of Nature bore any relation to the being of God, which his children could appreciate; but even these men could not understand the simple proposition of the opposite theory. Men may think that all nations, whose language has yet been discovered, have called youth *the morning of life*, by accident; but it is inconceivable that they should not understand the simple words in which other men say that there is *no accident in the world*, but all things relate to the spirit of God to which man also has relation and access. Perhaps, however, it is the second sentence which in unintelligible, "it appears to men, or it does not appear." In other words, *to people with open eyes there are colors; to people with shut eyes, at least, to those born blind, there are no colors.*

But having come to this fact, viz: "that the relation between mind and matter stands in the will of God," our poet grows silent with wonder and worship. The nature of this relation he acknowledges to be the yet unsolved problem. He names some of the principal men who have attempted a solution. Many readers of his book would have been glad, had he paused to tell us, in his brief comprehensive way, what was the solution of Pythagoras, and Plato, Bacon, Leibnitz, and Swedenborg, with remarks of his own upon each.

As to his own solution, some say he is unintelligible, talks darkly. They do not seem to have observed that he says nothing in the way of solution, so that nothing can be darkly said. This is what has disappointed the best lovers of his book. But if he does not give his own solution of the enigma, he does what is next best, he tells us the condition of solving it ourselves.

> A life in harmony with nature, the love of truth and of virtue, will purge the eyes to understand her text. By degrees we may come to know the primitive sense of the permanent objects of Nature, so that the world shall be to us an open book, and every form significant of the hidden life and final cause.

The chapter on Discipline is still more didactic than the one on Language. The first portion treats of the formation of the Understanding by the ministry of Nature to the senses, and faculty of deduction. The second section is in a higher strain. It treats of the development of the Reason and Conscience, by means of that relation between matter and mind, which "appears" so clearly to some men, and to all in a degree. It is a pity to give an extract from what is so fine in the whole, but a single sentence must give the hint to the character of this section:

> "The moral influence of Nature upon every individual, is the element of truth which it illustrates to him. Who can estimate this? Who can guess how much firmness the sea-beaten rock has taught the fisherman? How much tranquillity has been reflected to man

from the azure sky, over whose unspotted deep the winds forever
more drive flocks of stormy clouds, and leave no wrinkle nor stain?
flow much industry and providence and affection we have caught
from the pantomime of brutes? What a searching preacher of self-
command is the varying phenomenon of health?"

In the last part of this chapter on Discipline, the author makes a bold sally
at the cause of the analogy between the external world and the moral nature.
He implies that causes (the spiritual seeds of external things) are identical
with the principles that constitute our being; and that *virtues* (the creations
of our own heaven-aided wills) correspond to God's creations in matter; the
former being the natural growth in the moral world, the latter the natural
growth in the material world; or to vary the expression once more, Goodness
being the projection inward—Beauty the projection outward of the same all-
pervading Spirit.

Our author here leaves the didactic, and "the solemn harps harmonious
sound" comes full upon the ear and the heart from the next Canto of his
poem—Idealism. No part of the book has been so mistaken as this. Some
readers affect to doubt his Practical Reason, because he acknowledges, that
we have no evidence of there being essential outlying beings, to that which
we certainly see, by consciousness, by looking inward, *except 'a constant
faith' which God gives us of this truth*. But why should 'the noble doubt',
which marks the limit of the understanding, be so alarming, when it is found
to be but an introduction of the mind to the *superior certainty* residing in
that 'constant faith?' Do we not advance in truth, when we learn to change
the childish feeling by which we ascribe reality to the 'shows of things', for
a feeling involving a sense of GOD, as the only real—immutable—the All
in All?

The theory of Idealism has doubtless been carried to absurdity by
individuals who but half understood it; and has still more often been
represented in a way which was not only useless but injurious to minds
entirely dependent on what others say: for, to borrow two good compounds
from Coleridge, the *half-Ideas* of many would-be Idealist writers, have
passed, perforce, into the *no-Ideas* of many would-be Idealist readers. But
Mr. Emerson has sufficiently guarded his Idealism by rigorous and careful
expression, to leave little excuse for cavilling at his words or thoughts, except,
indeed, by professed materialists and atheists, to whom he gives no ground.

"The frivolous make themselves merry," he says, "with the Ideal
theory, as if its consequences were burlesque; as if it affected the

stability of nature. It surely does not. God never jests with us, and will not compromise the end of Nature, by permitting any inconsequence in its procession. Any distrust of the permanence of laws, would paralyse the faculties of man. Their permanence is sacredly respected, and his faith therein is perfect. The wheels and springs of man are all set to the hypothesis of the permanence of Nature. We are not built like a ship to be tossed, but like a house to stand."

He proceeds to give the progressive appearances of Nature, as the mind advances, through the ministry of the senses, to "the best and the happiest moments of life, those delicious awakenings of the higher powers,—the withdrawing of Nature before its God." The means by which Nature herself, Poetic genius, Philosophy, both natural and intellectual—and, above all, Religion and Ethics, work, to idealize our thought and being, are then minutely pointed out. No careful thinker can dispute a step of the process. We are tempted to quote all these pages and defy the materialist to answer them. But for those sober Christians, who ignorantly and inconsistently fear Idealism, one paragraph will answer the purpose:

> "The first and last lesson in religion is, *the things that are seen are temporal, the things that are unseen are eternal.* It puts an affront upon Nature. It does that for the unschooled, which philosophy does for Berkel[e]y and Viasa. The uniform language that may be heard in the churches of the most ignorant sects is, *contemn the unsubstantial shows of the world; they are vanities, dreams, shadows, unrealities; seek the realities of religion.* The devotee flouts Nature. *
> * * * * * They might all better say of matter, what Michael Angelo said of external beauty, *it is the frail and weary weed in which God dresses the soul, which he has called into time."*

Many philosophers have stopped at Idealism. But, as Mr. Emerson says, this hypothesis, if it only deny, or question the existence of matter "does not satisfy the demands of the Spirit. It leaves God out of me. It leaves me in the splendid labyrinth of my perceptions, to wander without end. Then the heart resists it, because it baulks the affections, in denying substantive being to men and women."

Mr. Emerson then proceeds to his chapter on Spirit, by which he means to suggest to us the substantial essence of which Idealism is the intellectual form. But this chapter is not full enough, for the purposes of instruction. One passage is indeed of great significance:

"But when, following the invisible steps of thought, we come to inquire, Whence is matter? and whereto?—many truths arise out of the depths of consciousness. We learn that the highest is present to the soul of man; that the great universal essence which is not wisdom, or love, or beauty, or power, but all in one and each entirely, is that for which all things exist, and that by which what they are; *that spirit creates*; that behind Nature, throughout Nature, *Spirit is present*, that Spirit is one and not compound; that Spirit does not act upon us from without, that is, in space of [*sic*] time, but spiritually or through ourselves. Therefore, that Spirit, that is the Supreme Being, does not build up Nature around us, but puts it forth through us, as the life of the tree puts forth new branches and leaves through the pores of the old. As a plant upon the bosom of God, he is nourished by unfailing fountains, and draws at his need inexhaustible power. Who can set bounds to the possibilities of Man? Once inspire the infinite, by being admitted to behold the absolute natures of justice and truth, and we learn that man has access to the entire mind of the Creator in the finite. This view, which admonishes me where the sources of wisdom and power lie, and points to virtue as

'The golden key
Which opes the palace of Eternity,'

carries upon its face, the highest certificate of truth, because it animates me to create my own world through the purification of my soul."

This is not only of refreshing moral *aura*, but it is a passage of the highest imaginative power, (taking the word *imaginative* in that true signification which farthest removes it from *fanciful*,) the mind must become purified indeed which can take this point of view, to look at the great shadow pointing to the sun behind us. Sitting thus at the footstool of God, it may realise that all that we see is created by the light that shines through ourselves. Not until thus purified, can it realise that those through whose being more light flows, see more than we do; and that others, who admit less light, see less. What assistance in human culture would the application of this test give us! How would our classifications of men and women be changed, did the positive pure enjoyment of Nature become the standard of judgment! But who may apply the standard? Not every mawkish raver about the moon, surely, but only a comprehender of Nature. And has there yet been any one in human form, who could be called a comprehender of Nature, save Him who had its secret, and in whose hands it was plastic, even to the raising of the dead?

Mr. Emerson must not accuse us of ingratitude, in that after he had led his readers to this high point of view, they crave more, and accuse him of stopping short, where the world most desires and needs farther guidance. We want him to write another book, in which he will give us the philosophy of his "orphic strains," whose meaning is felt, but can only be understood by glimpses.

He does, indeed, tell us that "the problem of restoring to the world original and eternal beauty," (in other words, of seeing Nature and Life in their wholeness), "is solved by the redemption of the soul." It is not unnecessary for the philosopher thus to bring his disciples round, through the highest flights of speculation, to the primitive faith of the humblest disciple, who sits, in the spirit of a child, at the feet of Jesus. But we should like to hear Mr. Emerson's philosophy of Redemption. It is very plain that it consists of broad and comprehensive views of human culture, worthy to employ the whole mind of one who seeks reproduction of Christ within himself, by such meditations as the following, which must be our last extract:

> "Is not Prayer also a study of truth—a sally of the soul into the unfound infinite? No man ever prayed heartily without learning something. But when a faithful thinker, resolute to detach every object from personal relations, and see it in the light of thought, shall, at the same time, kindle science with the fire of the holiest affections, then will God go forth anew into the creation."

—Elizabeth Palmer Peabody, "Nature—A Prose Poem,"
The United States Magazine and Democratic Review 1
(February 1838), pp. 319–29

PROSE: ESSAYS

Mary Moody Emerson (1844)

In this letter, Mary Emerson effuses over her nephew's *Essays: Second Series* (1844). She seems to have reconciled herself to Waldo's career as a writer (compare this newfound acceptance with the sentiments she expresses in earlier letters included in this volume.) Her enthusiasm is genuine. By the mid-1840s, Waldo had a successful, if not particularly financially rewarding, career as a lecturer, and his influence was widely felt.

Emerson's second book of essays involves more work on aesthetics and speculation on the activity of the Soul ("Experience," "Poetry," "Nature"), in keeping with the style of *Essays: First Series* (1841). Certainly Mary is proud of the book: "We never compliment an Angel on his divinity. So here R W E is one of the holy ones—a Seer Poet divine yet human."

Students interested in Emerson's career as an essayist, and in this group of essays in particular, might note this enthusiastic response. Students exploring Emerson's family relations, a rich field for scholars, might use this letter (along with the other letters in this volume) to gauge Mary's attitude toward Waldo. Her opinions about his career and manner were of great concern to him.

⟶•⟶ ⟶•⟶ ⟶•⟶

To Ralph Waldo Emerson

Dec 13 '44 Vale

I have this moment laid down your Essays having but few hours to run thro' them. You can better Judge of the state of mind this excited than I describe. And I somewhat bereft of power to judge and having nothing else to say, save the errand for w'h I write, will copy a line or so of the admiration of our Mountain Rustics notes w'h crowd the margin. "Experience." "What grit what bravery, what piercing eyes. How Jove like, grand & powerfull—He looks & smiles & shines surpassing Jupiter—with a strong fresh wind sweeps away our cobweb systems & we sail, swim or fly in the immensity of all." Now a sober conservative may sigh over the youths losses, perhaps. Under the chap "Nature." "Relentless, resistless as fate he takes the "wool from the eyes" that custom system & convention has put on. We hardly thank him, tho' he seems loving, human—a man of destiny tho' dear to gods & men—yet delusions are dearly hugged & like one awoke from sleep by his best friend to see the dawn of a golden day & age & "see men as trees walking not clearly." Under "Poetry." How grand, true, wise & beautifull—&c—exclaims the gratefull heart in it's Jubilant. But the calm of soul w'h follows is better. In your sympathy & surprise you feel that all compliment is surpurflous—who would compliment Shakespear? Who would dream of so doing to Him who is above naming as above every name? We never compliment an Angel on his divinity. So here R W E is one of the holy ones—a Seer Poet divine yet human. Those who have eyes will see & thank God for this and every "good gift". I have selected this venturing to say that if such be the effect of your writing, dearest Waldo, on many youth—there seems danger in their state of mental irreverence.

Tomorrow I give letters to C. Farrar & the ingraving of Marshall Ney to the cane of E.P.P. & that if you send me the essays & any thing immediately to her he will take them to Portland Stage as he returns not here. Did you have a letter from me directing your packet to T.W.H.? The man returned & said T. had left business. w'h I knew not tho' his family did. That you have not written nor lady Lid after my polite visit is not very flattering—So I owe you nothing for your hospitable cares and shall come whenever I like without waiting an invite. How do the Mother wife & children.

Good Eve

Your affectionate Aunt

MME.

I dont know how long C F may be in City. But well enough to send the packet to E P P & a letter of information by mail. I regret losing the only visitor in my young friend—whom I find much improved as a *talker*.

—Mary Moody Emerson,

Letter to Ralph Waldo Emerson (December 13, 1844)

MARGARET FULLER "EMERSON'S ESSAYS" (1844)

Margaret Fuller is a key figure in the study of the transcendentalists, as well as nineteenth-century American culture in general. Fuller taught at Bronson Alcott's Temple School before becoming the first editor of the the *Dial*, the transcendentalist journal, for which she wrote essays and poetry. She eventually became the literary critic for Horace Greeley's *New York Tribune*. Fuller was a close fiend of Emerson's and was one of Emerson's best readers and critics as well as one of Emerson's closest intellectual counterparts.

Fuller, in her commentary on Emerson's *Essays: Second Series*, claims that Emerson's essays are perhaps too given over to the perfect expression. Note the similes Fuller offers. These examples of artists seeking perfection without the leverage of the commonplace serve as adequate criticism of Emerson's prose style. Students examining Emerson's essays (especially "The Poet," from which Fuller quotes) should pay attention to Fuller's intention in this form of criticism.

Fuller does, however, perceive the lasting value of Emerson's work. He is held to be more for the "immortal"; that is, his work is more timeless than timely. Fuller's complaint may be that Emerson overlooks practical applications and observations, but she is willing to admit to Emerson's special status as one of "that band of whom there may be found a few in every age . . . who worship one God only, the God of Truth." For Fuller, this one god supercedes any religious orthodoxy. The phrase "God of Truth" presupposes a truth that can be known, or at least inferred. Emerson's essays, through that very quality of expression and immortality she discusses, suggest this kind of truth, which, for Emerson, comes in the form of aesthetics, beauty, the expression of the individual will, that which George Santayana refers to as "moral energy."

The essays have . . . been obnoxious to many charges. To that of obscurity, or want of perfect articulation. Of "Euphuism," as an excess of fancy in proportion to imagination, and an inclination at times to subtlety at the expense of strength, has been styled. The human heart complains of inadequacy, either in the nature or experience of the writer, to represent its full vocation and its deeper needs. Sometimes it speaks of this want as "underdevelopment" or a want of expansion which may yet be remedied; sometimes doubts whether "in this mansion there be either hall or portal to receive the loftier of the passions." Sometimes the soul is deified at the expense of nature, then again nature at that of man, and we are not quite sure that we can make a true harmony by balance of the statements. This writer has never written one good work, if such a work be one where the whole commands more attention than the parts, if such an one be produced only where, after an accumulation of materials, fire enough be applied to fuse the whole into one new substance. This second series is superior in this respect to the former, yet in no one essay is the main stress so obvious as to produce on the mind the harmonious effect of a noble river or tree in full leaf. Single passages and sentences engage our attention too much in proportion. These essays, it has been justly said, tire like a string of mosaics or a house built of medals. We miss what we expect in the work of the great poet or the great philosopher, the liberal air of all the zones: the glow, uniform yet various in tint, which is given to a body by free circulation of the heart's blood from the hour of birth. Here is undoubtedly the man of ideas, but we want the ideal man also; want the heart and genius of human life to interpret it, and here our satisfaction is not so perfect. We doubt this friend raised himself too early to the perpendicular and did not lie along the ground long enough to hear the secret whispers of our parent life. We could wish he might be thrown by conflicts on the lap of mother earth, to see if he would not rise again with added powers.

All this we may say, but it cannot excuse us from benefiting by the great gifts that have been given and assigning them their due place.

Some painters paint on a red ground. And this color may be supposed to represent the groundwork most immediately congenial to most men, as it is the color of blood and represents human vitality. The figures traced upon it are instinct with life in its fullness and depths.

But other painters paint on a gold ground. And a very different but no less natural, because also a celestial beauty, is given to their works who choose for their foundation the color of the sunbeam, which nature has preferred for her most precious product, and that which will best bear the test of purification, gold.

If another simile may be allowed, another no less apt is at hand. Wine is the most brilliant and intense expression of the powers of earth—it is her potable fire, her answer to the sun. It exhilarates, it inspires, but then it is liable to fever and intoxicate too the careless partaker.

Mead was the chosen drink of the northern gods. And this essence of the honey of the mountain bee was not thought unworthy to revive the souls of the valiant who had left their bodies on the fields of strife below.

Nectar should combine the virtues of the ruby wine, the golden mead, without their defects or dangers.

Two high claims our writer can vindicate on the attention of his contemporaries. One from his *sincerity.* You have his thought just as it found place in the life of his own soul. Thus, however near or relatively distant its approximation to absolute truth, its action on you cannot fail to be healthful. It is a part of the free air.

He belongs to that band of whom there may be found a few in every age, and who now in known human history may be counted by hundreds, who worship the one God only, the God of Truth. They worship not saints nor creeds nor churches nor relics nor idols in any form. The mind is kept open to truth, and life only valued as a tendency toward it. This must be illustrated by acts and words of love, purity, and intelligence. Such are the salt of the earth; let the minutest crystal of that salt be willingly by us held in solution.

The other is through that part of his life which, if sometimes obstructed or chilled by the critical intellect, is yet the prevalent and the main source of his power. It is that by which he imprisons his hearer only to free him again as a "liberating God" (to use his own words). But indeed let us use them altogether, for none other, ancient or modern, can worthily express how, making present to us the courses and destinies of nature, he invests himself with her serenity and animates us with her joy.

"Poetry was all written before time was, and whenever we are so finely organized that we can penetrate into that region where the air is music, we hear those primal warblings and attempt to write them down, but we lose ever and anon a word or a verse, and substitute something of our own, and thus mistreat the poem. The men of more delicate ear write down these cadences more faithfully, and these transcripts, though imperfect, become the songs of the nations.

"As the eyes of Lyncaeus were said to see through the earth, so the poet turns the world to glass, and shows us all things in their right series and procession. For through that better perception he stands one step nearer to things, and sees the flowing or metamorphosis; perceives that thought is multiform; that within the form of every creature is a force impelling it to ascend into a higher form; and following with his eyes the life, uses the forms which express that life, and so the speech flows with the flowing of nature."

Thus have we in a brief and unworthy manner indicated some views of these books. The only true criticism of these or any good books may be gained by making them the companions of our lives. Does every accession of knowledge or a juster sense of beauty make us prize them more? Then they are good indeed, and more immortal than mortal. Let that test be applied to these; essays which will lead to great and complete poems—somewhere.

—Margaret Fuller, "Emerson's Essays,"
New York Daily Tribune, December 7, 1844

CHARLOTTE BRONTË (1849)

Emerson's *Essays* I read with much interest, and often with admiration, but they are of mixed gold and clay—deep and invigorating truth, dreary and depressing fallacy seem to me combined therein.

—Charlotte Brontë, Letter to W.S. Williams (February 4, 1849)

PROSE: REPRESENTATIVE MEN

EDWARD FITZGERALD (1850)

I have also bought Emerson's *Representative Men,* a shilling book of Bohn's; with very good scattered thoughts in it: but scarcely leaving any large impression with one, or establishing a theory. So at least it has seemed to me: but I have not read very carefully.

—Edward FitzGerald, Letter to John Allen (March 4, 1850)

CHARLES ELIOT NORTON "EMERSON'S REPRESENTATIVE MEN" (1850)

Scholar and reformer Charles Eliot Norton was a friend to many New England writers, including Emerson and James Russell Lowell, and his letters are a valuable resource for students of nineteenth-century American literature. Norton also served as coeditor of the *North American Review* and was one of the founders of *The Nation*.

A significant point that Norton makes in his commentary and that students should note is that by 1850 (only fourteen years after the publication of "Nature") Emerson was already established among the firmament of American writers. Norton is also correct in surmising that Emerson's prose would outlive his poetry. The poetry is generally recognized as not up to the standards of his prose (though some of Emerson's poems in particular are highly regarded).

Note also Norton's concern over the deification of Emerson, the "conversion of a modern Yankee into a Pagan god." Emerson would no doubt have resisted the treatment himself, since he strove to reject the office of spiritual and intellectual master, insisting on the prominence of the individual will.

Students focusing on Emerson's prose style (and his use of figures and allusions) should note Norton's comparison of Emerson and Carlyle. The two writers are often mentioned in tandem, and while this comparison sheds light on the affinity between the two, Norton also offers a point of reference by which Emerson might be evaluated.

⸻

No American, perhaps we may add no English, reader needs to be told who and what Mr. Emerson is. In poetry and in prose, by spoken discourse and by written books, he has stamped his personality too deeply to be effaced upon the literature and speculations of the age. Some things he has published will live as long as the language itself; but much of his verse, constructed upon whims rather than under the influence of the spirit of poetry, will die out among the short-lived oddities of the day. Much of his prose, too, the production of imitation, unconscious perhaps, of vicious foreign models, can scarcely be expected to survive the charm which hangs about his person and lingers in the magic tones of his voice.

Mr. Emerson is a great writer, and an honest and independent thinker, on the whole. He is not, however, what one of the idolaters has lately called him, a Phoebus Apollo, descended from Olympus with hurtling arrows and the silver twanging bow. He is neither the god of the lyre, nor will his shafts deal death among the host of those who fail to reverence *his priest,* though Emerson, too, Phoebus-like, has often "walked in darkness like the Night." This conversion of a modern Yankee into a Pagan god is a dangerous attempt to apply the *rationalistic* principle to persons and things of the present day. Some disciple of the school of historical skepticism has been trying his hand at turning Mr. Emerson into a *myth.* We object to the proceeding altogether, not knowing where it will end, and whose turn will come next. Homer, Lycurgus, Solon, and other nebulous spots in the sky of antiquity, have already been resolved, and now Mr. Emerson is undergoing the same process. That great *realist,* Mr. Weller, Senior, hit the nail on the head and struck out the true principle for such cases. "Wot I like in that 'ere style of writing," said he, after listening to his son Sam's *walentine,* "is that there 'aint no callin' names in it,—no Wenusses, nor nothin' o' that kind; wot's the good o' callin' a young 'ooman a Wenus or a angel, Sammy?"

The present volume [*Representative Men*] is marked strongly both by the excellences and defects of Mr. Emerson's other writings. His style is often musical, clear, and brilliant; words are selected with so rare a felicity that they have the shine of diamonds, and they cut their meaning on the reader's mind as the diamond's edge leaves its trace deep and sharp on the surface of glass. But by and by, we fall upon a passage which either conveys no distinct sense, or in which some very common-place thought is made to sound with the clangor of a braying trumpet. Quaintness of thought and expression is his easily besetting sin; and here lies the secret of his sympathy with Carlyle, that highly gifted master of oddity and affectation. As a writer, Mr. Emerson is every way Carlyle's superior, would he but let the Carlylese dialect alone. He has more imagination, more refinement and subtlety of thought, more taste in style, more exquisite sense of rhythm. Perhaps his range of intellectual vision is not so broad. He has not the learning of Carlyle, nor the abundant humor, which sometimes reconciles us even to absurdity. But Mr. Emerson has a more delicate wit, a wit often quite irresistible by its unexpected turns, and the sudden introduction of effective contrasts. Carlyle has an extraordinary abundance of words, a store of epithets, good, bad, and indifferent, by which the reader is often flooded; Emerson is more temperate and artistic. And yet we catch him, every now and then, mimicking the Scotchman, as if Carlyle were the master, and Emerson the pupil. He imitates Carlyle's affectation of odd and quaint expressions; he imitates him in the structure of his sentences; he imitates him in borrowing from the Germans a transcendental coloring, and in putting on an air of indifference to all positive opinions, an assumption of even-handed impartiality towards all religious systems. The trick of grotesque illustration by common or vulgar objects, he has caught from the Platonic Socrates. But setting aside these imitations and affectations, there hovers over much of his writing a peculiar and original charm, drawn from no source but the delicate and beautiful mind of the author himself.

—Charles Eliot Norton, "Emerson's *Representative Men*,"
North American Review, April 1850, pp. 520–21

PROSE: GENERAL

WILLIAM P. TRENT (1903)

William Trent, professor of literature at Columbia University, wrote *A History of American Literature, 1607–1865* (1903). In the preface, Trent asserts that "American literature, so far as concerns not merely the outside world but the American people themselves, is a creation of the nineteenth century." Trent's book is not the first history of American literature, but Trent does establish grounds for the separation of history and literature in American writing.

Trent's analysis of Emerson occurs on the two fronts of style and substance. Of Emerson's style, Trent echoes a common refrain, that Emerson inadequately develops, or constructs, organized paragraphs, let alone complete essays. Students of Emerson's prose style should especially note Trent's phrase "pregnant sentence." This is an excellent description of that quality of Emerson's prose that seems so elusive to define. Emerson's style has been described as epigrammatic and poetic; Trent's expression captures the feeling engendered by Emerson's compacted expressions, of which F.O. Matthiesson writes, "[t]he problem that confronts us in dealing with Emerson is the hardest we shall have to meet, because of his inveterate habit of stating things in opposites."

Concerning substance, Trent makes the compelling argument that Emerson has created the condition for his own downfall as a thinker (Walt Whitman makes the same observation). For readers of the essays, this should seem familiar. Would the writer who encourages readers to reject all books and masters not include himself? Trent also claims that Emerson has "leavened the thought of America with his fine idealism," by which he most likely means "American thinking" and not the conceptual nature of the republic. In this second sense, however, the thought of America received a boost from Emerson; that is, Emerson (as Trent acknowledges) encouraged, and in some ways helped define, the democratic sense and identity of America that emerged in the nineteenth century.

—⁓⁓⁓— —⁓⁓⁓— —⁓⁓⁓—

What now shall be said of Emerson's prose? Was Matthew Arnold right when, as an experienced critic calmly judging the favourite author of his youth, he denied that the *Essays,* the lectures, and *English Traits* formed a body of prose of sufficient merit to entitle Emerson to be ranked as a great man of letters? It seems as if the time had come for Emerson's countrymen frankly to accept this verdict. Because of deficiencies both of style and of substance Emerson does not belong to the small class of the great masters of prose. His style, despite the fact that *Nature* and many of the essays contain pages of eloquent prose almost equal in power and beauty to noble poetry, was nearly always that of the lecturer or preacher rather than that of the writer. He too frequently lost the note of distinction and was content if he satisfied his far from exigent audiences. In diction, to be sure, he was a conscious and consummate master, and it need scarcely be said that few writers have surpassed him in the ability to compose a pregnant sentence. But, as is generally admitted and as is shown by his practice of piecing his notes together, he was rarely able to evolve a paragraph, much more a whole essay, in a masterly or even in a workmanlike fashion. It may be granted that critics have overemphasized his lack of coherence, that there is more logical unity in his essays than appears on first reading, that *English Traits* and the later volumes are far from being mere strings of "Orphic Sayings"; but the fact seems to remain that the prose style of Emerson from first to last lacks the firmness, the compass, the precision, the flexibility, the individuality, we demand of the prose writers whom we denominate masters.

In substance also he seems to be less great than he appeared to his contemporaries. This is partly due, paradoxically enough, to his own greatness. He has so leavened the thought of America with his fine idealism, his splendid belief in the capacity and the sacred rights and duties of the individual, his fearless democratic radicalism, that the latter-day reader receives as a matter of course utterances that thrilled the bosoms of youthful Americans two generations ago. The inspired seer is often in danger of seeming to be only a charming, somewhat impractical old gentleman. This attitude is obviously unjust to Emerson, and, to be candid, is probably seldom assumed by any sound-minded, sound-hearted reader of such nobly stimulating essays as those on "Self-Reliance" and "Spiritual Laws," or of the excellent, if less lofty, papers that make up *The Conduct of Life*, or of the homely discourse on "Civilization," in which, almost without warning, we are suddenly given the injunction—"Hitch your wagon to a star." But despite the continued sale of his works, despite popular votes that place him well to the front of American authors, it may fairly be held that not a few modern readers hold somewhat aloof from him both because of their familiarity with his leading ideas and because of his defects of substance. He is a great inciter to plain living and high thinking, but he is no longer an undisputed oracle on such subjects as "History," "Art," and the like, however charmingly and suggestively he may write about them. It is impossible not to perceive the discursiveness and the rashness of generalization displayed in *English Traits*. His defective sense of literary values, his excessive use of the speaker's privilege to plunder all the provinces of human culture, his relentless exploitation of his happy talent for discovering and presenting apt and telling illustrations, his irritating unwillingness to admit a pessimistic argument within the range of his mental vision, his almost fatal bias for stating half-truths only—these limitations of his genius detract sufficiently from the substantial value of his work to make it probable, if not certain, that his place is not with the world's masters of thought. On the other hand, it is equally true to maintain that no one can better gauge books and men when he understands them, that no one can range the fields of scholarship with more grace and divine right, that no one has better comprehended or employed the art of illustration, that no one can face unpleasant facts more bravely than Emerson when he thinks fit, or can more effectively express the scorn or reproach they deserve.

—William P. Trent, A *History of American Literature,*
1607–1865, 1903, pp. 333–36

POETRY

RALPH WALDO EMERSON (1855)

In this well-known letter, Emerson congratulates Whitman on the publication of *Leaves of Grass* in 1855. Emerson's own poetry relies on a formal, measured line and traditional stanza structure, while Whitman seeming to be only a charming, somewhat impractical old gentleman. This attitude is obviously unjust to Emerson, and, to be candid, is probably seldom assumed by any sound-minded, sound-hearted reader of such nobly stimulating essays as those on "Self-Reliance" and "Spiritual Laws," or of the excellent, if less lofty, papers that make up *The Conduct of Life,* or of the homely discourse on "Civilization," in which, almost without warning, we are suddenly given the injunction—"Hitch your wagon to a star." But despite the continued sale of his works, despite popular votes that place him well to the front of American authors, it may fairly be held that not a few modern readers hold somewhat aloof from him both because of their familiarity with his leading ideas and because of his defects of substance. He is a great inciter to plain living and high thinking, but he is no longer an undisputed oracle on such subjects as "History," "Art," and the like, however charmingly and suggestively he may write about them. It is impossible not to perceive the discursiveness and the rashness of generalization displayed in *English Traits.* His defective sense of literary values, his excessive use of the speaker's privilege to plunder all the provinces of human culture, his relentless exploitation of his happy talent for discovering and presenting apt and telling illustrations, his irritating unwillingness to admit a pessimistic argument within the range of his mental vision, his almost fatal bias for stating half-truths only—these limitations of his genius detract sufficiently from the substantial value of his work to make it probable, if not certain, that his place is not with the world's masters of thought. On the other hand, it is equally true to maintain that no one can better gauge books and men when he understands them, that no one can range the fields of scholarship with more grace and divine right, that no one has better comprehended or employed the art of illustration, that no one can face unpleasant facts more bravely than Emerson when he thinks fit, or can more effectively express the scorn or reproach they deserve.

—William P. Trent, A *History of American Literature,*
1607–1865, 1903, pp. 333–36

POETRY

Ralph Waldo Emerson (1855)

In this well-known letter, Emerson congratulates Whitman on the publication of *Leaves of Grass* in 1855. Emerson's own poetry relies on a formal, measured line and traditional stanza structure, while Whitman should seem familiar. Would the writer who encourages readers to reject all books and masters not include himself? Trent also claims that Emerson has "leavened the thought of America with his fine idealism," by which he most likely means "American thinking" and not the conceptual nature of the republic. In this second sense, however, the thought of America received a boost from Emerson; that is, Emerson (as Trent acknowledges) encouraged, and in some ways helped define, the democratic sense and identity of America that emerged in the nineteenth century.

What now shall be said of Emerson's prose? Was Matthew Arnold right when, as an experienced critic calmly judging the favourite author of his youth, he denied that the *Essays,* the lectures, and *English Traits* formed a body of prose of sufficient merit to entitle Emerson to be ranked as a great man of letters? It seems as if the time had come for Emerson's countrymen frankly to accept this verdict. Because of deficiencies both of style and of substance Emerson does not belong to the small class of the great masters of prose. His style, despite the fact that *Nature* and many of the essays contain pages of eloquent prose almost equal in power and beauty to noble poetry, was nearly always that of the lecturer or preacher rather than that of the writer. He too frequently lost the note of distinction and was content if he satisfied his far from exigent audiences. In diction, to be sure, he was a conscious and consummate master, and it need scarcely be said that few writers have surpassed him in the ability to compose a pregnant sentence. But, as is generally admitted and as is shown by his practice of piecing his notes together, he was rarely able to evolve a paragraph, much more a whole essay, in a masterly or even in a workmanlike fashion. It may be granted that critics have overemphasized his lack of coherence, that there is more logical unity in his essays than appears on first reading, that *English Traits* and the later volumes are far from being mere strings of "Orphic Sayings"; but the fact seems to remain that the prose style of Emerson from first to last lacks the firmness, the compass, the precision, the flexibility, the individuality, we demand of the prose writers whom we denominate masters.

In substance also he seems to be less great than he appeared to his contemporaries. This is partly due, paradoxically enough, to his own greatness. He has so leavened the thought of America with his fine idealism, his splendid belief in the capacity and the sacred rights and duties of the individual, his fearless democratic radicalism, that the latter-day reader receives as a matter of course utterances that thrilled the bosoms of youthful Americans two generations ago. The inspired seer is often in danger of experiments with the organic line. However, as this letter suggests, Emerson found value in Whitman's approach. Both recognized the need for a national literature, for America to realize its democratic promise.

However, this letter is interesting for what Emerson *doesn't* say; that is, he admires Whitman's courage, and praises the power of his work, but sidesteps comment on its form. Emerson wrote in "The Poet," "it is not metres, but metre-making argument, that makes a poem." The key for Emerson is meter, as evidenced by his own formal, measured verse. This letter might be interpreted as posing an aesthetic, and moral, question, and is valuable for students concerned with Emerson's poetic theory and practice. Those wishing to demonstrate that Emerson recognized order as a founding principle of poetic expression might refer to this letter.

As an afterword on *Leaves of Grass*, Emerson wrote to Carlyle the next May saying that "[o]ne book, last summer, came out in New York, a nondescript monster which has terrible eyes & buffalo strength, & was indisputably American,—which I thought to send you; but the book ... wanted good morals so much, that I never did." Emerson did end up sending Carlyle the book.

To Walt Whitman, Concord, July 21, 1855
Concord Masstts 21 July 1855

Dear Sir,

I am not blind to the worth of the wonderful gift of "Leaves of Grass." I find it the most extraordinary piece of wit & wisdom that America has yet contributed. I am very happy in reading it, as great power makes us happy. It meets the demand I am always making of what seemed the sterile & stingy Nature, as if too much handiwork or too much lymph in the temperament were making our western wits fat & mean. I give you joy of your free & brave thought. I have great joy in it. I find incomparable things said incomparably well, as they must be. I find the courage of *treatment*, which so delights us, & which large perception only can inspire.

I greet you at the beginning of a great career, which yet must have had a long foreground somewhere, for such a start. I rubbed my eyes a hide to see if this sunbeam were no illusion; but the solid sense of the book is a sober certainty. It has the best merits, namely, of fortifying & encouraging.

I did not know until I, last night, saw the book advertised in a newspaper, that I could trust the name as real & available for a Post-Office. I wish to see my benefactor, & have felt much like striking my tasks, & visiting New York to pay you my respects.

R. W. Emerson.

—Ralph Waldo Emerson, Letter to
Walt Whitman (July 21, 1855)

JAMES RUSSELL LOWELL (1883)

As for Emerson's verse (though he has written some as exquisite as any in the language) I suppose we must give it up. That he had a sense of the higher harmonies of language no one that ever heard him lecture can doubt. The structure of his prose, as one listened to it, was as nobly metrical as the King James version of the Old Testament, and this made it all the more puzzling that he should have been absolutely insensitive to the harmony of verse. For it was there he failed—single verses are musical enough. I never shall forget the good-humoredly puzzled smile with which he once confessed to me his inability to apprehend the value of accent in verse.

—James Russell Lowell,
Letter to James B. Thayer (December 24, 1883)

EDMUND CLARENCE STEDMAN
"RALPH WALDO EMERSON" (1885)

Edmund Stedman was an important figure in the New York literary world, and he wrote expansively on American authors of the nineteenth century. A poet and critic, Stedman was widely read by the time he produced the excerpt included here.

Stedman's essay was written just after Emerson's death, and the early sections read like a biography and a memorial. After providing what he views as the requisite background for Emerson's life and thought, Stedman gets to the business of evaluating Emerson's work as a poet. Stedman, like many of his contemporaries, finds strength in the imagery that characterizes Emerson's work. The value of this essay to students, though, is the detailed, specific critique of selected poems and of Emerson's sources.

Stedman emphasizes, and students should take note, the influence of Plato on Emerson. Stedman rightly begins with Platonic idealism as a source of Emerson's thought, before moving to a lesser-known my benefactor, & have felt much like striking my tasks, & visiting New York to pay you my respects.

R. W. Emerson.

—Ralph Waldo Emerson, Letter to
Walt Whitman (July 21, 1855)

JAMES RUSSELL LOWELL (1883)

As for Emerson's verse (though he has written some as exquisite as any in the language) I suppose we must give it up. That he had a sense of the higher harmonies of language no one that ever heard him lecture can doubt. The structure of his prose, as one listened to it, was as nobly metrical as the King James version of the Old Testament, and this made it all the more puzzling that he should have been absolutely insensitive to the harmony of verse. For it was there he failed—single verses are musical enough. I never shall forget the good-humoredly puzzled smile with which he once confessed to me his inability to apprehend the value of accent in verse.

—James Russell Lowell,
Letter to James B. Thayer (December 24, 1883)

EDMUND CLARENCE STEDMAN
"RALPH WALDO EMERSON" (1885)

Edmund Stedman was an important figure in the New York literary world, and he wrote expansively on American authors of the nineteenth century. A poet and critic, Stedman was widely read by the time he produced the excerpt included here.

Stedman's essay was written just after Emerson's death, and the early sections read like a biography and a memorial. After providing what he views as the requisite background for Emerson's life and thought, Stedman gets to the business of evaluating Emerson's work as a poet. Stedman, like many of his contemporaries, finds strength in the imagery that characterizes Emerson's work. The value of this essay to students, though, is the detailed, specific critique of selected poems and of Emerson's sources.

Stedman emphasizes, and students should take note, the influence of Plato on Emerson. Stedman rightly begins with Platonic idealism as a source of Emerson's thought, before moving to a lesser-known experiments with the organic line. However, as this letter suggests, Emerson found value in Whitman's approach. Both recognized the need for a national literature, for America to realize its democratic promise.

However, this letter is interesting for what Emerson *doesn't* say; that is, he admires Whitman's courage, and praises the power of his work, but sidesteps comment on its form. Emerson wrote in "The Poet," "it is not metres, but metre-making argument, that makes a poem." The key for Emerson is meter, as evidenced by his own formal, measured verse. This letter might be interpreted as posing an aesthetic, and moral, question, and is valuable for students concerned with Emerson's poetic theory and practice. Those wishing to demonstrate that Emerson recognized order as a founding principle of poetic expression might refer to this letter.

As an afterword on *Leaves of Grass*, Emerson wrote to Carlyle the next May saying that "[o]ne book, last summer, came out in New York, a nondescript monster which has terrible eyes & buffalo strength, & was indisputably American,—which I thought to send you; but the book . . . wanted good morals so much, that I never did." Emerson did end up sending Carlyle the book.

⚡ ⚡ ⚡

To Walt Whitman, Concord, July 21, 1855
Concord Masstts 21 July 1855

Dear Sir,

I am not blind to the worth of the wonderful gift of "Leaves of Grass." I find it the most extraordinary piece of wit & wisdom that America has yet contributed. I am very happy in reading it, as great power makes us happy. It meets the demand I am always making of what seemed the sterile & stingy Nature, as if too much handiwork or too much lymph in the temperament were making our western wits fat & mean. I give you joy of your free & brave thought. I have great joy in it. I find incomparable things said incomparably well, as they must be. I find the courage of *treatment*, which so delights us, & which large perception only can inspire.

I greet you at the beginning of a great career, which yet must have had a long foreground somewhere, for such a start. I rubbed my eyes a hide to see if this sunbeam were no illusion; but the solid sense of the book is a sober certainty. It has the best merits, namely, of fortifying & encouraging.

I did not know until I, last night, saw the book advertised in a newspaper, that I could trust the name as real & available for a Post-Office. I wish to see source, Plotinus. Stedman's discussion of Plotinus is significant because, while Plato is often identified as a touchstone for Emerson's idealism, Plotinus is less frequently mentioned but, according to Stedman, no less important. Stedman offers a compelling argument that a translation of Plotinus (published in 1817 and 1834) was available to Emerson. Students discussing "Nature" should pay particular attention, because Emerson, the expert epigrammatic writer, chose an epigram from Plotinus to preface the first edition, in 1836, of his first major work.

Stedman's essay is most effective in the last three sections, as he launches into detailed criticism of the poetry. Stedman, a strong critic, sets out his claims, defines his terms, and pursues his analysis in a logical, orderly manner. This is especially important for students working through what can be confusing terminology and complicated evaluations of Emerson's poetry. Stedman clarifies the terms by which an effective evaluation may proceed. His commentary, while exact, rarely escalates to language too technical for students to follow.

Unlike much criticism, which tries to associate Emerson's work with a particular theoretical framework or a particular school of thought, Stedman's instead considers the poetry on its own terms, arguing that Emerson did not compose according to a theory. Stedman's commentary on Margaret Fuller's reviews of Emerson leads him into an informative discourse on didacticism. His definition of the term, and its application to Emerson, are among the most valuable aspects of this essay.

Rather than composing from a theory, as Stedman argues, Emerson started first with the inspiration—the natural force or symbol—and worked outward to create the appropriate vehicle for his vision. Emerson does not seem to have started with formal concerns from which he then proceeded to establishing the content. While this may account for what many critics determine to be a weakness of his poetry, Stedman argues that this is the essential nature of his poetry, an indispensable quality inseparable from the poem itself. The vision, the inspiration *is* the complete poem. As Stedman claims, "the thought of Style . . . should enter into the mind of neither writer nor reader. Style makes itself, and Emerson's is the apothegmatic style of one bent upon uttering his immediate thoughts,—hence, strong in sentences, and only by chance suited to the formation of an essay." Thus, "Emerson's whole argument is poetic." Stedman's explanation of this quality should be of special interest to students writing on the imagistic and metaphorical, in other words, poetic qualities of Emerson's unique writing style.

I

The grasses had scarcely taken root on Emerson's grave among the pines when a discussion of his genius began, to which so many have contributed, that we already are asking Lowell's question concerning Shakespeare,—Can anything new be said of him? One thing, it seems to me, may be said, at least in a new way and as a clew to his work as a poet. While, of all his brotherhood, he is the radiant exemplar of his own statement, that in spirit "the true poet and the true philosopher are one," nevertheless, of all verse his own shows most clearly that the Method of the poet not only is not one with that of the philosopher, but is in fact directly opposed to it. The poet, as an artist, does not move in the direction which was Emerson's by instinct and selection. The Ideal philosophy scrutinizes every phase of Nature to find the originating sense, the universal soul, the pure identity; it follows Nature's trails to their common beginning, inverting her process of evolution, working back from infinite variety to the primal unity. This, too, is the spirit of the poet,—to find the soul of things. But in method he is an artist: his poetry is an art that imitates Nature's own habit. He works from unity to countless results and formations, from the pure thought to visible symbols, from the ideal to the concrete. As a poet, Emerson found himself in a state, not of distraction, but often of indecision, *between the methods of philosophy and art.* To bear this in mind is to account more readily for the peculiar beauties and deficiencies of his verse,—and thus to accept it as it is, and not without some understanding of its value.

Hermann Grimm recurs to the dispute whether our sage was a poet, a philosopher, or a prophet. The fact is that he was born with certain notes of song; he had the poet's eye and ear, and was a poet just so far as, being a philosopher, he accepted poetry as the expression of thought in its rare and prophetic moods, and just so far as, in exquisite moments, he had the mastery of this form of expression.

Emerson's prose is full of poetry, and his poems are light and air. But this statement, like so many of his own, gives only one side of a truth. His prose is just as full of every-day sense and wisdom; and something different from prose, however sublunary and imaginative, is needed to constitute a poem. His verse, often diamond-like in contrast with the feldspar of others, at times is ill-cut and beclouded. His prose, then, is that of a wise-man, plus a poet; and his verse, by turns, light and twilight, air and vapor. Yet we never feel, as in reading Wordsworth, that certain of his measures are wholly prosaic. He was so careless of ordinary standards, that few of his own craft have held his verse at its worth. It is said that his influence was chiefly, like that of Socrates, upon the sensitive and young, and such is the case with all fresh influences; but I take it that those who have fairly assimilated Emerson's poetry in their youth have been not so much born poets as born thinkers of a poetic cast. It is inevitable, and partakes of growth by exercise, that poets in youth should value a master's sound and color and form, rather than his priceless thought. They are drawn to the latter by the former, or not at all. Yet when poets, even in this day of refinement, have served their technical apprenticeship, the depth and frequent splendor of Emerson's verse grow upon them. They half suspect that he had the finest touch of all when he chose to apply it. It becomes a question whether his discords are those of an undeveloped artist, or the sudden craft of one who knows all art and can afford to be on easy terms with it. I think there is evidence on both sides;—that he had seasons when feeling and expression were in circuit, and others when the wires were down, and that he was as apt to attempt to send a message at one time as at the other. But he suggested the subtilty and swiftness of the soul's reach, even when he failed to sustain it.

I have said that of two poets, otherwise equal, the one who acquires the broadest knowledge will draw ahead of him who only studies his art, and the poet who thinks most broadly and deeply will draw ahead of all. There can be little doubt of Emerson as a thinker, or as a poet for thinkers satisfied with a deep but abstract and not too varied range. Yet he did not use his breadth of culture and thought to diversify the purpose, form, symbolism, of his poems. They are mostly in one key. They teach but one lesson; that, to be sure, is the first and greatest of all, but they fail to present it, after Nature's method, in many forms of living and beautiful interest,—to exemplify it in action, and thus bring it within universal sympathy. That this should be so was, I say, inevitable from the field of Emerson's research,—that of pure rather than of applied philosophy. Thus far, however, he represents Thought in any adjustment of our poetic group, and furthermore,—his thought being independent and emancipatory,—the American conflict with superstition, with servility to inherited usage and opinion.

We shall see that he had himself a noble and comprehensive ideal of what a typical poet should be, and was aware that his own song fell short of it. Still, he called himself a poet, and the consent of the best minds has sustained him in his judgment. His prose alone, as Lowell said, showed that he was essentially a poet; another with reason declared of his spoken essays that they were "not so much lectures as grave didactic poems, theogonies," adorned with "odes" and "eclogues." Thirty years later a cool and subtle writer looks back to find them the "most poetical, the most beautiful, productions of the American mind." For once the arbiters agree, except in a question akin to the dispute whether all things consist solely of spirit or solely of matter. Common opinion justified

Mr. Sanborn's fine paradox that, instead of its being settled that Emerson could not write poetry, it was settled that he could write nothing else. We know his distaste for convention, his mistrust of "tinkle" and "efficacious rhymes." But his gift lifted him above his will; even while throwing out his grapnel, clinging to prose as the firm ground of his work, he rose involuntarily and with music. And it well may be that at times he wrote verse as an avowal of his nativity, and like a noble privileged to use the language of the court. Certainly he did not restrict himself to the poet's calling with the loyalty of Tennyson and Longfellow. In verse, however careful of his phrase, he was something of a rhapsodist, not apt to gloss his revelations and exhortings with the nice perfection of those others. He must be reviewed as one whose verse and parable and prophecy alike were means to an end,—that end not art, but the enfranchisement and stimulation of his people and his time. When Longfellow, the poet of graceful art and of sympathy as tender as his voice, took his departure, there went up a cry as from a sense of fireside loss. People everywhere dwelt upon the story of his life and recalled his folk-songs. Emerson glided away almost unperceived under the shadow of the popular bereavement. But soon, and still multiplying from the highest sources, tributes to his genius began to appear,—searching, studying, expounding him,—as when a grand nature, an originating force, has ceased to labor for us. This is the best of fame: to impress the selected minds, which redistribute the effect in steadfast circles of extension. More than his associates, Emerson achieved this fame. He had the great man's intellect, which, according to Landor, "puts in motion the intellect of others." He was, besides, so rare a personage, that one who seeks to examine his writings apart from the facts and conduct of his life needs must wander off in contemplation of the man himself. Yet anything that others can write of him is poor indeed beside a collect of his own golden sayings. He felt his work to be its own and best interpreter, and of recent authors who have justly held this feeling he doubtless was the chief.

II

His writings, then, are the key to his biography—the scroll of a life which, as for essential matter, and as he said of Plato's, was chiefly "interior." To quote his own language further, "Great geniuses have the shortest biographies." Among the external points of significance in Emerson's story are those derived from his ancestral strain, for he was of pure and even gentle English blood, "through eight generations of cultured, conscientious, and practical ministers." He himself, as we know, assumed the profession of his father and forefathers, and for a time was a Unitarian preacher in Boston; this, after the stated courses at Harvard, where he read and wrote philosophy, nor failed to cultivate the Muse—for whose art he had shown a rare aptness even in childhood. The office and honors of the Class Poet fell to him, as to Lowell in after years. In letters he had Everett, Ticknor, and Edward Channing for instructors. In theology he was deeply influenced by Channing, the divine,—the true founder, through the work of Emerson and lesser pupils, of our liberal religious structure. Emerson projected the lines of the master so far beyond their first draft that he was unable long to remain within the Unitarian limits of that day. Some one has cleverly said that his verse, "Good-bye, proud world!" came from one whose future gave no cause for epigrams like that of Madame de Sevigne on Cardinal de Retz—of whom she wrote that he pretended to retire from a world which he saw was retiring from him. The separation from the church, and the retreat to Concord, were the beginning of Emerson's long career as poet, lecturer, essayist, thinker and inspirer. The details of his social, domestic, and civic relations are all upon record. Nothing could be more seemly than his lifelong abode in the New England village of Concord, the home of his line, the birth-place of our liberties; and it became, largely through his presence, the source of our most resultful thought. Here he blended, in his speech and action, the culture of the university, nigh at hand, with the shrewd prudence of the local neighborhood, as became a poet and sage imbued with patriotism, morals, and the wisdom of practical life. Here, though crossing the ocean more than once, and inspecting other lands with the regard that sees for once and all, he otherwise exemplified during half a century his own conception of the clear spirit—that needs not to go afar upon its quests, because it vibrates boundlessly, and includes all things within reach and ken. For the rest, the life of Emerson appertained to the household, the library, the walk, the talk with all sorts and conditions of men, communion with rare natures, the proper part in local and national movement. As a lecturer, his range was the country at large, but the group that drew about him made Concord a modern Academe. Unconsciously he idealized them all with the halo of his own attributes. To him they all were of the breed so exquisitely characterized in his reference to Margaret Fuller's "Friends." "I remember," he says, "these persons as a fair, commanding troop, every one of them adorned by some splendor of beauty, of grace, of talent, or of character, and comprising in their band persons who have since disclosed sterling worth and elevated aims in the conduct of life." Thus year after year a tide, that ceases not with the death of him who mainly attracted it, has set toward Concord,—a movement of pilgrims craving spiritual exaltation and the interplay of mind

with mind. The poet's moral and intellectual experiences are revealed
in discourses, always beginning with the memorable sermon on the Lord's
Supper, which prefigured his emancipation from dogma,[1] and the essay on
Nature, wherein he applied a new vision to the world about us. These were
the Alpha of his conviction and insight; his after-speech followed consistently
and surely, "as the night the day." He created his own audience, whose demand
for his thought grew by what it fed on, beginning in a section, and spreading
not only through a country but over many lands. If it is true that "he was
not the prince of transcendentalists but the prince of idealists," the history
of New England transcendentalism is no less a corollary to the problem of
Emerson's life.

Our starry memories of the places and people that once knew Emerson
radiate always from one centre—the presence of the sage himself. Many
pupils, catching something of his own sure and precise art of delineation,
have drawn his image for us, dwelling upon the sinewy bending figure,
the shining and expectant face, the union of masculinity and sweetness in
his bearing. His "full body tone" is recalled, "full and sweet rather than
sonorous, yet flexible, and haunted by many modulations." Persuasion sat
upon his lips. The epithet "sun-accustomed" is applied to Emerson's piercing
eyes by one, a woman and a poet, who marked the aquiline effect of his noble
profile. I, too, remember him in this wise, and as the most serene of men:
one whose repose, whose tranquillity, was not the contentment of an idler
housed in worldly comforts, but the token of spiritual adjustment to all the
correspondences of life; as the bravest and most deferential, the proudest in
self-respect, yet recognizing in deep humility the supremacy of universal law.
No man so receptive, and none with so plain and absolute a reservation of
his own ground. Even in the shadow and silence of his closing years, he bore
the mien of one assured that

> the gods reclaim not from the seer
> Their gift, although he ceases here to sing,
> And, like the antique sage, a covering
> Draws round his head, knowing what change is near.

III

It is not my province to take part in the discussion of Emerson's
philosophy, his system or lack of system. Some notion of this, however, must
affect our thoughts of him as a poet, since of all moderns he most nearly
fulfilled Wordsworth's inspired prediction, uttered sixty years ago, of the

approaching union of the poet and the philosopher. He deemed the higher office that of the poet,—of him who quaffs the brook that flows fast by the oracles,—yet doubtless thought himself not so well endowed with melody and passion that his teaching should be subordinate to his song. But the latter was always the flowering of his philosophic thought, and it is essential to keep in view the basis of that pure reflection. He looked upon Nature as pregnant with Soul; for him the Spirit always moved upon the face of the waters. The incomprehensible plan was perfect: whatever is, is right. Thus far he knew, and was an optimist with reverent intent. It was in vain to ask him to assert what he did not know, to avow a creed founded upon his hopes. If a theist, with his intuition of an all-pervading life, he no less felt himself a portion of that life, and the sense of omnipresence was so clearly the dominant sense of its attributes, that to call him a theist rather than a pantheist is simply a dispute about terms; to pronounce him a Christian theist is to go beyond his own testimony. Such a writer must be judged by the concurrence of his books; they are his record, and the parole evidence of no associate can weigh against his written manifest for an instant. His writings assure us that he accepted all bibles and creeds for what good there was in them. One thing for him was "certain": "Religions are obsolete when lives do not proceed from them." He saw that "unlovely, nay frightful, is the solitude of the soul which is without God in the world"; but the creeds and dogmas of anthropomorphic theology were merely germinal. "Man," thus far, has "made all religions, and will yet make new and even higher faiths."

Emerson, a man of our time, while a transcendentalist, looking inward rather than to books for his wisdom, studied well the past, and earlier sages were the faculty of his school. A latter-day eclectic, he took from all literatures their best and essential. A Platonic idealist, he was not averse to the inductive method of Aristotle; he had the Alexandrian faith and ecstasy, the Epicurean zest and faculty of selection; like the Stoics, he observed morals, heroism, self-denial, and frugality. There is much in his teachings that recalls the beautiful ethics of Marcus Aurelius, and the words of Epictetus, as reported by Arrian. This spiritual leanings never stinted his regard of men and manners. He kept a sure eye on the world; he was not only a philosopher, but the paragon of gentlemen, with something more than the Oriental, the Grecian, or the Gallic, tact. He relished to the full the brave distinctions, the portraitures and tests of Plutarch, and found the best of all good company in the worldly wise, the cheery and comfortable Montaigne. One may almost say that he refined and digested what was good in all philosophies, and nothing more. He would get hold of Swedenborg, the mystic, yet not be Swedenborg exclusively, nor imitate the rhetoric of the Sophists, the pride of the Cynics. From all he learned what each confesses in the end,—the limitations of inquiry,—that the Finite cannot measure, though it may feel, the Infinite. No more would he formulate a philosophy, but within it he could recognize nature, art, taste, morals, laws, religion, and the chance of immortality. When it was said that he had no new system, he thought that he needed none, and was sceptical of classification.

It appears that he found the key to his own nature in Plato, being an idealist first of all. His intuitive faculty was so determined that ideality and mysticism gave him the surest promise of realities; his own intellect satisifed him of the power of intellect. Plainly hearing an interior voice, he had no doubt that other men were similarly monished. Plato, the guide of his youth, remained his type of philosopher and man. To Plato's works alone should Omar's saying of the Koran be applied: "Burn the libraries, for their value is in this book." Nowhere else was there such a range of speculation. "Out of Plato come all things." And thus he held to the last. "Of Plato," he said, years afterward, "I hesitate to speak, lest there should be no end. . . . Why should not young men be educated on this book? It would suffice for the tuition of the race." Yet Emerson's philosophy was a greater advance from Neo-Platonism than the Alexandrians were able to make upon the lines indicated by their elemental master. In personal life and bearing, Plotinus, with whom our poet seems to have been most in sympathy, was very closely his prototype. There is first to be noted the curious resemblance between the eclectic, investigating Alexandrian age and our present time; and secondly, it is Plotinus of whom we are told that "He lived at the same time with himself and with others, and the inward activity of his spirit ceased only during his hours of sleep. . . . His written style was close, pregnant, and richer in thought than in words, yet enthusiastic, and always pointing to the main object. He was more eloquent in his oral communications, and was said to be very clever in finding the appropriate word, even if he failed in accuracy on the whole. Besides this, the beauty of his person was increased when discoursing; his countenance was lighted up with genius." Taylor's translations of selections from the Works of Plotinus, published in 1817 and 1834, must have fallen into Emerson's hands, and I am satisfied of their impression upon his mind. As one examines the lives and writings of the two men, the likeness is still more notable, especially with respect to their views of fate, will, ethics, the "higher law," the analysis of the beautiful, and in the ardor with which young students, and many of the elderly and wise, listened to their respective teachings. Emerson was a Plotinus reanimate after the lapse of sixteen centuries of Christianity. He has now, like the Neo-Platonist, "led back the Divine principle within" him "to the God who is all in all."

To the great thinkers of the past, the New England teacher, without fear or boasting, well might feel himself allied. The accepted great, free of the ordinary bounds of place and time, recognize one another across the vague, like stars of the prime magnitude in the open night. Emerson knew the haps and signs of genius: "Whenever we find a man higher by a whole head than any of his contemporaries, it is sure to come in doubt what are his real works." We cannot say "What is master, and what school." "As for their borrowings and adaptings, they know how to borrow. A great man is one of the affinities, who takes of everything." But they are not above the law of perfect life; virtue, simplicity, absolute sincerity, these are their photosphere. "Live as on a mountain. Let men see, let them know, a real man, who lives as he was meant to live." To this Roman standard the New Englander subjoined the shrewd, kindly wisdom of his stock and region. He was eminent among those whose common sense is the most telling point to be made against Locke's negation of innate ideas,—whose judgment is so apt that, granting Locke's theory, it can be accounted for only by the modern theory of ideas prenatal and inherited. His written wisdom is more effective than Montaigne's, being less dependent on citations. He knew by instinct what our novelists learn from observation and experience; or is it that they study chiefly their own time and neighborhood, while he sat aloof and with the ages? Thus strong in equipment, sound in heart, and lofty of intellect, we find him revered by his pupils, and without a living peer in the faculty of elevating the purpose of those who listened to his buoyant words. We must confess that a differentiation between master and school, and between members of the school, after awhile became manifest. That such a process was inevitable is plain, when Emerson's transcendental and self-reliant laws of conduct are kept in mind.

One may say, in illustration, that his philosophical method bears to the inductive or empirical a relation similar to that between the poetry of self-expression and the poetry of aesthetic creation,—a relation of the subjective to the objective. The former kind of verse often is the more spontaneous, since it has its birth in the human need for utterance. It is the cry of adolescence and femininity, the resource of sensitive natures in which emotion outvies the sense of external beauty or power. It was the voice of Shakespeare's youth, nor was it ever quieted throughout the restless careers of Byron, Heine, and de Musset. But we accept as the great works of the poets their intellectual and objective creations, wherein the artist has gone beyond his own joy and pain, his narrow intro-vision, to observe, combine, transfigure, the outer world of nature and life. Such the epics, idyls, dramas, of the masters. When subjective poetry is the yield of a lofty nature, or of an ideal and rapturous womanhood like Mrs. Browning's, it is a boon and revelation to us all; but when, as too often, it is the spring-rise of a purling, commonplace streamlet, its egotism grows pitiful and repulsive. This lesson has been learned, and now our minor poets, in their fear of it, strive to give pleasure to our sense of the beautiful, and work as artists,—though somewhat too delicately,—rather than to pose as exceptional beings, "among men, but not of them."

As with the subjective poets, so with many of the transcendental acolytes. The force of Emerson lay in the depth and clearness of his intentions. He gave us the revelation and prophecy of a man among millions. Such a teacher aids the self-development of noble minds; his chief peril is that of nurturing a weaker class that cannot follow where he leads. Some of its enthusiasts will scarcely fail to set too high a value upon their personal impulses. They "still revere," but forget to "still suspect" themselves "in lowliness of heart." For the rest, the down-East instinct is advisory and homiletic; New Englanders are prone to teach, and slower to be taught. Emerson, however, grew to be their superior man, the one to whom all agreed to listen, and from whom all quote. His example, also, has somewhat advanced the art of listening, in which he was so perfect, with forward head and bright, expectant visage. His inculcations were of freedom, of the self-guidance that learns to unlearn and bears away from tradition; yet this, too, will breed false liberty of conceit in minor votaries, whose inward light may do well enough for themselves, yet not suffice for the light of the world. Hence the public, accepting Emerson, has been less tolerant of more than one Emersonian, with his *ego, et rex mew*. After all is said, we must see that our transcendentalists were a zealous, aspiring band of seekers after the true, the beautiful, and the good; what they have lacked in deference they have made up in earnestness and spirituality. There have been receptive natures among them, upon whom, as indeed upon the genius of his people far and wide, the tonic effect of Emerson's life and precept has been immeasurable. Goethe's declaration of himself that he had been "to the Germans in general, and to the young German poets in particular, their liberator," may, with perfect truth, be applied to Emerson, and to a generation that has thriven on his word. He has taught his countrymen the worth of virtue, wisdom, courage,—above all, to fashion life upon a self-reliant pattern, obeying the dictates of their own souls.

IV

Recognizing Emerson's high mood as that of a most original poet, I wish chiefly to consider his relations to poetry and the poetic art. His imaginative essays are not poems. Speech is not song; the rarest mosaic lacks the soul of the canvas swept by the brush. The credentials that he presented from time to time, and mostly in that dawn when poets sing if ever, are few and fragmentary, but they will suffice. They are the trophies, the wreaths and golden vessels, the *spolia opima*, which he set before the shrine of the goddess. They are the avowal of a rare spirit that there are things which cannot be rendered in prose; that Poetry claims a finer art, a supremer utterance, for her service, and that she alone can stamp the coins and bronzes which carry to the future the likeness of her viceroy.

In his verse, Emerson's spiritual philosophy and laws of conduct appear again, but transfigured. Always the idea of Soul, central and pervading, of which Nature's forms are but the created symbols. As in his early discourse he recognized two entities, Nature and the Soul, so to the last he believed Art to be simply the union of Nature with man's will—Thought symbolizing itself through Nature's aid. Thought, sheer ideality, was his sovereign; he was utterly trustful of its guidance. The law of poetic beauty depends on the beauty of the thought, which, perforce, assumes the fittest, and therefore most charming, mode of expression. The key to art is the eternal fitness of things; this is the sure test and solvent. Over and again he asserted his conviction: "Great thoughts insure musical expression. Every word should be the right word. . . . The Imagination wakened brings its own language, and that is always musical. . . . Whatever language the poet uses, the secret of tone is at the heart of the poem." He cites Moller, who taught that the building which was fitted accurately to answer its end would turn out to be beautiful, though beauty had not been intended. (The enforced beauty of even the rudest sailing craft always has seemed to me the most striking illustration of this truth.) In fine, Emerson sees all forms of art symbolizing but one Reason, not one mind, but The Mind that made the world. He refers "all production at last to an aboriginal Power." It is easy to discern that from the first he recognized "the motion and the spirit," which to Wordsworth were revealed only by the discipline of years; but his song went beyond the range of landscape and peasant, touching upon the verities of life and thought. "Brahma" is of the presentation of the truth manifest to the oldest and most eastern East, and beyond which the West can never go. How strange that these quatrains could have seemed strange! They reveal the light of Asia, but no less the thought of Plato—who said that in all nations certain minds dwell on the "fundamental Unity," and "lose all being in one Being." Everywhere one stuff, under all forms, this the woven symbolism of the universal Soul, the only reality, the single and subdivided Identity that alone can "keep and pass and turn again," that is at once the doubter and the doubt, the slayer and the slain, light and shadow, the hither and the yon. Love is but the affinity of its portions, the desire for reunion, the knowledge of soul by soul, to which the eyes of lovers are but windows. Art is the handiwork of the soul, with materials created by itself, building better than it knows, the bloom of attraction and necessity.

Thus far the theory of Emerson's song. It does not follow that he composed upon a theory. At times I think him the first of our lyric poets, his turns are so wild and unexpected; and he was never commonplace, even when writing for occasions. His verse changes unawares from a certain tension and angularity that were congenital, to an ethereal, unhampered freedom, the poetic soul in full glow, the inner music loosed and set at large. Margaret Fuller wrote that his poems were "mostly philosophical, which is not the truest kind of poetry." But this depends upon the measure of its didacticism. Emerson made philosophical poetry imaginative, elevating, and thus gave new evidence that the poet's realm is unbounded. If he sought first principles, he looked within himself for them, and thus portrays himself, not only the penetrative thinker, but the living man, the citizen, the New England villager, whose symbols are drawn from the actual woods and hills of a neighborhood. Certainly he went to rural nature for his vigor, his imagery and adornments. An impassioned sense of its beauty made him the reverse of the traditional descriptive poet. Most poetry of nature justly is termed didactic; most philosophical verse the same. Miss Fuller failed to make distinctions. All feel what didacticism signifies, but let us try to formulate it.

Didacticism is the gospel of half-truths. Its senses are torpid; it fails to catch and convey the soul of truth, which is beauty. Truth shorn of its beauty is tedious and not poetical. We weary of didactic verse, therefore, not because of its truth, but because of its self-delusive falsehood. It flourishes with a dull and prosaic generation. The true poet, as Mrs. Browning saw, is your only truth-teller, because he gives the truth complete in beauty or not at all.

Emerson doubts his power to capture the very truth of nature. Its essence—its beauty—is so elusive; it flees and leaves but a corpse behind; it is the pearly glint of the shells among the bubbles of the latest wave:—

> I fetched my sea-born treasures home;
> But the poor, unsightly, noisome things

Had left their beauty on the shore,
With the sun, and the sand, and the wild uproar.

But such poems as the "Forerunners" show how closely he moved, after all, upon the trail of the evading sprite. He seemed, by the first intention, and with an exact precision of grace and aptness, to put in phrases what he saw and felt,—and he saw and felt so much more than others! He had the aboriginal eye, and the civilized sensibility; he caught both the external and the scientific truth of natural things, and their poetic charm withal. As he triumphed over the untruthfulness of the mere verse-maker, and the dulness of the moralist, his instant, sure, yet airy transcripts gave his poems of nature a quality with out a counterpart. Some of his measures had at least the flutter of the twig whence the bird has just flown. He did not quite fail of that music music-born,

> a melody born of melody,
> Which melts the world into a sea.
> Toil could never compass it;
> Art its height could never hit.

He infused his meditations with the sheen of Day itself,—of

> one of the charmed days
> When the genius of God doth flow;
> The wind may alter twenty ways,
> A tempest cannot blow;
> It may blow north, it still is warm;
> Or south, it still is clear;
> Or east, it smells like a clover-farm;
> Or west, no thunder fear.

He returns with delight to Nature's blending of her laws of beauty and use, perceiving that she

> beats in perfect tune,
> And rounds with rhyme her every rune,
> Whether she work in land or sea,
> Or hide underground her alchemy.
> Thou canst not wave thy staff in air,
> Or dip thy paddle in the lake,
> But it carves the box of beauty there,
> And the ripples in rhymes the oar forsake.

"Woodnotes" is full of lyrical ecstasy and lightsome turns and graces. To assimilate such a poem of nature, or "The Problem," that masterpiece of religion and art, is to feed on holy dew, and to comprehend how the neophytes who were bred upon it find the manna of noontide somewhat rank and innutritious. "May-Day" is less lyrical, more plainly descriptive of the growth and meaning of the Spring, but not in any part didactic. It is the record of the poet's training, a match to Wordsworth's portrayal of his subjective communing with Nature in youth; its spirit is the same with Lowell's woodland joyousness, one of child-like and unquestioning zest. Finally, this poet's scenic joinery is so true, so mortised with the one apt word, as where he says that the wings of Time are *"pied* with morning and with night," and the one best word or phrase is so unlooked for, that, as I say, we scarcely know whether all this comes by grace of instinct, or with search and artistic forethought. It seems "the first fine careless rapture"; the labor, which results in the truth of Tennyson's landscape and the pathos of Longfellow's, may be there, but is not to be detected, and in these touches, if not otherwise, he excelled his compeers. His generalizations pertain to the unseen world; viewing the actual, he puts its strength and fineness alike into a line or epithet. He was born with an unrivalled faculty of selection. Monadnock is the "constant giver," the Titan that "heeds his sky-affairs"; the tiny humming-bee a "voyager of light and noon," a "yellow-breeched philosopher," and again an "animated torrid zone"; the defiant titmouse, an "atom in full breath." For a snow-storm, or the ocean, he uses his broader brush, but once only and well. His minute truth and sense of values are held in honor by his pupils Whitman and Burroughs, our poetic familiars of the field, and by all to whom the seasonable marvels of the pastoral year are not unwelcome or unknown.

Thus keenly Emerson's instinct reponded to the beauty of Nature. I have hinted that her secure laws were the chief promoters of his imagination. It coursed along her hidden ways. In this he antedated Tennyson, and was less didactic than Goethe and kindred predecessors. His foresight gave spurs to the intellect of Tyndall and other investigators,—to their ideal faculty, without which no explorer moves from post to outpost of discovery. Correlatively, each wonder-breeding point attained by the experimentalists was also occupied by our eager and learned thinker from the moment of its certainty. Each certainty gave him joy; reasoning *a priori* from his sense of a spiritual Force, the seer anticipated the truths demonstrated by the inductive workers, and expected the demonstration. Even in "The Sphinx," the first poem of his first collection, the conservation of force, the evolution from the primordial atom, are made to subserve his mystical faith in a broad Identity. Here, thirty years before Tennyson made his most compact expression of the central truth,—

> Flower in the crannied wall
> Little flower—but if I could understand
> What you are, root and all, and all in all,
> I should know what God and man is,
>
> Emerson had put it in this wise:—
>
> Thorough a thousand voices
> Spoke the universal dame:
> "Who telleth one of my meanings,
> Is master of all I am."

The reference, in "Bacchus," to the ascent of life from form to form, still remains incomparable for terseness and poetic illumination:—

> I, drinking this,
> Shall hear far Chaos talk with me;
> Kings unborn shall walk with me;
> And the poor grass shall plot and plan
> What it will do when it is man.

And in "Woodnotes" he discoursed of

> the genesis of things,
> Of tendency through endless ages,
> Of star-dust and star-pilgrimages,
> Of rounded worlds, of space and time,
> Of the old flood's subsiding slime;

but always thinks of the universal Soul as the only reality,—of creation's process as simply the metamorphosis which

> Melts things that be to things that seem,
> And solid nature to a dream.

Even in the pathetic "Threnody" he stays his anguish with faith in the beneficence of Law. With more passion and less method than afterward gave form to *In Memoriam*, he declared that the "mysteries of Nature's heart" were "past the blasphemies of grief." He saw

> the genius of the whole,
> Ascendant in the primal soul,
> Beckon it when to go and come."

Such a poet was not like to go backward. The "Song of Nature" is his paean to her verities, still more clearly manifest in his riper years. This superb series of quatrains, cumulative as thunder-heads and fired with lyric glory, will lend its light to whatsoever the poetry of the future has in reserve for us.

It should be noted that Emerson's vision of the sublime in scientific discovery increased his distaste for mere style, and moved him to contentment with the readiest mode of expression. It tempered his eulogy of "Art," and made him draw this contrast: "Nature transcends all moods of thought, and its secret we do not yet find. But a gallery stands at the mercy of our moods, and there is a moment when it becomes frivolous. I do not wonder that Newton, with an attention habitually engaged on the paths of planets and suns, should have wondered what the Earl of Pembroke found to admire in 'stone dolls.'"

Right here we observe (deferring matters of construction) that our seer's limitations as a poet are indicated by his dependence on out-door nature, and by his failure to utilize those higher symbols of the prime Intelligence which comprise the living, acting, suffering world of man. With a certain pride of reserve, that did not lessen his beautiful deference to individuals, he proclaimed "the advantage which the country life possesses for a powerful mind over the artificial and curtailed life of cities." He justified solitude by saying that great men, from Plato to Wordsworth, did not live in a crowd, but descended into it from time to time as benefactors. Above all he declared—"I am by nature a poet, and therefore must live in the country." But here a Goethe, or de Musset, or Browning might rejoin: "And I am a poet, and need the focal life of the town." If man be the paragon of life on this globe, his works and passions the rarest symbols of the life unseen, then the profoundest study is mankind. Emerson's theorem was a restriction of the poet's liberties. One can name great poets who would have been greater but for the trammels of their seclusion. I believe that Emerson's came from self-knowledge. He kept his range with incomparable tact and philosophy. Poets of a wider franchise— with Shakespeare at their front—have found that genius gains most from Nature during that formative period when one reads her heart, if ever, and that afterward he may safely leave her, as a child his mother, to return from time to time, but still to do his part among the ranks of men.

Emerson makes light of travel for pleasure and observation, but ever more closely would observe the ways of the inanimate world. Yet what are man's works but the works of Nature by one remove? To one poet is given the ear to comprehend the murmur of the forest, to another the sense that times the heartbeats of humanity. Few have had Emerson's inward eye, but it is well that some have not been restricted to it. He clung by attraction, no less than by circumstance, to "a society in which introspection," as Mr. James has shrewdly written, "thanks to the want of other entertainment, played almost the part of a social resource." His verse, in fact, is almost wholly void of the epic and dramatic elements which inform the world's great works of art. Action, characterization, specific sympathy, and passion are wanting in his song. His voice comes "like a falling star" from a skyey dome of pure abstraction. Once or twice, some little picture from life,—a gypsy girl, a scarcely outlined friend or loved one,—but otherwise no personage in his works except, it may be, the poet himself, the Saadi of his introspective song: even that wise and joyous bard restored in fragments, suggested rather than portrayed. Emerson would be the "best bard, because the wisest," if the wisdom of his song illustrated itself in living types. He knew the human world, none better, and generalized the sum of its attainments,—was gracious, shrewd, and calm,—but could not hold up the mirror and show us to ourselves. He was that unique songster, a poet of fire and vision, quite above the moralist, yet neither to be classed as objective or subjective; he perceived the source of all passion and wisdom, yet rendered neither the hearts of others nor his own. His love poetry is eulogized, but it wants the vital grip wherewith his "Concord Fight" and "Boston Hymn" fasten on our sense of manhood and patriotism. It chants of Love, not of the beloved; its flame is pure and general as moonlight and as high-removed. "All mankind love a lover," and it is not enough to discourse upon the philosophy of "Love," "Experience," "Power," "Friendship." Emerson's "Bacchus" must press for him

> wine, but wine which never grew
> In the belly of the grape.

His deepest yearnings are expressed in that passionate outburst,—the momentary human wail over his dead child, and in the human sense of lost companionship when he tells us,—

> In the long sunny afternoon,
> The plain was full of ghosts.

Oftener he moves apart; his blood is ichor, not our own; his thoughts are with the firmament. We reverence his vocation, and know ourselves unfitted for it. He touches life more nearly in passages that have the acuteness, the practical wisdom of his prose works and days; but these are not his testimonials as a poet. His laying on of hands was more potent; a transmitted heat has gone abroad through the ministry of his disciples, who practise as he preached, and sometimes transcend both his preaching and his practice.

All the same, the originator of a force is greater than others who add four-fold to its momentum. They are never so manifestly his pupils as when they are "scarifying" and "sounding and exploring" him, "reporting where they touch bottom and where not," on ground of their own, but with a pleasant mockery of the master's word and wont. There was a semblance between the poets Emerson and Rossetti, first, in the small amount of their lyrical work, and again in the positive influence which each exerted upon his pupils. In quality the Concord seer, and the English poet who was at once the most spiritual and sensuous of his own school, were wholly unlike. Rossetti was touched with white fire, but dreamed of souls that meet and glow when disembodied. The spirits of his beatified thrill with human passion. Our seer brought something of heaven to earth, while Rossetti yearned to carry life through death to heaven. . . .

Popular instinct, recognized by those who compile our anthologies, forbids an author to be great in more than one way. These editors go to Emerson for point and wisdom, and too seldom for his truth to nature and his strictly poetic charm. Yet who excels him in quality? That Margaret Fuller had a fine ear, and an independent one, proved by her admission that "in melody, in subtilty of thought and expression," he took the highest rank. He often captures us with absolute beauty, the poetry that poets love,—the lilt and melody of Shelley (whose vagueness irked him) joined to precision of thought and outline. Poe might have envied "Uriel" his lutings of the spangled heaven; he could not have read "Woodnotes," or he would have found something kindred in the bard who said,—

> Quit thy friends as the dead in doom,
> And build to them a final tomb;
> Let the starred shade that nightly falls
> Still celebrate their funerals,
> And the bell of beetle and of bee
> Knell their melodious memory.

Emerson "listened to the undersong," but rejoiced no less in the "divine ideas below" of the Olympian bards,

> Which always find us young
> And always keep us so.

His modes of expression, like his epithets, are imaginative. The snow is "the north-wind's masonry"; feeling and thought are scarcely deeper than his speech; he puts in words the "tumultuous privacy of storm," of the "sweet varieties of chance." With what high ecstasy of pain he calls upon the deep-eyed boy, the hyacinthine boy, of his marvellous "Threnody!" Time confirms the first impression that this is the most spontaneous, the most elevating, of lyrical elegies,—that it transcends even the divine verse of Bishop King's invocation to his entombed wife. How abrupt, how exquisitely ideal, the opening phrase! Afterward, and throughout, the pure spirit of poetry rarefied by the passion of its theme: the departed child is the superangelic symbol of the beauty, the excellence, that shall be when time ripens and the harmonies of nature are revealed,—when life is no longer a dream within a dream. Read the "Threnody" anew. What grace! What Eolian music, what yearning! What prophecy and exaltation! See how emotion becomes the soul of art. Or is it that true passion cannot but express itself in verse at once simple and sensuous, thus meeting all the cardinal points of Milton's law?

One readily perceives that "Merlin" conveys Emerson's spirited conception of the art and manners of the bard. His should be no trivial harp:—

> No jingling serenader's art,
> Nor tinkle of piano strings;
>
> . . .
>
> The kingly bard
> Must smite the cords rudely and hard,
> As with hammer or with mace;
>
> . . .
>
> He shall not his brain encumber
> With the coil of rhythm and number;
> But leaving rule and pale forethought,
> He shall aye climb
> For his rhyme.

Thus fearlessly should a poet compel the Muse; and even to a broader liberty of song one, at least, of Emerson's listeners pushed with deliberate zeal. Walt Whitman was stimulated by this teaching, and by the rugged example of Carlyle, to follow resolutely the method which suited his bent and project; and Emerson's "Mithridates," we may say, is at once the key-note and best defence of Whitman's untrammelled, all-heralding philosophy. The descriptive truth, the lusty Americanism, of the democratic chanter took hold upon the master's expectant heart. A later modification of the first welcome, and the omission of the new songs from "Parnassus," had no bearing upon the question of their morals or method; Emerson was moved solely by his taste,—and New England taste has a supreme dislike of the unsavory. The world, even the Concord world, is not wholly given over to prudery. It has little dread, nowadays, of the voluptuous in art, ancient or modern. But to those of Puritan stock cleanliness is even more than godliness. There is no "fair perdition" tempting us in the "Song of Myself" and the "Children of Adam." But here are things which, whether vessels of honor or dishonor, one does not care to have before him too often or too publicly, and which were unattractive to the pure and temperate seer, whose race had so long inhabited the clean-swept keeping-rooms of the land of mountain breezes and transparent streams. The matter was one of artistic taste and of the inclinations of Emerson's nature, rather than of prudery or censorship.

As for his own style, Emerson was impressed in youth by the free-hand manner of the early dramatists, whom he read with avidity. He soon formed his characteristic measure, varying with "sixes," "sevens," and "eights," resembling Ben Jonson's lyrical style, but even more like that of Milton, Marvell, and other worthies of the Protectorate. In spirit and imagery, in blithe dithyrambic wisdom, he gained much from his favorite Orientals—Saadi and Hafiz. One stately and various measure he rarely essayed, but showed that it was well suited to his genius. In "Musketaquid" and "Sea-Shore" we see the aptness of his ear and hand for blank verse. The little poem of "Days," imitated from the antique, is unmatched, outside of Landor, for compression and self-poise:—

> Daughters of Time, the hypocritic Days,
> Muffled and dumb like barefoot dervishes,
> And marching single in an endless file,
> Bring diadems and fagots in their hands.
> To each they offer gifts after his will,
> Bread, kingdoms, stars, and sky that holds them all.
> I, in my pleached garden, watched the pomp,
> Forgot my morning wishes, hastily
> Took a few herbs and apples, and the Day
> Turned and departed silent. I, too late,
> Under her solemn fillet saw the scorn.

We could wish that Emerson had written more blank verse,—a measure suited to express his highest thought and imagination. Probably, however, he said all that he had to say in verse of any kind. He was not one to add a single line for the sake of a more liberal product.

He is thought to have begun so near the top that there was little left to climb. None of his verse is more pregnant than that which came in the first glow, but the later poems are free from those grotesque sayings which illustrate the fact that humor and a lively sense of the absurd often are of slow development in the brain of an earnest thinker. There was, it must be owned, a tinge of provincial arrogance, and there were expressions little less than ludicrous, in his early defiance of usage. He was too sincere a personage to resort to the grotesque as a means of drawing attention. Of him, the leader, this at least could not be suspected. Years afterward he revised his poems, as if to avoid even the appearance of affectation. On the whole, it is as well that he left "The Sphinx" unchanged; that remarkable poem is a fair gauge of its author's traits. The opening is strongly lyrical and impressive. The close is the flower of poesy and thought. The general tone is quaint and mystical. Certain passages, however, like that beginning "The fiend that man harries," are curiously awkward, and mar the effect of an original, almost an epochal, poem. This would not be admitted by the old-fashioned Emersonian,—never, by any chance, a poet pure and simple,—who makes it a point of faith to defend the very passages where the master nods. Just so the thick-and-thin Browningite, who testifies his adoration by counting the *m's* and *n's* of the great dramatist's volumes, and who, also, never is a poet pure and simple, celebrates Mr. Browning's least poetic experiments as his masterpieces. I think that the weakness of "transcendental" art is as fairly manifest in Emerson's first and chief collection of verse as were its felicities,—the former belonging to the school, the latter to the seer's own genius. Poe, to whom poetry was solely an expression of beauty, was irritated to a degree not to be explained by contempt for all things East. He extolled quaintness, and justly detested obscurity. He was prejudiced against the merits of such poets as Channing and Cranch by their prophetic bearing, which he berated soundly as an effort to set up as poets "of *unusual* depth and *very* remarkable powers of mind." Admitting the grace of one, he said that it was "laughable to see that the transcendental poets, if beguiled for a minute or two into respectable English and common-sense, are always sure to remember their cue just as they get to the end of their song, and round off with a bit of doggerel." Their thought was the "cant of thought," in adopting which "the cant of phraseology is adopted at the same time." This was serviceable criticism, *et ab hoste*, though Poe's lack of moral, and keenness of artistic, sense made him too sure of the insincerity of those who place conviction above expression. And Mr. James sees that Emerson's philosophy was "drunk in by a great many fine moral appetites with a sense of intoxication." The seer himself was intoxicated at times, and spoke, like the hasheesh-eaters, with what then seemed to him music and sanity. In a more reflecting season he excluded from his select edition certain pieces from which too many had taken their cues,—for example, the "Ode" to W. H. Channing, "The World-Soul," and "Tact." The Ode begins finely with a manner caught from Ben Jonson's ode "To Himself," and we can ill spare one passage ("The God who made New Hampshire"); but was it the future compiler of "Parnassus" who preceded this with laughter-stirring rhymes, and shortly avowed that "Things are of the snake," and again that "Things are in the saddle, And ride mankind"? Well, he lived to feel that to poets, "of all men, the severest criticism is due," and that "Poetry requires that splendor of expression which carries with it the proof of great thoughts."

But the forte of bardlings is the foible of a bard. Emerson became his own censor, and did wisely and well. We have seen that his art, even now, upon its constructive side, must often seem defective,—unsatisfactory to those whose love of proportion is a moral instinct. Many poets and critics will feel it so. The student of Emerson learns that he, too, moved upon their plane, but would not be confined to it. More than other men, he found himself a vassal of the unwritten law, whether his impulse lifted him above, or sent him below, the plane of artistic expression. If he could not sustain the concert-pitch of his voice at his best, he certainly knew what is perfection, and said of art much that should be said. He was not, he did not wish to be, primarily an artist: he borrowed Art's aid for his lofty uses, and held her at her worth. His essay on Art would be pronounced sound by a Goethe or a Lessing, though such men probe less deep for the secret principle of things, and deal more featly with the exterior. Elsewhere he insists that we must "disabuse us of our superstitious associations with place and time, with number and size. Where the heart is, there the muses, there to gods sojourn. . . . A great man makes his climate genial in the imagination of man, and its air the beloved element of all delicate spirits." And again (like Arnold) he speaks of the modernness of all good books: "What is well done, I feel as if I did; what is ill done, I reck not of." He revised his prose less carefully, for republication, than his verse, and doubtless felt surer of it. He himself would have been the first to declare, as to the discordant and grotesque portions of his verse or prose, that the thought was proportionately defective,—not strong and pure enough to insure the beauty of the art which was its expression. Above all he knew, he confessed, that it is the first duty of a poet to express his thoughts naturally, counting among "the traits common to all works of the highest art,—that they are universally intelligible, that they restore to us the simplest state of mind." This was his own canon. Where he failed of it, he might not surely know; where he knew, there he rebuked himself. He struck out, in his self-distrust, many things of value to those who loved his verse. We dwell with profit on the fact that he retained so little that should be stricken out.

V

It is but a foolish surmise whether Emerson's prose or verse will endure the longer, for they are of the same stuff, warp and woof, and his ideality crosses and recrosses each, so that either is cloth-of-gold. Of whichever a reader may first lay hold, he will be led to examine the whole fabric of the author's work. Few writers, any one of whose essays, met with for the first time, seems more like a revelation! It will not be, I think, until that time when all his prose has passed into a large book, such as the volume we call Montaigne, that its full strength and importance can be felt. In certain respects it dwarfs other modern writing, and places him among the great essayists. These are not the efforts of a reviewer of books or affairs, but chapters on the simplest, the greatest, the immemorial topics, those that lie at the base of life and wisdom: such as Love, Experience, Character, Manners, Fate, Power, Worship—lastly, Nature herself, and Art her ideal counterpart. If to treat great themes worthily is a mark of greatness, the chooser of such themes begins with the instinct of great design. Bacon's elementary essays excepted, there are none in English of which it can be more truly averred that there is nothing superfluous in them. Compare them with the rest in theme and method. Carlyle, outside of *Sartor Resartus* and *Hero-Worship*, usually reviews books, histories, individuals, at extreme length, and with dramatic comment and analysis. Emerson treats of the principles behind all history, and his laconic phrases are the very honey-cells of thought. There are let-downs and surplusage even in Landor. Throughout Emerson's writings each word is of value; they are the discourse of one who has digested all the worthy books, and who gives us their results, with latter-day discoveries of his own. He is the citizen of a new world, observing other realms and eras from an unrestricted point of view.

The intent of our essayist is the highest, and by no means that of writing for the exercise or glory of authorship. "Fatal," he declares, "to the man of letters is the lust of display. . . . A mistake of the main end to which they labor is incidental to literary men, who, dealing with the organ of language learn to enjoy the pride of playing with this splendid engine, but rob it of its almightiness by failing to work with it." He estimates books at their worth. They "are for nothing but to inspire. I had better never see a book than to be warped by its attraction clean out of my own orbit, and made a satellite instead of a system."

Thus the thought of Style, it may be, should enter into the mind of neither writer nor reader. Style makes itself, and Emerson's is the apothegmatic style of one bent upon uttering his immediate thoughts,—hence strong in sentences, and only by chance suited to the formation of an essay. Each sentence is an idea, an epigram, or an image, or a flash of spiritual light. His letters to Carlyle show that he was at one time caught by the manner of the author whose character, at least, seemed of the most import to him. This was but a passing trace. When he was fresh from the schools, his essays were structural and orderly, but more abstract than in latter years. During his mature and haply less spiritual period, had he cared to write a history, the English would have been pure English, the narrative racy and vigorous. Portions of the *English Traits* make this plain. Since De Foe, where have we found anything more idiomatic than his account of Wordsworth delivering a sonnet?

> This recitation was so unlooked for and surprising,—he, the old Wordsworth, standing apart, and reciting to me in a garden-walk, like a schoolboy declaiming,—that I at first was near to laugh; but recollecting myself, that I had come thus far to see a poet, and he was chanting poems to me, I saw that he was right and I was wrong, and gladly gave myself up to hear.

Note also Emerson's account of an ocean voyage. For charm of landscape-painting, take such a passage as that, in the second essay on Nature, beginning: "There are days which occur in this climate." But terseness is the distinctive feature of his style. "Men," he said, "descend to meet." "We are all discerners of spirits." "He [a traveller] carries ruins to ruins." No one has compressed more sternly the pith of his discourse.

No poet, let us at once add, has written prose and shown more incontestably his special attribute. Emerson's whole argument is poetic, if that work is poetic which reaches its aim through the analogies of things, and whose quick similitudes have the heat, the light, the actinism, of the day-beam, and of which the language is rhythmic without degeneracy,—clearly the language of prose, always kept from weakness by the thought which it conveys. No man's writing was more truly his speech, and no man's speech so rhythmic: "There are Muses in the woods to-day, and whispers to be heard in the breezes"; and again, "Hawthorne rides well his horse of the night." As he spoke, so he wrote: "Give me health and a day, and I will make the pomp of emperors ridiculous"; "The conscious ship hears all the praise"; of young idealists, "The tough world had its revenge the moment they put the horses of the sun to plough in its furrow"; of Experience, "was it Boscovich who found out that bodies never come in contact? Well, souls never touch their objects. An innavigable sea washes with silent waves between us and the things we aim at and converse with." In the same essay,—"Dream delivers us to dream, and there is no end to illusion. Life is a train of moods like a string of beads, and as we pass through them, they prove to be many-colored lenses which paint the world their own hue."[2] And of Love's world, with the cadences of Ecclesiastes,—"When the day was not long enough, but the night, too, must be consumed. When the moonlight was a pleasing fever, and the stars were letters, and the flowers ciphers, and the air was coined into song; when all business seemed impertinence, all the men and women running to and fro in the streets mere pictures." But to show the poetry of Emerson's prose is to give the whole of it; these essays are of the few which make us tolerate the conceit of "prose poems." Their persistent recourse to imagery and metaphor, their suggestions of the secret relations of things, at times have subjected them to the charge of being obscure. The fault was not in the wine:—

> Hast thou a drunken soul?
> Thy bane is in thy shallow skull, not in my silver bowl!

In mature years the essayist pays more regard to life about him, to the world as it is; he is more equatorial, less polar and remote. His insight betrays itself in every-day wisdom. He is the shrewd, the benignant, the sagacious, Emerson, writing with pleasant aptitude, like Hesiod or Virgil, of domestic routine, and again of the Conduct of Life, of Manners, Behavior, Prudence, Grace. This is in the philosophic order or progress, from the first principles to the application of them. Some of his followers, however, take him to task, unwilling that the master should venture beyond the glory of his cloud. As for his unique treatises upon Behavior, it was natural that he should be led to think upon that topic, since in gentle bearing, in his sweetness, persuasiveness, and charm of smile and voice, he was not excelled by any personage of our time, and what he said of it is of more value than the sayings of those who think such a matter beneath his regard. His views of civic duty and concerning the welfare of the Republic are the best rejoinder to his early strictures upon Homer and Shakespeare for the temporal and local features of their master-works. As a critic he was ever expectant, on the lookout for something good and new, and sometimes found the one good thing in a man or work and valued it unduly. When he made a complete examination, as in his chapter on Margaret Fuller, he excelled as a critic and delineator. *Parnassus* is not judicial, but oddly made up of his own likings, yet the best rules of criticism are to be found in its preface. With the exception of *English Traits,* he published no long treatise upon a single theme. His general essays and lectures, however, constitute a treatise upon Man and Nature, and of themselves would serve as America's adequate contribution to the English literature of his period. We are told of an unprinted series of his essays that may be grouped as a book on the Natural History of the Intellect. Should these see the light, it would be curious to compare them with the work of some professional logician—with the standard treatise of President Porter, for instance—upon a similar theme. Something in quantity may yet be added to Emerson's literary remains. But it will not differ in quality; we have had the gist of it: for he was a writer who, though his essays were the fruit of a prolonged life, never wrote himself out. Often an author has gained repute by one or two original works, while his ordinary efforts, if not devoted to learned or scientific research, have been commonplace. The flame of Emerson's intellect never fades or flickers, and never irks us. It burns with elemental light, neither of artifice nor of occasion, serene as that of a star, and with an added power to heat the distance which receives it.

VI

In summing up the traits of Emerson one almost ceases to be critical, lest the highest praise may not be quite undue. More than when Bion died, the glades and towns lament him, for he left no heir to the Muse which he taught his pupils. In certain respects he was our most typical poet, having the finest intuition and a living faith in it,—and because there was a sure intellect behind his verse, and because his influence affected not simply the tastes and emotions, but at last the very spirit, of his countrymen. He began where many poets end, seeking at once the upper air, the region of pure thought and ideality. His speech was wisdom, and his poesy its exhalation. When he failed in either, it seemed to be through excess of divining. His triumphs were full of promise for those who dare to do their best. He was as far above Carlyle as the affairs of the soul and universe are above those of the contemporary, or even the historic, world. His problem, like that of Archimedes, was more than the taking of cities and clash of arms. The poet is unperturbed by temporal distractions; yet poets and dreamers, concerned with the ideal, share in the world's battle equally with men of action and practical life. Only, while the latter fight on the ground, the idealists, like the dauntless ghosts of the Huns and Romans, lift the contest to the air. Emerson was the freest and most ideal of them all, and what came to him by inheritance or prophetic forecast he gave like a victor. He strove not to define the creeds, but to stimulate the intellect and purpose of those who are to make the future. If poetry be that which shapes and elevates, his own was poetry indeed. To know the heart of New England you must hear the songs of his compeers; but listening to those of Emerson, the east and west have yielded to the current of its soul.

The supreme poet will be not alone a seer, but also a persistent artist of the beautiful. Of those who come before the time for such a poet is ripe, Longfellow on the whole has done the most to foster the culture of poetry among us as a liberal art. Emerson has given us thought, the habit of thinking, the will to think for ourselves. He drained the vats of politics and philosophy, for our use, of all that was sweet and fructifying, and taught his people self-judgement, self-reliance, and to set their courses by the stars. He placed chief value upon those primitive laws which are the only sure basis of national law and letters. And as a poet, his verse was the sublimation of his rarest mood, that changed as water into cloud, catching the first beams of sunrise on its broken edges, yet not without dark and vaguely blending spots between. Emerson and Longfellow came at the parting of the ways. They are of the very few whom we now recognize as the true founders of an American literature. No successors with more original art and higher imagination can labor to more purpose. If the arrow hits its mark, the aim was at the bowstring; the river strengthens and broadens, but the sands of gold wash down from near its source.

Not a few are content with that poetry which returns again and again to its primal conceptions, yet suggests infinite pathways and always inspires,— the poetry of a hermitage whose Lar is Nature, and whose well-spring flows with clear and shining Thought. To such,—who care less for sustained flights of objective song, who can withdraw themselves from passion and dramatic life, who gladly accept isolated cadences and scattered, though exquisite, strains of melody in lieu of symphonic music "wandering on as loth to die,"—Emerson will seem the most precious of our native poets. He will not satisfy those who look for the soul incarnate in sensuous and passionate being. Such readers with Professor Dowden, find him the type of the New World transcendentalist, the creature of the drying American climate, one "whose nervous energy has been exalted," so "that he loves light better than warmth." He is not the minstrel for those who would study men in action and suffering, rather than as heirs to knowledge and the raptured mind. He is not a warrior, lover, raconteur, dramatist, but an evangelist and seer. The greatest poet must be all in one, and I have said that Emerson was among the foremost to avow it. Modern bards poorly satisfy him, being meagre of design, and failing to guide and console. Wordsworth was an exception, yet he had "written longer than he was inspired." Tennyson, with all his tune and color, "climbs no mount of vision." Even Shakespeare was too traditional, though one learns from him that "tradition supplies a better fable than any invention can." In face of the greatest he felt that "the world still wants its poet-priest, a reconciler, who shall not trifle with Shakespeare the player, nor shall grope in graves with Swedenborg the mourner; but who shall see, speak, and act with equal inspiration." Thus clearly he conceived of the poet's office, and equally was he assured that he himself was not, and could not be, the perfect musician. He chose the part of the forerunner and inspirer, and when the true poet shall come to America, it will be because such an one as Emerson has gone before him and prepared the way for his song, his vision, and his recognition.

Notes

1. Definitely set forth in his Address before the Senior Class in Divinity College, Cambridge, July 15, 1838.
2. Life, like a dome of many-colored glass, Stains the white radiance of eternity. (Shelley's *Adonais.*)

—Edmund Clarence Stedman, "Ralph Waldo Emerson,"
Poets of America, 1885, pp. 133–79

C.C. Everett "The Poems of Emerson" (1887)

Charles Carroll Everett taught theology and preached at the Divinity School at Harvard. Everett also served as dean, though after Emerson's time there.

The significance of Everett's passage to students of Emerson's poetry is that Everett defends Emerson's poetry against charges of obscurity. This is an exception to the general criticism of Emerson's poetry, both then and now.

The poetic (that is, the compact and imagistic) qualities of Emerson's prose often results in an unfair comparison between the essays and the poetry, and the poetry suffers. Everett makes two important points: that Emerson's poetry is visual (he "deals with pictures"), and that the poetry "appeals not directly to the understanding but to the imagination of the reader." Emerson might have chosen to explain the images of his poems, but he *chose* to create poetry as a separate, organic medium. Everett makes the almost too obvious distinction clear for readers, and this is part of the significance of the essay: we often hear general terms in criticism of poetry, but Everett makes these basic ideas approachable and understandable.

Many find the poems of Emerson obscure. This obscurity results very largely from the fact of their strength. So far as the content of the poems is concerned, this consists of the thoughts and images that would present themselves to a poetic nature that had caught the fullest intellectual and spiritual impulse of his time. To the comprehension of these the poet, if he be indeed such, can furnish little help. If he utters a thought it is not simply as a thought that he utters it. As we have seen, the ideas in the poetry of Emerson rarely present themselves except as creations of the imagination. In other words, the poet deals with pictures. If one recognizes what is placed before him, well and good; if he does not, he must study it out for himself. Emerson speaks in one case of "leopard-colored rills." When I first read these poems in my youth, I remember that I was troubled with this phrase. I had never seen enough, or had never observed enough, to recognize the beauty and truth of the epithet. I could only wait till the thing recalled the words. If Emerson had supposed that any reader would not recognize the meaning he could have explained it and told how the effect was produced. He could have said that, given a bottom of reddish sand with shadows or ripples playing over it, we should have something that might suggest the skin of a leopard; but in this case we should have an approach to prose. So if Emerson had explained the spiritual imagery of his poems, he might have made them more clear, but with a like defect. It is the province of the imagination to gather up into single living forms whatever is offered to its view. The horizon will vary according to the position or the insight of the poet. If what it presents be familiar, all will recognize and comprehend; so far as it is less familiar, will there be obscurity. The question to ask in this latter case is, whether the thought of the poet be fantastic or fanciful; that is, whether it be his private thought; or, on the other hand, whether it lie in the pathway of the race. If when we reach it we find it human and normal, then it is not the fault of the poet, but to his praise, that we have found it at first obscure. It is, I repeat, because he is a poet that he appeals not directly to the understanding but to the imagination of the reader, which he assumes to be in harmony with his own. Even the essays of Emerson were at first found obscure. One writer compared the reading of them to the making one's way through a swamp. You put your foot upon some little hummock that bears its weight, and then look about you to find a resting place for the next step. Rarely now are his essays found obscure. Indeed, we can scarcely understand to-day the difficulty that beset their first reading. The difference is that at the time the style and the range of the thought were new; now, thanks largely to Emerson himself, they have become familiar. In the poetry the difficulty is greater, partly because the thought is higher and subtler; partly because, as has just been shown, poetry appeals to the imagination rather than to the understanding. To this it must be added that because the style of Emerson is so strong and epigrammatic the thought is doubly barred. So far as the expression is concerned, we must pronounce our judgment not according to the degree of the difficulty in comprehending, but according to the fitness of the expression as felt when comprehension has been reached. It will often be found, when the meaning flashes upon the mind, that the very difficulty is the beauty of the phrase.

—C.C. Everett, "The Poems of Emerson,"
Andover Review, March 1887, pp. 239–40

Charles F. Richardson (1887)

Charles Richardson's two-volume work, *American Literature, 1607–1885,* is the first comprehensive history of American literature. In it, Richardson calls for American literature to be held to the same standards applied to literature of every age and country.

Like Everett, Richardson defends Emerson's poetry against his contemporary critics. However, Richardson contrasts Emerson with more highly regarded English poets (such as William Wordsworth and William Cowper). Richardson's claim that Emerson is "the singer of the upward march of nature" is important for students of Emerson's poetry, but also to students writing about "Nature." Students should note that the 1838 edition of "Nature" is prefaced with a six-line poem that exactly demonstrates Richardson's claim, and is one of the most compelling examples of Emerson's poetic abilities.

Richardson makes another significant point: "The perfection of verbal melody exists when the reader or hearer cannot conceive of any other way of singing the thought." This may seem obvious, but the underlying assumption should not be missed. Poetry is not a variation or a subspecies of prose but is a separate, organic unit of expression. The poet, in this case Emerson, writes in a manner that cannot be expressed in any other medium. Poetry, then, is both medium and message. One reason that Emerson's poetry is held in lesser esteem than his prose is that Emerson's medium—that is, his difficulty with the formal qualities of poetry—subverts the power of his imagery. Poetry has formal qualities that may be evaluated objectively—this is the process Richardson refers to by the term *scansion*—but the form and content of Emerson's poems cannot be anything else but poetry. Thus, the poems must be considered on their own merit, as the "song" the poet sings cannot exist in any other form.

The poetry of Emerson, whatever its special manner or theme, is the poetry of acquiescence, optimism, idealism, spiritualism, individualism. It often has a didactic and magisterial tone, rather than the moralizing tone of Wordsworth or Cowper. "Do this," "shun that," it swiftly says. "Be not a fool, not a money-maker, but a poet and a lover of the beautiful and the good." Nature, rightly understood, is a fit and lovely thing, and so is the soul at its best. Poetry notes and intensely describes some of the qualities of each, or of both. It was no wonder that Emerson anticipated, in half-a-dozen poems, the later conclusions of the evolutionists. He was the singer of the upward march of nature and the onward march of man. His poetic field was too broad to be tilled thoroughly in many parts. He was too proverbial to be a great constructive artist. He gives us saws, sayings, admonitions, flashes, glimpses, few broad constructed pictures. With these we are content, and do not ask him for epics, tragedies, or "Excursions," having poems like those already named; or "Good-bye, Proud World," "The Sphinx," and the "Concord Hymn"; or lines like

> He builded better than he knew;
> Earth proudly wears the Parthenon
> As the best gem upon her zone;
> The silent organ loudest chants
> The master's requiem;
> And conscious law is king of kings;
> Or music pours on mortals
> Its beautiful disdain.

Emerson's poetic art was at times of exquisite quality, a lovely presentation of noble thought. The perfection of verbal melody exists when the reader or hearer cannot conceive of any other way of singing the thought; and not a few of Emerson's lines or poems well bear this test. When this art gives place to grim force we do not feel, as Lowell said of Whittier, that Emerson as poet is

> Both singing and striking in front of the war
> And hitting his foes with the mallet of Thor,

for Emerson's stern strength is not that of a Taillefer but rather that of a Saxon law-maker. He announces, with all his force, but does not wage war in defence of the sayings he has uttered with oracular positiveness. Emerson is one more illustration of the fact, too often forgotten, that a poet can be forcible and lyrical at the same time; rooted in cold, deep thought and giving to the warm winds the loveliest flowers of beauty. Emerson, more than any

American poet, severely tests and almost defies the laws of poetics, as they have been deduced from other languages and applied to English scansion; but yet from his work may be selected many an example proving anew that English is capable of fine and deliberate metrical and melodious effects. He who recognizes Emerson's aims and methods will attempt neither to prove all his failures to be glorious successes, which men are too blind to see; nor to declare him rugged or unmelodious or obscure,—the poet who, when he would, could sing so sweet and clear a song.

—Charles F. Richardson, *American Literature,*
1607–1885, 1887, Vol. 2, pp. 169–71

Edmund Gosse
"Has America Produced a Poet?" (1889)

A librarian, writer, translator, and critic, Edmund Gosse wrote literary histories and biographies of Thomas Grey, John Donne, and Henrik Ibsen. Gosse served as librarian to the House of Lords and was knighted in 1925.

Gosse offers an interesting critique of Emerson the poet by employing the extended metaphor of the ship starting out strongly, under the full wind of inspiration, and gradually losing its power. The metaphor is appropriate because of the linguistic and symbolic connection between wind and inspiration (the Latin word *spiritus,* from which we get the term *inspire,* can mean "spirit," "breath," or "wind"). Thus, Gosse suggests that Emerson's inspiring visions for his poems are substantial, but he labors with the form, a reasonable enough criticism. Gosse's regret that Emerson's "technical shortcomings" compromise the effectiveness of his visions is in line with the general trend of criticism of Emerson's poetry. Students writing about Emerson's poetry might utilize this kind of thinking to help determine the poems that succeed, or suffer, from what Gosse refers to as "mere cacophonous eccentricity."

If Emerson had been frequently sustained at the heights he was capable of reaching, he would unquestionably have been one of the sovereign poets of the world. At its very best his phrase is so new and so magical, includes in its easy felicity such a wealth of fresh suggestion and flashes with such a multitude of side-lights, that we cannot suppose that it will ever be superseded or will lose its charm. He seems to me like a very daring but purblind diver, who flings himself headlong into the ocean, and comes up bearing, as a rule, nothing but sand and common shells, yet who every now and then rises grasping some wonderful and unique treasure. In his prose, of course, Emerson was far more a master of the medium than in poetry. He never became an easy versifier; there seems to have been always a difficulty to him, although an irresistible attraction, in the conduct of a piece of work confined within rhyme and rhythm. He starts with a burst of inspiration; the wind drops and his sails flap the mast before he is out of port; a fresh puff of breeze carries him round the corner; for another page, the lyrical *afflatus* wholly gone, he labours with the oar of logic; when suddenly the wind springs up again, and he dances into a harbour. We are so pleased to find the voyage successfully accomplished that we do not trouble to inquire whether or no this particular port was the goal he had before him at starting. I think there is hardly one of Emerson's octo-syllabic poems of which this will not be found to be more or less an accurate allegorical description. This is not quite the manner of Milton or Shelley, although it may possess its incidental advantages.

It cannot be in candour denied that we obtain a very strange impression by turning from what has been written about Emerson to his own poetry. All his biographers and critics unite, and it is very sagacious of them to do so, in giving us little anthologies of his best lines and stanzas, just as writers on *Hudibras* extract miscellanies of the fragmentary wit of Butler. Judged by a chain of these selected jewels, Emerson gives us the impression of high imagination and great poetical splendour. But the volume of his verse, left to produce its own effect, does not fail to weaken this effect. I have before me at this moment his first collected *Poems,* published, as he said, at "the solstice of the stars of his intellectual firmament." It holds the brilliant fragments that we know so well, but it holds them as a mass of dull quartz may sparkle with gold dust. It has odes about Contocook and Agischook and the Over-God, long nebulous addresses to no one knows whom, about no one knows what; for pages upon pages it wanders away into mere cacophonous eccentricity. It is Emerson's misfortune as a poet that his technical shortcomings are for ever being more severely reproved by his own taste and censorship than we should dare to reprove them. To the author of "The World-Soul," in shocking verses, we silently commend his own postulate in exquisite prose, that "Poetry requires that splendour of expression which carries with it the proof of great thoughts." Emerson, as a verse-writer, is so fragmentary and uncertain that we cannot place him among the great poets; and yet his best lines and stanzas seem as good as theirs. Perhaps we ought to consider him, in relation to Wordsworth and Shelley, as an asteroid among the planets.

—Edmund Gosse, "Has America Produced a Poet?"
(1889), *Questions at Issue*, 1893, pp. 86–88

CHRISTOPHER P. CRANCH "EMERSON'S LIMITATIONS AS A POET" (1892)

Christopher Pearse Cranch was a minister, poet, author, caricaturist, and a tireless contributor to transcendentalist publications, including the *Dial*. Cranch did not have the poetic talents of his colleagues Emerson, Thoreau, and Jones Very, but was an excellent and insightful critic.

Cranch's critique is similar to that of Richardson, Everett, and Gosse in that he recognizes the beauty of Emerson's imagery but the weakness of his formal abilities. Students should note, however, that those critics each identify different poems as among the ones they consider Emerson's strongest. This suggests that, while these critics agree on a general tendency of Emerson as a poet, they recognize different groups of poems as best illustrating Emerson's strengths. Thus, the criticism is subjective. Students should note that Emerson's strength as a poet might be recognized in any number of poems, and not to take it for granted that specific poems necessarily are failures.

Cranch also writes that "every complete poet should be an artist too," that poetry demands "a perfect soul in a perfect body." The idea is fairly common among Emerson's critics, but Cranch's expression uniquely illustrates a value that Emerson as well as other transcendentalists revered: the ideal connection between soul and body, the spiritual and the physical, as an inherent property of nature. This is the quality of pantheism Emerson is often accused of promoting, and is evident, for Cranch, as a formal requirement for poetry, which Emerson certainly would have understood.

It seems to me that, with Emerson, verse was not, as a general thing, so natural and congenial a form of expression that it drew him magnetically and irresistibly. I admit that marked exceptions must be made to this statement. And there are noble poems and parts of poems which seem the pure and spontaneous prompting of the Muse. Notably those where he is plainly swayed by a strong tide of emotion, or touched by some vivid fancy or natural picture—as in his 'Threnody,' the 'Rhodora,' 'The Amulet,' 'Rubies,' 'Each and All,' 'The Snow-storm' and parts of the 'Wood-Notes.' His poem, The Problem'—almost matchless as it is—is less an outflow of lyric expression than a brilliant mosaic of thoughts concisely and poetically expressed; a poem (in this respect, though not otherwise) like Gray's *Elegy*, where many of the couplets, as there the quatrains, might change places without seriously dislocating the whole structure.

Though perhaps never guilty of writing *invita Minerva*, he is naturally more epigrammatic than lyric. It is only in the fusion of an emotion or an ideal that he *flows*. And even then his stream is roughened and impeded by serious technical limitations. For such long elemental wave-sweeps as Milton or Byron or Shelley or Keats delighted in, he was unfit. He lacked one essential element, the sensuous—and this includes the rhythmical sense. The form is slighted—the thought or the picture only prized. But every complete poet should be an artist too, and know how to wed beautiful thoughts to beautiful forms, and in the most harmonious union. Here, I think, was Emerson's deficiency. I am sure that in all times of literature, those poems will live longest that best fulfill the demand for a perfect soul in a perfect body.

But what then? Shall we quarrel with our poet because he is not a complete rhythmical artist? Shall we not rather trust to the impression he makes by the rare thought and original diction shining through lines which are incomplete, which are halting, odd, extravagant, or obscure, but which are so much a natural way he has of expressing himself that they may be said to be full of 'an art that Nature makes'? The imperfect structure of many of his poems can never hide from us those wonderfully graphic touches wherein he is so alive to Nature—those memorable couplets or those 'skyey sentences' (a term he so felicitously applies to Shakespeare),—or those happy condensations of thoughts into phrases that have become as household words to us.

As to the question of rank of this or that poet, or of comparison of one with another, my feeling is that there can be little profit in such speculation, even in the form of professional criticism. I don't think that musicians hold many warm debates about the respective merits of Beethoven, Mendelssohn, Schubert or Schumann. When we see, hear, feel Beauty, we acknowledge and applaud it. I think we grow less and less inclined to be dogmatically critical as to the relative greatness of the plays of Shakespeare; and we don't stand debating whether the sunset of last evening was finer than that of a week ago.

Whatever the technical imperfections of Emerson's verse, it is beyond question that we are lifted by his rare though broken music into chambers of thought and mystical sentiment, to which few poets of our day have the key. If he is not a great poetic artist, he is a great seer and inspirer—and of prose-poets our first.

—Christopher P. Cranch, "Emerson's Limitations
as a Poet," *Critic*, Feb. 27, 1892, p. 129

Chronology

1803	Born May 25 in Boston to William Emerson and Ruth Haskins Emerson.
1811	May 12, Emerson's father, William, dies.
1812	Emerson enters Boston Public Latin School.
1817	Begins studies at Harvard College.
1820	Begins keeping his journal.
1821	Graduates Harvard. Teaches at his brother William's school in Boston.
1822	Publishes his first article, "Thoughts on the Religion of the Middle Ages," in *The Christian Disciple*.
1825	Enters Harvard Divinity School.
1826–27	Officially sanctioned to preach as a Unitarian minister. Sails to South Carolina and Florida in an effort to improve his health.
1828–29	Becomes engaged to Ellen Louisa Tucker. Ordained at Second Church in Boston. Marries Ellen on September 10, 1829.
1831	Ellen dies of tuberculosis on February 8 at the age of 19.
1832	Resigns from post at Second Church. Travels in Europe.
1833	Meets Wordsworth, Coleridge, and Carlyle during travels abroad. Returns to Boston. Delivers his first public lecture, "The Uses of Natural History."
1834	Settles in Concord.
1835	Lectures on biography. Marries Lydia Jackson, whom he renames Lidian, on September 14.
1836	Meets Margaret Fuller; helps form Transcendental Club; publishes "Nature" anonymously. Birth of son Waldo.

1837 Delivers the "American Scholar" at Harvard before the Phi Beta Kappa Society. Writes "The Concord Hymn."

1838 Delivers the "Divinity School" address at Harvard, which causes him to be banned from speaking at the university.

1839 Birth of daughter Ellen Tucker.

1841 Publication of first series of *Essays*. Thoreau comes to live with the Emersons. Birth of daughter Edith.

1842 Death of Waldo. Emerson succeeds Margaret Fuller as editor of *The Dial*.

1844 Birth of son Edward. Delivers "Emancipation of the Negroes in the British West Indies." Publication of *Essays: Second Series*.

1845 Thoreau moves to Walden Pond. Delivers series of lectures on "Representative Men."

1846 Publication of *Poems*.

1847 Travels to Europe for most of the year.

1849 Publication of *Nature; Addresses, Lectures*.

1850 Publication of *Representative Men*. Margaret Fuller dies.

1851 Delivers series of lectures on "The Conduct of Life."

1853 Death of Emerson's mother.

1854 Lectures on poetry at Harvard Divinity School. Thoreau publishes *Walden*.

1855 Whitman publishes *Leaves of Grass*; Emerson writes letter to Whitman in praise of his accomplishment.

1856 Publication of *English Traits*.

1860 Publication of *The Conduct of Life*.

1862 Henry David Thoreau dies.

1865 Eulogizes Abraham Lincoln.

1867 Publication of *May Day and Other Pieces*. Named Overseer of Harvard College. Delivers "The Progress of Culture" address to the Phi Beta Kappa Society.

1870 Publication of *Society and Solitude*.

1871 Travels to California and meets naturalist John Muir.

1872 Travels to Europe and the Mediterranean.

1875 Publishes *Letters and Social Aims*.

1882 Dies April 27 of pneumonia in Concord, Massachusetts.

Index